Technological Change and Organization

Technological Change and Organization

Edited by
Rod Coombs

Professor of Technology Management, Manchester School of Management, UMIST, UK.

Kenneth Green

Senior Lecturer in Technology Management, Manchester School of Management, UMIST, UK.

Albert Richards

Research Associate, CROMTEC, Manchester School of Management, UMIST, UK.

Vivien Walsh

Senior Lecturer in Technology Management, Manchester School of Management, UMIST, UK.

Edward Elgar
Cheltenham, UK • Northampton, MA, USA

Published by
Edward Elgar Publishing Limited
Glensanda House
Montpellier Parade
Cheltenham
Glos GL50 1UA
UK

Edward Elgar Publishing, Inc.
136 West Street
Suite 202
Northampton
Massachusetts 01060
USA

This book has been printed on demand to keep the title in print.

A catalogue record for this book
is available from the British Library

Library of Congress Cataloguing in Publication Data
Technological change and organization / edited by Rod Coombs ... [et al.].
    Papers from a conference held in Manchester in April 1996.
    Includes bibliographical references.
    1. Technological innovations—Management—Congresses.
2. Industrial organization—Congresses.   3. Industrial management—Congresses.   I. Coombs, Rod.
HD45.T392   1998
658.5'14—dc21   97–35416
                                                      CIP

ISBN 1 85898 589 7

Typeset by Manton Typesetters, 5–7 Eastfield Road, Louth, Lincolnshire LN11 7AJ, UK.

Contents

Figures

Tables

Contributors

Dr Pascal Byé, Institut National de la Recherche Agronomique, Département Economique, Montpellier, France

Dr Vittorio Chiesa, Politecnico di Milano, Consiglio Nazionale delle Ricerche–Instituto di Tecnologie Industriali e Automazione (CNR-ITIA), Italy

Dr Jens-Frøslev Christensen, Department of Industrial Economics and Strategy, Copenhagen Business School, Denmark

Dr Simon Collinson, Assistant Director and Senior Research Fellow, Institute for Japanese–European Technology Studies, Edinburgh University, Scotland, UK

Professor Rod Coombs, Professor of Technology Management, Manchester School of Management, UMIST, UK

Dr Margarida Fontes, Instituto Nacional de Engenharia e Tecnologia Industrial, Lisbon, Portugal

Dr Kenneth Green, Manchester School of Management, UMIST, UK

Dr Paolo Guerrieri, Università Degli Studi Di Roma 'La Sapienza', Italy

Dr Bastiaan de Laat, CSI, Ecole Nationale Supérieure des Mines de Paris, France

Dr Philippe Larédo, CSI, Ecole Nationale Supérieure des Mines de Paris, France

Dr Nicola De Liso, IDSE, Milano, Italy

Dr Robert Magnaval, European Commission, Research and Technological Development Framework Programme, Brussels, Belgium

Professor Stan Metcalfe, Stanley Jevons Professor of Political Economy and Cobden Lecturer, Department of Economics, University of Manchester, UK

Dr Alfredo Molina, Director, TechMaPP and Senior Research Fellow, Department of Business Studies, Edinburgh University, Scotland, UK

Dr Albert Richards, Manchester School of Management, UMIST, UK

Professor Peter Swann, Manchester Business School, UK

Professor Andrew Tylecote, Sheffield University Management School, UK

Dr Vivien Walsh, Manchester School of Management, UMIST, UK

K. Matthias Weber, Institute for Prospective Technological Studies, World Trade Center, Seville, Spain

Preface

This book arose from a conference held in Manchester in April 1996, the third in a series of conferences on 'Advances in the Social and Economic Analysis of Technology'. The conference brought together a broad international group of scholars at a time when research on innovation and technical change was entering a new phase of synthesis and integration, drawing on new concepts in the theory of the firm, in evolutionary economics, and in the analysis of national and sectoral 'systems' of innovation.

The editors had the difficult job of selecting, from a large number of papers delivered at the conference, a set which would best represent the key theme of this synthesis. The papers chosen were developed by the authors into the chapters for this volume. In re-reading them some time after the conference, it is clear that they continue to give an accurate picture of the important trends in thinking about the analysis of innovation.

We are very grateful to the contributors for their work on these chapters, and to all the participants at the conference for their contributions. We look forward to continuing to bring the international community of innovation scholars to Manchester from time to time to continue the work of synthesizing economic and social analysis of innovation and technological change.

Rod Coombs
Ken Green
Albert Richards
Vivien Walsh

1. Introduction

Rod Coombs, Kenneth Green, Albert Richards and Vivien Walsh

The chapters in this volume analyse how the processes of innovation and technological change depend on the organizational contexts in which they take place. These contexts are various. They include, for example: the business unit; the larger corporate entity of which a business may be a part; the surrounding milieu of other firms, government agencies and other actors within which an innovating firm is operating; and the capital and labour markets. These organizational dimensions of technical change are not to be seen as a passive 'environment' which is 'impacted' by innovations. Rather they are intrinsic and active parts of the innovation process itself.

In recent years our understanding of innovation has already made considerable headway in this direction, in parallel with the death of 'linear' models of innovation – whether of the technology-push or demand-pull variety. Benchmarks in this progress include such diverse contributions as Rothwell's five serial models of the innovation process (Rothwell, 1992), which incorporate more and more rounded accounts of the innovating firm and its organizational setting; Pavitt's sectoral taxonomy of innovation processes (Pavitt, 1984), actor–network analysis of technical change (for example: Mangematin; 1996, Larédo and Mustar, 1996; Callon, 1996; Callon et al., 1986), and the extensive literature on national systems of innovation (for example, Lundvall, 1992; Nelson, 1993).

However, the challenges of incorporating these organizational parameters into theories of innovation and technological change are significant. A major difficulty concerns the loss of focus on the unit of analysis and on precisely what is being explained. As soon as we introduce into the analysis of specific innovations such wide-ranging bodies of material as, for example, historical accounts of the development of industrial sectors, or the peculiarities of capital markets or business elites in particular countries, then we run the risk of being seen to make more ambitious claims than simply giving an account of technological change. Instead we seem to move in the direction of proposing broader social and/or economic theories which are distinguished by having technological change as their central pivot. To the extent that social

sciences in general have neglected the significance of innovation and technology, such ambitious steps by students of innovation can be seen as justified.
But a superior analysis of innovation and technology can only ever be a
partial basis for larger-scale progress in social science. Other shifts and
currents in the disciplines need to be taken into account. We need to experi-
ment by casting our interpretations of innovation within these new currents
and theories, and exploring the connections and common threads thereby
generated.

Some prominent examples of this approach have already borne fruit. The
original concept of a technological trajectory as an empirical observation
concerning sequences of related innovations has gradually merged with the
notion of path-dependence in innovation and become embedded in the account of the firm as a collection of routines which is central to evolutionary
economics. In this volume, several of the chapters contribute further to this
broad topic, by developing various aspects of the model of the firm as a
collection of technological capabilities and the processes which deploy them.
Other chapters focus less on the capabilities within the firm, and more on the
firm's access to and articulations with capabilities outside the firm, in the
wider organizational context. The remainder of this introductory chapter will
summarize the contributions of and connections between the chapters, organized into these two broad categories.

ORGANIZATION, CAPABILITIES AND THE INNOVATING FIRM

The chapter by Metcalfe and De Liso (Chapter 2) provides a careful exposition of the connections between a capabilities model of the firm and the
notion of constrained variety generation, which is central to an evolutionary
account of innovation. In employing a capabilities model the authors are
explicitly establishing a connection to a resource-based theory of the firm.
However, they go beyond the normal components of such theories by emphasizing the importance of the specific organizational characteristics of individual firms which create a distinctive knowledge base and a specific way of
perceiving and tackling innovation opportunities. Thus it not simply a static
concept of capabilities; it is a dynamic model of capabilities and the organizational ability to mobilize those resources which together are seen to have
the potential to generate innovation and competitive advantage. As we shall
see later, in discussion of other chapters, this perspective is complementary to
the emphasis on strategic intent as an adjunct to core competences in the
Prahalad and Hamel (1990) model of strategy determination which has become so influential in recent years.

Chapter 3, by Byé and Magnaval, focuses on collaborative R&D activity, the factors which motivate the partners, and the procedures which are used to regulate it. They argue that the upstream aspects of R&D which are prone to more genuine scientific uncertainty cannot be governed by any obvious price-based or even quasi-market relationships. In consequence the partners are forced to adopt more strategic and interpretive stances towards understanding the merits of collaborative projects and managing their conduct. By contrast, as R&D projects become more market-focused, the possibility of a harder-edged contractual approach becomes greater, as the values and risks associated with particular technical activities become more open to calculation. Thus we can see in upstream collaborative R&D another example of firm behaviour which is best interpreted as capability-building rather than as purely contractual in nature.

Chapter 4, by Chiesa, is concerned with analysing the factors promoting and controlling the tendency for large multinational companies to locate a modest but increasing proportion of their R&D in countries outside their home country. A related concern is whether the 'external' R&D is principally aimed at tailoring existing products to local markets, or whether it is used to provide sources of novel technology from those locations, and then transfer it into the core innovating processes of the company. This topic has already been studied by scholars of the organization of multinational companies and foreign direct investment. But Chiesa's approach casts new light on the issue by choosing one industrial sector (telecommunications equipment) and looking explicitly at the balance between factors internal to that industry and factors which are specific to each firm, in explaining variances in their behaviour with respect to the location and role of their R&D units. He finds that firm-specific competences and their historical underpinnings, together with the embedding of those competences in national institutional structures, are very important moderators of the industry-level 'drivers' which might otherwise be expected to produce common behaviour. Once again, then, a resource-based or capabilities perspective on the firm provides powerful insights into the organizational aspects of innovation processes.

In Chapter 5, Christensen is also concerned with large firms, in particular their divisional structure. He adopts a resource-based view and focuses on the technological capabilities which form part of the resource base, and which bear on the innovative potential of the firm. He asks the question about how technological capabilities that span more than one division get mobilized (or not) in the innovation processes of the firm. He examines the received Chandlerian ideas on strategy and structure which have been the traditional way of analysing the corporate management of multidivisional organizations and finds that they have little to say about this question of the organization of

corporate innovation and technology resources. Christensen proceeds to try
to fill this gap by elaborating the capabilities perspective.

Chapter 6, by Collinson and Molina, looks at the different organizational
approaches to radical innovation of two large electronics companies. The
two case studies are Philips and the Photo-CD device, and Sony and the
'Discman'. The perspective they employ is the 'sociotechnical constituencies' approach which has been developed by Molina in earlier work. This
perspective goes well beyond an internal focus on the firm and embraces a
wide sweep of factors and agencies outside it. However, those parts of the
perspective which do look at the internal aspects of the firm are very
consistent with the capabilities perspective. What is most revealing in their
analysis is the different approach to cross-functional integration within
the two firms. Compared to Philips, Sony possesses many more specific
organizational routines which permit technological and market knowledge
in different parts of the corporate structure to be combined to achieve a
radical innovation. Thus we see again that capabilities and the procedures
which mobilize them are an important determinant of the firm-specific
nature of innovation opportunities.

The capabilities perspective is reinforced from a totally different, and
somewhat surprising, direction in Chapter 7 by Swann. His argument begins
with the issue of the alleged short-termism of decisions concerning investment in innovation and technology. The chapter gives a concise summary of
the debates about whether the responsibility for short-termism lies with the
influence of the capital markets on managers, or with managers themselves.
However, Swann then analyses more precisely just what would constitute a
decision which could be demonstrated to be short-termist. In what sense it is
genuinely 'irrational' from the point of view of the longer-term interests of
the firm? He finds that there are some short-termist stances which are rational
and some which are not. Among those which are not rational are those cases
where payback periods are based on the one-product life cycle directly related to the investment in question, even though it is clear that returns will
continue to accrue from subsequent product life cycles which enjoy spillovers from the technology of the earlier product. He says that where firms do
invest in a way which takes account of subsequent product life cycles, they
are consciously choosing to invest in those intangibles which contribute to
the development of their specific innovative capabilities. Subsequently he
demonstrates how this approach is consistent with the core competence approach to strategy formulation of Prahalad and Hamel.

These six chapters, then, despite their widely differing primary points of
departure, have one common thread. This is the treatment of firm-specific
knowledge, and firm-specific organizational routines, as the contributing components of the particular firm capabilities which shape their innovative oppor-

tunities. Thus organizational factors are seen as primary features of the generative process of technological change.

CAPABILITIES IN SPECIFIC SECTORAL, REGULATORY AND NATIONAL CONTEXTS

The other four chapters in this volume focus on the interactions between firms' behaviour and the contexts in which they are set.

Chapter 8 by Fontes examines the role of new technology-based firms (NTBFs) in the Portuguese economy. Her analysis demonstrates a significant variety of types into which these firms fall, depending on the nature of their initial technological endowments, their forms of external technological networking, and the sophistication or otherwise of their customers. This investigation of NTBFs in an economy which is not fully mature, like Portugal's, shows that their ability to act as a dynamic component of a specific national system of innovation is profoundly influenced by the underdeveloped character of other parts of that system, in particular the lack of sophistication of the local customer base. NTBFs are therefore not an invariant form of firm which can be transplanted from one location to another. They are very dependent on their surrounding context for their ability to express their potential technological capabilities.

In Chapter 9, by de Laat and Larédo, the primary topic is the interesting recent phenomenon of 'technology foresight' programmes in different countries. These programmes are interesting because of their scope, the number of firms and individuals involved, and their apparent intention of securing consensus on directions for future innovative activity within industrial sectors. The authors examine a number of cases of this sort, and uncover the paradox that despite the high level of activity in 'foresighting', there are no real theories or concepts to substantiate or even guide the activity in a rational way. They argue that foresight activities fall into several categories depending on whether there are strong unitary perspectives among the actors which permit consensus, or whether, at the other extreme, there are sharply contrasting scenarios of the future held by different groups of firms or actors within a given foresighting community. Employing the actor–network framework of Callon and Latour, de Laat and Larédo argue that it is therefore often appropriate to view foresight activities as simply novel arenas in which alternative scenarios, and therefore alternative future innovation trajectories, are battling for hegemony. The aims of the participants may therefore be rather more like pre-emptive strikes than consensus.

In Chapter 10, Guerrieri and Tylecote apply a sharp test to the robustness of the concept of a national system of innovation. They argue from the mass of received theory on innovation that the central determinant of innovative success is cross-functional coordination within firms. They then argue that there are two primary sources of influence on whether or not firms have access to these abilities to achieve such coordination. One is the industry they operate in, and its ability to foster certain common approaches and procedures and expectations about innovation. This factor is proxied in the analysis by using Pavitt's taxonomy of sectors. The other source of influence is the national system in which the firm is embedded. The key features of this system are the nature of the science base, the quality of the labour force, and the nature of the sources of finance. What the authors aim to demonstrate is that within specific countries the strength of the sectoral influence is moderated by the actions of the relevant national factors. This leads to consistent patterns, with certain industries being expected to be more capable of expressing their 'natural' innovative approaches in some countries than in others. These patterns are supported by a variety of quantitative and qualitative data. This analysis is therefore a powerful alternative approach to the issue of the relationship between technology and national competitive advantage.

In Chapter 11, Weber provides a detailed account of the interactions between government actions and the more familiar dynamics of economics and technology. His chosen case study is the development of the combined heat and power technology (CHP) in the UK over the past 15 years. Weber shows that the liberalization and privatization initiatives of the Conservative government in the 1980s inadvertently created an environment in which CHP initially appeared more attractive to privately owned electricity generators, despite being previously an underdeveloped technology. Subsequently, however, the intensification of competition in the electricity industry created a degree of short-termism which militated against the investment in CHP. The point here is that a variety of direct and indirect consequences of government actions can interact in complex ways with the other determinants of the direction of technical change.

Thus in the four chapters discussed in this section, we see a rich pattern of interactions between the internal organizational processes which govern firms' innovative capabilities and the 'external' organizational contexts in which they attempt to sustain and express them. Taken together with the other six chapters, they constitute a significant addition to our understanding of the co-evolution of technology and organizational forms. This is consistent with the long-term project of placing technology and innovation firmly at the centre of an understanding of economic and social change, rather than regarding them as exogenous variables.

REFERENCES

Callon, M. (1986), 'The sociology of an actor–network: the case of the electric vehicle', in Callon et al. (1986).

Callon, M., Law, J. and Rip, A. (eds) (1986), *Mapping the dynamics of science and technology: sociology of science in the real world*, London: Macmillan, pp. 19–34.

Larédo, P. and Mustar, P. (1996), 'The technoeconomic network: a socioeconomic approach to state intervention in innovation', in Coombs, R., Richards, A., Saviotti, P.-P. and Walsh, V. (1996), *Technological Collaboration: The Dynamics of Cooperation in Industrial Innovation*, Cheltenham, UK: Edward Elgar.

Lundvall, B.-A. (ed.) (1992), *National Innovation Systems*, London: Pinter.

Mangematin, V. (1996), 'The simultaneous shaping of organization and technology within cooperative systems', in Coombs, R., Richards, A., Saviotti, P.-P. and Walsh, V. (1996), *Technological Collaboration: The Dynamics of Cooperation in Industrial Innovation*, Cheltenham, UK: Edward Elgar.

Nelson, R.R. (ed.) (1993), *National systems of innovation: a comparative analysis*, New York: Oxford University Press.

Pavitt, K. (1984), 'Sectoral patterns of technological change: towards a taxonomy and a theory', *Research Policy*, **13**, 843ff.

Prahalad, C.K. and Hamel, G. (1990), 'The core competence of the corporation', *Harvard Business Review*, **90**(3), May/June, 79–93.

Rothwell, R. (1992), 'Successful industrial innovation: critical factors for the 1990s', *R&D Management*, **22**(3), 221–40.

2. Innovation, capabilities and knowledge: the epistemic connection

Stan Metcalfe and Nicola De Liso

INTRODUCTION

Our purpose in this chapter[1] is to make connections between two rapidly developing literatures: one concerned with a capabilities perspective on the firm; the other placing the development of the firm in a context of evolutionary competition. We shall argue that a capabilities perspective provides a useful bridge between evolutionary economics, which is concerned with the coordination of diverse behaviours, and the origins and articulation of novel behaviours in relation to questions of organization management and strategy. Naturally, a concern with innovation, whether technological or organizational, plays a central role in this story. We shall also show that there are interesting connections with evolutionary epistemology and with the concept of competitive advantage. These are perspectives quite different from those embodied in a contractual approach to the firm (Foss, 1996) but, of course, they do link closely to perspectives which make knowledge and the creation of knowledge the distinctive feature of firm behaviour.

Before turning to the details, let us be clear about the purpose of the argument. It is to help us understand the differences in behaviour between firms – not their similarities – for it is the differences which matter to the competitive process. No source of differentiation is more powerful than that of differential innovative behaviour; it is the wellspring from which the immense diversity of firm behaviour flows. In stressing the differences between firms we are of course directing the argument towards what evolutionists call a population perspective. In this perspective the emphasis is on the differences between entities which define the population, in contrast to essentialism where the differences are a nuisance, hiding the essential features of the phenomena under investigation. For an essentialist it is a natural step to emphasize and seek to explain similarities in behaviour, a path which leads him/her uncomfortably to the idea of uniform entities or agents. For the populationist this is anathema; he/she is seeking to explain why and how entities differ, what are the sources of variety and what are the constraints on the generation of variety. Let us begin with a brief review of some innovative literature.

INNOVATIONS: A VARIETY OF APPROACHES

In our view it should not be controversial to suggest that a theory of innovation is unfinishable business in that we shall never be able to predict the timing and form of specific innovative events. Novelty cannot be bounded in such a rationalistic way. By contrast, we can of course expect to gain much greater insight into the activity of innovation and the processes which are established to generate innovations. Here there are four elements in our understanding: the opportunities to innovate; the resources available to do so; the capabilities to manage the innovation process; and the incentives to innovate. What an evolutionary theory of innovation thus seeks to explain is the distribution of these elements across different firms. In this chapter we shall be concerned with only two of these matters – opportunities and management capabilities – which we believe are particularly significant as explanations of the differential ability to innovate between firms.

For many years now, the complexity of innovation phenomena has been documented by a range of scholarly studies which speak to the theme of differential performance at innovating. Each study typically takes its own frame of reference and unit of analysis which can range from the genesis of individual innovations, the development of whole technologies interpreted as a sequence of related innovations, the behaviour of innovating organizations, typically firms, to the activities of individual innovators. All have found their mark in the literature. In their path-breaking work in the 1950s, Carter and Williams (1957) undertook many case studies of innovation which led them to a characterization of the progressive firm in no less than 24 dimensions. In this they prefigured much of the subsequent interest of scholars by drawing attention to the importance of a firm's external connections with the world of science and technology, the quality of its training and recruitment activities, and the degree to which its selling policy and technical services to customers supported its innovative efforts. They pointed to the importance of trained, lively and receptive management, and judged that the technically progressive firm would be of good quality in general. In reaching their conclusions they had also identified the wide differences between firms in their innovativeness and the apparent lack of a clear relationship between progressiveness and performance. None the less, they felt confident enough to conclude in a way that is thoroughly modern in its ring. The progressive firm linked its R&D closely with production and sales policies, it enjoyed close connections with suppliers and customers, and it paid close attention in its recruitment policy to attracting good minds. Success, such firms agreed, built on success and, conversely, backwardness had a tendency to be self-perpetuating, the low-quality firm having neither the resources nor the reputation to attract and keep creative minds. The recent study by Kunkle (1995) on the comparative records of GE and RCA at developing a commercial electron microscope in the USA is a clear-cut example of the Carter and Williams thesis. The studies of Langrish et al. (1972) and Freeman (1974) came to remarkably similar conclusions on the role of external connections and the internal connectedness of R&D with marketing activities.

Writing twelve years later than Carter and Williams, Jewkes, Sawyers and Stillerman (1969), in their study of 57 important inventions, had also concluded that the forces making for technological creativity were too complex and intricate to provide any simple summary. While recognizing that large and small firms would have comparative advantages in different types of innovation, they also emphasized the continuing importance of the lone innovator whose motives and persistence could not be reduced to the simply economic. Like Carter and Williams, they clearly saw and identified the great diversity which characterizes innovative activity and drew the obvious implication that no one channel or institutional form could be expected to provide an ideal framework of innovation. Almost four decades later, Freeman (1994) has written a comprehensive survey of the innovation literature which draws on many of the themes established by Jewkes et al. But, of course, the evidence is now more impressive and he is able to address a wide variety of sources in distinguishing between the roles of external and internal learning in the innovation process. Now the progressive firm has become the 'learning firm', but the broad messages remain the same. Let us briefly review some other recent studies of innovation which emphasize the diversity of approaches and units of analysis.

Consider first an approach based upon case studies of organizational performance at innovation, Margaret Graham's (1986) study of RCA's attempts at inventing the consumer video recorder – an attempt which ultimately failed. RCA had a strong record as a consumer electronics innovator and had a self-image of technological leader which it embedded in a separate research centre set up to drive the knowledge base free from pressures associated with operating units. The route chosen by RCA was one of ten or so tried internationally by companies in the 1960s and 1970s. It settled for a disk-based technology, but the two technologies which ultimately triumphed, VHS and Beta-Max, were based on magnetic tape technology, being design analogies to the cassette recorder, not the record player. Within RCA different research teams followed different technological paths, posing problems for the internal selection environment with conflict emerging between discipline-driven work and practical problem-solving activity, and the relations between the research centre and the consumer electronics division. After a number of abortive product launches, the company made its final choice of design and technology in 1979 and launched this on the market in March 1981. By April 1984, the product was withdrawn: Japanese competitors had established an insurmountable market advantage based on technology which RCA had rejected as infeasible.

Several interesting lessons follow from this study of a major, failed innovation in a very large company. The first is the importance of the process which generates the range of possible paths to innovation and the process which ultimately concentrates effort around the chosen option. These processes have to manage the tensions between unchallenged R&D, driving the long-term knowledge base of the company in isolation from other aspects of strategy, and the shorter-term customer- and problem-driven needs of the operating divisions. For whatever reason RCA defined the 'wrong agenda' and placed its bets on the 'wrong' options. The technologies which triumphed were themselves subject to a fierce competitive process, with the VHS design driving out the early market leader – the Beta-Max design. As Cusumano et al. (1992) show, the success of the VHS option did not depend on any technological superiority within the family of tape-based technologies, but rather on the ability of the companies concerned to accumulate the complementary marketing and productive assets necessary to build market positions more quickly than rivals.

From a different perspective, Henderson (1994) has explored the theme of strategic diversity in the pharmaceuticals industry, focusing on the development of cardiovascular drugs. In this sector, the crucial competitive issue is the ability to design compounds to produce specified effects on the cardiovascular system. The traditional knowledge base in this area was built around the technology of diuretics but, following a number of scientific breakthroughs, a range of new possibilities became available. The British company, ICI, successfully exploited the beta-blocker route while other companies explored quite different design paths, principally around calcium channel blockers and Angiotensin Converting Enzyme (ACE) inhibitors. Each of these design paths had a different rationalization and provided the companies concerned with the opportunity to develop a family of clearly related designs to control particular body mechanisms. A second theme which Henderson explores is the ability of companies to integrate quite different bodies of knowledge and their disciplines to achieve competitive advantage. In particular, she draws attention to the links which companies enjoyed with the external science knowledge base and the way in which their internal organization integrated the wide range of disciplines required to take a drug from design to market. From our perspective, what is interesting about this study is that it shows clearly how companies can take very different and non-substitutable paths to serve the same market.

Quite different approaches to the study of individual innovations have been provided by historians of technology. Vincenti's study (1990) of flush riveting in the construction of metal-skinned aircraft is a good case in point. This apparently simple innovation required an immense amount of trial-and-error learning before success was attained, with companies following different routes to a solution, sharing that knowledge in a variety of ways and finally settling on a uniform design solution. Science played no direct role in reaching this solution, according to Vincenti; it was reached entirely as a result of empirical engineering, the progressive search for a design by sequential trial and error, with the resulting knowledge not easily codifiable or communicable. Thus in building the industry knowledge base there was an element of collective invention, with the movement of personnel and an important role being played by a group of key suppliers, the tool manufacturers. McBride's study (1992) of the development of warship propulsion technology, following the introduction of the Parsons turbine at the end of the nineteenth century, provides another perspective. Three rival solutions to the problems which arose in coupling a high-speed turbine to the ship's propellers were developed – reduction gearing, fluid drive and electric drive – each with its own distinctive knowledge base. The adoption of electric drive brought a new entrant into the ship construction industry, General Electric, and for a short period this technology met the strategic needs of the US navy to improve the operating range of the Pacific fleet. Two factors led to the eclipse of this technology: the need for faster ships to counter the growth of the Japanese fleet, and improvements in metallurgy and machinery technology which jointly led to the readoption of the rival technology, reduction gearing.

Other literature deals with the ability of firms to change technological direction in response to technological threats. Cooper and Schendel's study (1976) was one of the first to explore this question and they found systematic support for the view that such changes are very difficult to accomplish; a corollary of this is the importance of new entrants in establishing radically different designs, a theme explored in greater depth in Utterback (1994). New technology threatens skills and established accumulations of human and knowledge capital, and there is a clear tendency for management to emphasize the shortcomings of new technologies and downplay their potential advantages. When firms do attempt to develop the new technology, strategy and resources appear to be divided, with a continuing commitment to the old technology, and often this division is reflected in organizational separation of the old from the new. It is this divided loyalty which reflects the difficulties of building new skills and strategic perspectives appropriate to the new technology. An interesting case study of technological rejection is provided by Clark (1994) in his study of Bell Laboratories' response to magnetic recording technology. In the 1930s, Bell built a considerable knowledge base and technological capabilities which enabled it to construct machines superior to those of the German competitor firms. None the less, AT&T's management refused to sanction commercial innovation because they considered that recording would create a loss of privacy and reduce the demand for telephone calls. Moreover, it was part of the AT&T strategic model to control the entire system and prevent the attachment of devices whose use would be outside its control. Consequently when, post 1945, the market for tape machines for telephone recording purposes was developed, Bell had lost its lead and was unable to respond to a market opportunity which was supplied by rival firms.

We see in each of these studies a number of themes central to the study of innovation in an evolutionary context. Put simply, resources and incentives to innovate do not appear to be a problem for industries as a whole although they may be a problem for individual firms. Rather, the issues appear to centre around questions of opportunities and capabilities, and what is of central importance here is the fact that different competing forces follow a wide range of technological and strategic routes to compete in the same market. The ability to generate sequences of linked innovations appears to be of particular significance. As Nelson (1991) has emphasized, there are non-discretionary differences in firm behaviour at innovation which cannot be explained in terms of economic factors. Individual firms coalesce around particular but different technological designs and it is these differences which provide the basis for an evolutionary theory of competition. Thus the central question for innovation research is not whether firms are similar but whether they are different. The similarities cannot be the basis of competitive advantage; only the differences can play that role. Thus how and why differences in behaviour arise is what must be explained. In the long term every position is vulnerable and this is perhaps the most important lesson to be learnt from Schumpeter's (1912) emphasis on creative destruction. This is a process of evolutionary change which has been played out on a global scale increasingly since 1945.

In explaining further the generation and regeneration of difference, we shall explore the following four themes: bounded cognition, differential accumulation of capabilities, technological trajectories and technological systems.

BLIND VARIATION AND SELECTIVE RETENTION: A METAPHOR FOR INNOVATION?

Innovations are discoveries which entail the growth of knowledge, and in this present us with a puzzle: one cannot have prior knowledge of something which is yet to be discovered. We believe that this creates insuperable objections to a rational theory of innovation and at the same time opens up interesting connections with evolutionary epistemology. Consider first the matter of rationality. This is a complex matter and no serious student of the innovation process has ever put much faith in the extreme idea of rationality, which is otherwise so prevalent in modern economic theory. We can begin by accepting a far less restrictive version of rationality as reasoned behaviour: the directed, intentional behaviour of firms seeking competitive advantage by committing resources to innovation. Such behaviour is motivated; it involves striving (Winter, 1984) and entails no more than an ability to choose with the aim of making the best of the resources at the command of the firm or innovating business unit. Unfortunately, where innovations are concerned, neither what is considered best nor the resources considered to be available are free from ambiguity. Thus one must confront the complexity of innovative activity, its future orientation and its inherent degree of non-quantifiable uncertainty in relation to events which must be considered unique.

As Langlois (1990), for example, along with many others in the Simon tradition (1955), has pointed out, the fundamental problems which arise in compiling the list of potential choices relate to the imagination required to produce the relevant choice set and the computational problems entailed in translating between objectives and options. Problems soon become too complex to be solved analytically, and when this happens one is reduced to judgement and the guiding hand of experience. Complexity implies that there is no single motive to reduce choices to a comparable basis, that there is computational indeterminacy and an ineluctable range of ignorance, which means that decisions are made on the basis of expectation and hunch. Brian Arthur (1994) expresses the matter perceptively when he emphasizes the resort to inductive reasoning and pattern recognition in the face of complexity. New information is evaluated by reference to previous experience, and this gives to the knowledge generation process an inherently path-dependent character. History matters because history determines the knowledge which is constructed from particular items of information. Thus, to the extent that optimization occurs at all, it does so within local domains in which the choice set and the evaluation of that choice set is historically contingent: of itself this is quite enough to underpin the diversity of firm behaviour, which is the chief empirical characteristic of the innovation process in modern capitalism. Winter (1987) puts this very clearly when he distinguishes between fragmented conceptualizations of the relevant choices and the difficulties of implementing solutions to the particular chosen problem. At this point we turn to ideas developed in evolutionary epistemology, for they relate directly to the question of the exercise of imagination and the perception and construction of innovation possibilities. The major contributor to this literature has been the psychologist Donald Campbell (1974, 1987), who has insisted that all generic knowledge can only be the product of what he calls blind variation and selective retention. In its structure this is, of course, an evolutionary argument; there are sources of variations, mechanisms for accepting some of these variations and rejecting others, and mechanisms for propagating the survivors (Gamble, 1983). By far the most controversial of these ideas has been that related to the alleged blindness of the variations. On this Campbell expresses strong views. Blind does not mean random; there is nothing in his argument which implies equiprobability or statistical independence of variations. What the notion does mean can be summed up in terms of three propositions:

- variations are independent of the environmental conditions of the occasion of their occurrence;
- successful trials are no more likely to occur than unsuccessful trials in any such sequence; and
- errors from previous trials do not result in subsequent trials being conceived as corrections.

Now it is unfortunate that acceptance of these strong conditions has been the basis for acceptance or rejection of the entire variation and selection approach to the growth of knowledge. For the strength of this approach is its appeal to a sophisticated falsificationism and its implicit emphasis on the social context of selection processes. Blindness should not be the defining issue; it is after all only one possible hypothesis about the origins of variation. What is acceptable about the notion is the idea that every attempt to gain knowledge is a genuine leap in the dark. One may have prior expectations but, as Shackle famously opined (1961), expectations lie in the imagination; they cannot be knowledge; knowledge can only relate to the present. In other words, all knowledge generation processes are full of surprises and one does not need much acquaintance with the innovation literature to accept the validity of this statement. In this regard 'blindness' is acceptable as a starting-point but its drawback is that it closes off from investigation too many interesting influences on variety generation, in particular, those which are consequences of the selection process. Again it is important to be clear what is at stake – understanding the precise content of variations in knowledge or understanding the process by which they are generated.

In this regard, Campbell certainly accepts the idea of constraints on the process of knowledge development, not only in terms of the background of received wisdom, but also in terms of heuristics which limit the search space. This is a familiar idea. The development of knowledge cannot be random since the space of options is immeasurably vast, as students of *Gulliver's Travels* will recall. To make progress we have to limit progress, and this requires us to adopt mental frameworks which limit and guide our search processes. They are devices for escaping from the tyranny of combinatorial explosion. In their actual evaluation of evolutionary epistemology, Stein and Lipton (1989) place particular attention on what they call mechanisms for pre-adaptation – those heuristics and focusing devices which shape the generation of reasonable hypotheses. They suggest that the heuristics can be of three general types: abstract rules or general principles of enquiry; concrete rules, specific ways of generating hypotheses in a discipline context; and exemplars, canonical solutions or concrete models of solutions to specific problems. What is important about this argument is that epistemic variations, which all innovations are at some point, while they may necessarily be blind, in that their economic performance can only be anticipated, are not random. The mental frameworks within which innovative ideas arise are predominantly shaped by past experience and by the limits imposed by the particular sets of heuristics in play. In this sense innovations are never entirely novel; they are always prefigured in some of their dimensions. In a number of important writings, Vincenti has explored these ideas in relation to cumulative sequences of engineering innovations in the development of the aeronautical industry (1990).

An emphasis on the diversity of mental frameworks raises the question of whether there exists a true model of the reality of any given innovative context, or whether there are as many divergent representations as there are diverse behaviours of firms. Wilson (1990) tackles this question by distinguishing two approaches: where the generation of ideas is based on some model of reality to enable vicarious experimentation, and where it is based on what he calls adaptive imaginary representations or fictional worlds, which simplify complex reality and provide a set of instructions on how to behave in particular circumstances. He places all models of rationality, including bounded rationality, in the first group. However, a fictional world limits and motivates behaviour and it is to be judged by its operational effectiveness, not by its relation to the truth – in the scientific sense appropriate to a model of reality. Thus if models of reality are 'scientific', adaptive imaginary representations are 'technological': like engineering knowledge they are tested by their utility, accumulated by trial and error and are the epitome of rule-guided behaviour. It seems to us that managerial ideas about innovation are more adaptive imaginary representations than models of reality, and in this they equate to technology and engineering rather than to science.

Accepting variations as necessarily guided, we come now to a more substantial objection to Campbell's strong claims, namely that variations cannot be considered as reflecting a prior awareness of the likelihood of success. What this misses is that the heuristics which guide variation do not only relate to the prior development of scientific and technological knowledge; they also relate to the environment in which these advances are to be tested.

Whatever may be true of science, technology is tested by its practical utility, and utility is a matter of fit with the economic and social environment. Thus many heuristics important for the competitive process are matters of understanding the economic and social environment. The conjectures which generate possible innovations are unlikely to be independent of a perception of the field of application of that innovation. They cannot, then, be blind in Campbell's sense. Nor does this damage the approach; rather it enriches it by pointing to other stimuli and constraints on the growth of knowledge, additional to those which are internal to the knowledge enterprise. We shall see that this is important when we come to consider the capabilities of the firm, for organization places constraints on the generation of innovation conjectures.

The final comment we wish to make concerns the antipathy between the notion of blindness and that of learning, specifically if we restrict the notion of learning to some concept of reinforcement. In this regard learning does mean error correction; learning from mistakes means that past trials shape the candidates for future trials. Failure is as significant as success: both shape perceptions of what might reasonably be tried next. Having been to this degree critical of Campbell's concept of blind variation, we none-the-less accept the variation–selection framework for analysing the growth of knowledge and hence innovation. It rules out the random and it rules out Olympian rationality; it is the necessary middle ground of reasonable behaviour in the development of knowledge within organizations. Before turning to capabilities and organization, we should note that the discussion of variation and selection fits comfortably with paradigm-related notions of the growth of knowledge. But those are importance differences to attend to when applying paradigms to technology and innovation as distinct from pure science.

The general thrust of a paradigmatic perspective is cognitive: to paraphrase Vincenti, what technologists know and how they come to know it. Such a paradigm indicates fruitful directions for technological change, defines concepts of progress, establishes tests to judge performance, and has a powerful exclusion effect on the collective thinking of engineers, technologists and the organizations they represent. Technological paradigms are sets of heuristics which reflect both the antecedents and potential applications of new knowledge. A technological paradigm builds cumulatively by suggesting a sequence of puzzles sometimes guided by theory but often solved entirely empirically. A progressive technology generates many performance-enhancing puzzles and in this routine aspect it is akin to normal science. However, technological design and development is more concerned with puzzle solving than with hypothesis testing – more with verifying what works than with theoretical falsification. A technological puzzle is solved when the performance standards of an artefact are improved or become more predictable, not when a puzzle solution yields a better understanding of a natural phenomenon (Vincenti, 1990). Moreover, technologies involve practice as well as knowledge, and this is why it is necessary to investigate the development of a technology in three dimensions: the growth of codified knowledge, the acquisition of tacit skills and the development and application of product and process artefacts (Layton, 1974). It is because of these different dimensions of technology that it is so difficult to distinguish satisfactorily between radical and incremental forms of innovation. What is radical in terms of a change in knowledge may yet be trivial in terms of the performance of technological artefacts, and conversely. Advances in scientific knowledge may result in the development of a new design configuration based on previously unknown principles and requiring a new community of practitioners to articulate a new paradigm. Technological change is always a mix of the familiar and the new in proportions which vary along the knowledge–artefact spectrum.

Thus the creation of a new paradigm represents an agenda for the growth of knowledge and organizational capability. Such a device serves to delimit the field, setting the initial conditions and boundaries for new conjectures and providing a conceptual scheme within which theoretical speculation is bounded. Thus a paradigm defines an unexplored opportunity, an opportunity which has self-defining limits on the possible patterns of discovery. In short, paradigms constitute a consistent starting-point subjected to further refinement in the research process. They provide the frameworks which link together sequences of innovations to explore a technological opportunity. As such they are a key element in defining the capability of a firm. Within their constraints we can give full run to blind trial-and-error, but only within these constraints. They provide the basis for a shared view of the world and the lens through which that world is perceived. Capabilities are accumulated, learnt by working with the design configuration and by exploring the opportunities that it represents. Hence all business units are specialized and the source of that specialization is this design configuration (Loasby, 1995a, 1995b). Morover, their patterns of innovation develop within the localized context of the specific design configuration, each with its own set of practices and standard solutions to design problems, and each with its own technology support system of users, suppliers and other practitioners within an appropriate network.

CAPABILITIES AND THE FIRM

Firms are intentional organizations and if they are to survive, let alone prosper, their intentions must be matched by their ability to act in support of such intentions. This is the starting-point for the capabilities view of the firm and for its connection with evolutionary epistemology. In considering the productive opportunities of the firm, one is led naturally to enquire into the basis for its knowledge of these opportunities and how they develop differentially across firms. The firm is defined by what it knows; its knowledge determines what it can do and how. In recent literature this has become known as the capabilities view of the firm, and it is of considerable interest in any study of the sources and conduct of innovation-related activities; for the essence of innovation is that it requires a change of knowledge within the firm (Kogut and Zander, 1992).

Several recent contributions to the management literature provide an underpinning to this approach. Barney (1991), for example, emphasizes the importance of firm resource heterogeneity as a basis for competitive advantage, and distinguishes in broad fashion between the physical, human and organizational resources of the firm. To be the basis of differential advantage, the bundle of resources must be deployed to create differences in effectiveness and efficiency, there must be no strategic substitutes available to rivals, and the resource bundle must not easily be imitated. Imperfect mobility in imperfect resource markets is one reason for imperfect imitability, but equally significant are the complexity of the links between particular resource bundles and competitive advantage. These give rise to observational difficulty and causal ambiguity (Dierickx and Cool, 1989), and to the social complexity of the resource bundles when viewed internally, in terms of organizational structures, and externally, in terms of customer–supplier linkages. Amit and Schoemaker (1993) explore similar themes but emphasize the imperfect tradability of the resources which yield strategic advantages and the consequences that they must be accumulated internally, together with the related implications that the specialized nature of the assets means that they are open to sudden obsolescence and that they are a basis for inertia in responding to new opportunities. Of course, bundles of resources themselves do not constitute strategic assets. Strategic assets are resources which are utilized for a purpose in the context of specific capabilities, such that the resource and the capability become a unity. It is clear from this resource-based perspective that a great deal of the competitive value of a capability depends on matters of organization and the organization of knowledge. A number of different elements contribute to this theme. The first is to see the firm as a collection of individuals, each with their own knowledge and aptitude, brought together in teams which are focused around activities (Richardson, 1972; Penrose, 1959). Only individuals know, but what they know can be shared in a collective understanding. These activities may be grouped in different functional ways – production, marketing, and so on – but from an evolutionary perspective it is useful to define them in relation to three broad groupings concerned with current operations, the growth or replication of current operations, and the development of qualitatively different operations through innovation. Of

course, the firm is much more than simply the sum of the individuals contained within it and the knowledge and skills that they possess as individuals.
First, the individuals operate with the help of other complementary productive assets (Teece, 1987) and second, the individuals are organized. The
organization of the firm creates its distinctive signature by coordinating the
internal division of labour and, equally importantly, by transforming the
knowledge and skills of the individual members into a collective capability,
what McKelvey (1982) has suggestively called a competence pool. A moment's reflection on the nature of any team sport will illustrate the point
perfectly, and reinforce the idea that an important management task is the
effective choice and allocation of individuals to teams. The organization
further forms the context in which any new knowledge is acquired; it is the
framework for learning and creativity. In terms of our previous discussion, it
is the framework within which the firm's distinctive adaptive imaginary representations of its world emerge. The same teams of individuals placed in
different organizational contexts are expected to know different things and
learn in different ways, while a change in the individual members of the
organization may equally be expected to change what it knows and how it
learns. Thus what individuals know and can achieve depends on their context.
In this way it is possible to sum up the organization as an operator transforming the individual into the collective; it is a device for benefiting from the
division of labour in the generation of knowledge and skill, a device which
gives the firm or business unit its individual and indissoluble character. In
this context several authors have emphasized the role of the top management
team in a business unit in shaping the nature of the collective enterprise
(Eliason, 1990; Castanias and Helfat, 1991). This team defines the direction
in which the business unit develops and the organization of its operations. It
is the top team's capabilities which determine the ability of the organization
to conjecture alternative futures and to test internally the alternatives and
select among them. And, of course, innovation is a matter of conjecturing
alternative futures, of imagining how the future can be different from the
past. If one accepts this argument, one is in danger of ignoring too much the
role of the individual. This would be a mistake: firms are composed of
individuals and indeed any discussion of entrepreneurship emphasizes that
point. So this line of argument is not meant to deny the importance of the
individual but rather to emphasize that individuals always operate in an
organizational context. However distinctive the individual may be, context is
still important. Clearly, in closely coupled organizations there is far less
scope for individual creative behaviour than in more open loosely-coupled
organizations. It is a familiar theme in the management literature as to where
one sets the balance, close-coupling being beneficial for efficiency but loose-
coupling being beneficial for innovation.

The second strand of the capabilities approach explains the nature of the distinctive organizational resource or organizational operator in terms of its sets of decision rules or routines. Each routine relates to some task, cognitive or physical, within a specific activity, and provides the instructions for action according to the circumstances prevailing (Nelson and Winter, 1992). But routines do not operate in isolation, and the important point is that the firm's behaviour depends on the interaction within its bundle of routines; capability relates to the integration and joint operation of routines. Hence it is not always possible to link specific behaviours to single routines. Arrow (1974) has usefully developed this idea by specifying the firm's internal language or communication code as the element which shapes the integration of routines. Who talks to whom, with what frequency, on what topics and with what authority, both internally and externally – with suppliers, customers and the wider community of technological support – is a rather simple-minded way of specifying this integration function of an organization. However, no organization is simply reducible to its set of routines. For one thing, routines vary considerably in the specificity of the action they stimulate and in the nature of the information by which they are triggered. Certain routines may brook no deviation from a performance template; others may admit a great deal of interpretative flexibility so that the outcome varies with the individual or team performing the routine and the other teams with which they interact. This is particularly likely with respect to the sets of higher-level routines, such as those which guide innovative activities, since their purpose is to encourage and accommodate creativity. Other routines may be entirely automatic in their application, being deeply ingrained rules applied without thought and invoked purely by habit. Equally important is the fact that routines do not denote purpose or intent, the strategic objectives of the firm. Thus the collective capability is a bundle of routines operated by teams of individuals for a strategic purpose. In this way the collective capability is an image of the firm's theory of its own activity and purpose. This is a view which has been stressed by Pralahad and Hamel (1990) when they emphasize the importance of strategic intent, and the failure of a resource-based perspective to account for these differences in firm performance which reflect, they argue, a mismatch between resources and ambitions. In short, productive opportunities are conjectured connections between capabilities and intentions (Loasby, 1991, 1994).

Capability is much more than the individual assets; if it were not, the firm would be no more than a bundle of bilateral contracts between owner and employee, and rent could not exceed the differences between current and next-best-use-value. One thing this tells us is that the organization must possess a memory, or tradition of practice, so that losses in personnel can be matched with new employees who can be trained in the firm's routines.

Indeed Penrose (1959) pointed out that one of the major constraints on the rate of growth of the firm is the rate at which it can absorb and train new staff. Thus an individual may be difficult to replace when s/he leaves one organization and of much lower effectiveness when working in another organization – the importance of context again. Now it is with respect to knowledge that non-tradability becomes particularly significant. For well-known reasons markets in knowledge, managerial or technological, are highly imperfect, and this reinforces the bias towards growth of capability through internal accumulation. The tacitness of much of the knowledge, its indivisibility in use, the uncertainty of its valuęs in different contexts, its proprietary nature, and the fact that much of what is known is jointly produced by the firm's activities – and indeed decays if the activity ceases – mean that innovation-related capabilities cannot easily be augmented through trade and market relationships. However, there is a clear danger in this internalist approach – the danger of overlooking that the business unit is embedded in a wider matrix of organizations which support the generation of technology. Constant's (1980) idea of the community of practitioners is still perhaps the best way to sum this up. Thus in Freeman's recent survey (1994) the external connections of the firm with a wider knowledge base are given considerable emphasis, and this is also the theme which underpins the idea of national or sectoral innovation systems and technology support systems. However, this is not a new idea: industrial districts, Marshallian external economies and informal knowledge trading (Von Hippel, 1988) are familiar examples in which capabilities spread beyond the boundary of the individual organization. Of course this is a reflection of how knowledge accumulates when the generation of knowledge itself has become subject to a division of labour. Hence the processes of knowledge accumulation internal to the firm must be augmented through inter-organizational arrangements, such as joint R&D ventures, although the success of these arrangements often founders on an incompatibility between the members of the different organizations.

One way of summarizing the capabilities perspective as articulated thus far is as follows. The ability to act aptly implies competence, and competence is a combination of capabilities and intention, while capability is a combination of resources and routines, these last in a specific organizational context. However, the ability to act aptly also presupposes intelligence and knowledge of a cognitive framework within which all the firm's activities are carried out. It does not matter what we call this cognitive framework/design configuration/paradigm theory of business – all are equally instructive in their own ways. What matters is the sense of commitment to a cognitive framework: that it be shared among the members of the organization in an appropriate fashion. Along with Loasby it seems reasonable to presume that one cognitive framework excludes another; it is a mark of a division of labour between organizations. Now what matters for our purpose is that the cognitive framework is the context in which variation and selection with respect to the generation of knowledge occurs. Following Witt's (1993) persuasive terminology, it shapes both pre-revelation processes and post revelation processes *within* the organization as a key element of a theory of the innovative process.

By what criteria might one judge the value of different cognitive frameworks? One is by their adaptability, their propensity to respond aptly to new circumstances and opportunities; presumably a broad framework is superior to a narrow framework in a fashion analogous to the way we judge scientific theories. The Lakatosian notion of a progressive framework which generates a stream of fruitful hypotheses is surely appropriate here. Firms with degenerative business frameworks are more than likely on the way to extinction. Another relevant criterion is the screening ability of the framework, its capability to draw upon external sources of new hypotheses. All mental frameworks are limiting; they guide at the price of exclusion and so the capacity to respond to external information becomes one way in which degeneracy can be avoided, though not without difficulty, as the frequency with which managers refer to the 'not invented here' syndrome suggests.

Thus in understanding why firms are different one must look seriously at their rival cognitive frameworks and the way in which they interact with organization to shape variation and selection. Who is allowed to propose variations and with what authority? Who selects and by what criteria from the rival options that emerge? Who determines the resources which support the variation process and how? These are natural questions which arise when we combine the capabilities perspective with that from evolutionary epistemology. Thus firms differ because they have different variation, selection and retention procedures – procedures which should be central features of a theory of innovation.

In breaking open the black box of variation, selection and retention, it is also necessary to treat seriously the existence of different categories of knowledge. Some of this knowledge will be codified, capable of being transmitted other than by speech or observation; other important elements will be tacit and reflect the complexity of what is involved in the firm's operations. Some of the knowledge will be procedural, akin to engineering knowledge; other knowledge will be formal and contain a theoretical understanding of the task or activity (Vincenti, 1990). Different kinds of knowledge will be accumulated by different mechanisms on different timescales. In some cases the scientific method may yield results; in others what is required is a sequence of trial-and-error experiments. Much of the knowledge which is required is the result, not of an independent research programme, but of the operation of the routines themselves, in what is probably the most important practical example of joint production.

ON BEING DIFFERENT, ON BEING COMPETITIVE

All of this matters because being competitive depends on being advantageously different from one's rivals, and at root depends on a superior capacity for innovation. Hence the triad of capabilities referred to above, in relation to operating current activities, in relation to growing these activities, and in relation, fundamentally, to changing those activities to one's advantage. From this follows our claim that the bridging together of capabilities and an evolutionary epistemological perspective on innovation is isomorphic to an evolutionary theory of competition.

We have at our disposal a rich framework to comprehend the origin of competitive advantage. It depends on a firm's cognitive framework and the intention and capability with which that framework is operated. No two firms are ever alike on any of their dimensions. They perform differently at a point in time and over time; hence the ever-changing structure of market relationships which is symptomatic of competitive capitalism. Competitiveness is, of course, a chain relationship, not an absolute. One is more or less competitive only in comparison with a set of rivals who operate in the same market environment. Hence the emphasis in virtually all management literature on being competitive by having better products or better methods of production than one's rivals, and preferably sustaining these differences over time.

In explaining these differences in performance, one can turn to the perception of opportunities, the resources available, the incentives for change and the managerial ability to innovate. All these are brought together by recognizing that the ability to act also presupposes a cognitive framework and that this framework is the context for variation, selection and retention in the innovative process. What distinguishes modern capitalism is that such cognitive frameworks are widely distributed across different firms in an economy. Even if each framework may ultimately be limited in perspective, there are plenty of others with which it competes. It is this decentralized capability to generate new varieties of business plan which is surely the foundation of economic growth.

NOTE

1. This chapter draws on and develops arguments presented in De Liso and Metcalfe (1995) and Metcalfe (1996). We are grateful to Rod Coombs and Fred Steward for comments on an earlier draft, and to Professor Witt and colleagues at the Max-Planck Institute for Research into Economic Systems: Evolutionary Economics Unit, Jena, where the final version was drafted. The assistance of Sharon Boardman and Kieran Flanaghan is gratefully acknowledged. We gratefully acknowledge the support of Engineering and Physical Sciences Research Council (EPSRC) in the conduct of this research from which this paper is drawn.

REFERENCES

Amit, R. and Shoemaker, P.J.H. (1993), 'Strategic Assets and Organizational Rent', *Strategic Management Journal*, **14**, 32–46.

Arrow, K. (1974), *The Limits of Organization*, New York: Norton.

Arthur, W.B. (1994), 'Inductive Reasoning and Bounded Rationality', *American Economic Review*, **84** (May), 406–11.

Barney, J. (1991), 'Firm Resources and Sustained Competitive Advantage', *Journal of Management*, **17**, 99–120.

Campbell, D.T. (1974), 'Evolutionary Epistemology', in Schlipp, P.N. (ed.), *The Philosophy of Karl Popper*, Illinois: La Salle.

Campbell, D.T. (1987), 'Blind Variation and Selective Retention in Creative Thought as in other Knowledge Processes', in Radnitzky, G. and Bartley, W., *Evolutionary Epistemology, Theory of Rationality and the Sociology of Knowledge*, New York: Open Court.

Carter, C. and Williams, B.R. (1957), *Industry and Technical Progress*, London: Oxford University Press.

Castanias, R.A. and Helfat, C.E. (1991), 'Management Resources and Rents', *Journal of Management*, **17**, 155–71.

Clark, M. (1994), 'Suppressing Innovation: Bell Laboratories and Magnetic Recording', *Technology and Culture*, **34**, 516–38.

Constant, E.W. (1980), *The Origins of the Turbojet Revolution*, Baltimore, MD: Johns Hopkins University Press.

Cooper, A.C. and Schendel, D. (1976), 'Strategic Responses to Technological Threats', *Business Horizons*, **19**, 61–9.

Cusumano, M.A., Mylonadis, Y. and Rosenbloom, R.S. (1992), 'Strategic Manoeuvring and Mass Market Dynamics: The Triumph of VHS over Beta', *Business History Review*, **66**, 51–94.

De Liso, N. and Metcalfe, J.S. (1995), 'On Technological Systems and Technological Paradigms: Some Recent Developments in the Understanding of Technological Change', in Helmstadter, E. and Perlman, M. *Behavioral Norms, Technological Progress and Economic Dynamics: Studies in Schumpeterian Economics*, Michigan: University of Michigan.

Dierickx, I. and Cool, K. (1989), 'Asset Stock Accumulation and Sustainability of Competitive Advantage', *Management Science*, **33**, 1504–13.

Eliason, G. (1990), 'The Firm as a Competent Team', *Journal of Economic Behaviour and Organization*, **13**, 273–98.

Foss, N. (1996), 'Capabilities and the Theory of the Firm', mimeo, Danish Research Unit for Industrial Dynamics, Copenhagen Business School.

Freeman, C. (1974), *The Economics of Industrial Innovation*, London: Penguin Books.

Freeman, C. (1994), 'The Economics of Technical Change', *Cambridge Journal of Economics*, **18**, 463–514.

Gamble, T.J. (1983), 'The Natural Selection Model of Knowledge Generation: Campbell's Dictum and Critus', *Cognition and Brain Theory*, **6**, 353–63.

Graham, M.B.W. (1986), *The Business of Research: RCA and the Video Disk*, London: Cambridge University Press.

Henderson, R. (1994), 'The Evolution of Integrative Capability: Innovation in Cardio Vascular Drug Discovery', *Industrial and Corporate Change*, **3**, 607–30.

Jewkes, J., Sawyers, D. and Stillerman, R. (1969), *The Sources of Invention* (2nd edn), New York: Norton.

Kogut, B. and Zander, U. (1992), 'Knowledge of the Firm, Combination Capabilities and the Replication of Technology', *Organization Science*, **3**, 383–96.
Kunkle, G.C. (1995), 'Technology in the Seamless Web: "Success" and "Failure" in the History of the Electron Microscope', *Technology and Culture*, **36**, 80–103.
Langlois, R.N. (1990), 'Bounded Rationality and Behaviourism: A Clarification and a Critique', *Journal of Institutional and Theoretical Economics*, **146**, 691–5.
Langrish, J., Gibbons, M., Evans, W.J. and Jevans, F.R. (1972), *Wealth From Knowledge*, London: Macmillan.
Layton, E.T. (1974), 'Technology as Knowledge', *Technology and Culture*, **15**(1), January, 31–41.
Loasby, B.J. (1991), *Equilibrium and Evolution: An Exploration of Connecting Principles in Economics*, Manchester: Manchester University Press.
Loasby, B.J. (1994), 'The Organization of Knowledge and the Organization of Industry', mimeo, University of Stirling.
Loasby, B.J. (1995a), 'The Organization of Capabilities', mimeo, University of Stirling.
Loasby, B.J. (1995b), 'The Concept of Capabilities', mimeo, University of Stirling.
McBride, W.M. (1992), 'Strategic Determinism in Technology Selection: The Electric Battleship and U.S. Naval–Industrial Relations', *Technology and Culture*, **33**, (2 April), 248–77.
McKelvey, W. (1982), *Organizational Systematics*, Berkeley: University of California Press.
Metcalfe, J.S. and De Liso, N. (1996), 'Innovation, Capabilities and Knowledge: The Epistemic Connection', in De la Mothe, J. and Paquet, G., *Evolutionary Economics and the New International Political Economy*, London: Pinter.
Nelson, R. (1991), 'Why No Firms Differ, and How Does it Matter', *Strategic Management Journal*, **12**, 61–74.
Nelson, R.R. and Winter, S. (1992), *An Evolutionary Theory of Economic Change*, Cambridge, MA: Harvard University Press.
Penrose, E. (1959), *The Theory of the Growth of the Firm*, Oxford: Basil Blackwell.
Prahalad, C.K. and Hamel, G. (1990), 'The Core Competence of the Corporation', *Harvard Business Review*, May/June, 79–91.
Richardson, G.B. (1972), 'The Organization of Industry', *Economic Journal*, **82**, 372–83.
Schumpeter, J.A. (1912, Engl. tr. 1961), *The Theory of Economic Development*, New York: Oxford University Press (first English translation 1934).
Shackle, G.L.S. (1961), *Decision, Order and Time in Human Affairs*, Cambridge: Cambridge University Press.
Simon, H.A. (1955), 'A Behavioural Model of Rational Choice', *Quarterly Journal of Economics*, **69**, 99–118.
Stein, E. and Lipton, P. (1989), 'Where Guesses Come From: Evolutionary Epistemology and the Anomaly of Guided Variation', *Biology and Philosophy*, **4**, 33–56.
Teece, D.J. (1987), 'Capturing Value from Technological Innovation: Integration, Strategic Patterning and Licensing Decisions', in Brooks, H. and Guide, B.R. (eds), *Technology and Global Industry*, Washington, DC: National Academy Press.
Utterback, J.M. (1994), *Mastering the Dynamics of Innovation*, Cambridge, MA: Harvard Business School Press.
Vincenti, W.G. (1990), *What Engineers Know and How They Know it*, Baltimore, MD: Johns Hopkins University Press.
Von Hippel, E. (1988), *The Sources of Innovation*, Baltimore, MD: MIT Press.

Wilson, D.S. (1990), 'Species of Thought: A Comment on Evolutionary Epistemology', *Biology and Philosophy*, **5**, 37–62.

Winter, S. (1984), 'Schumpeterian Competition in Alternative Technological Regimes', in Day, R. and Eliason, G. (eds), *The Dynamics of Market Economies*, Amsterdam: North-Holland.

Winter, S. (1987), 'Knowledge and Competence as Strategic Assets', in Teece, D. (ed.), *The Competitive Challenge: Strategies for Industrial Innovation and Renewal*, Cambridge, MA: Ballinger.

3. Research procedures induced by non-market variables

Pascal Byé and Robert Magnaval

INTRODUCTION

It is generally accepted that the early stages of research activities require different strategies to those of the later stages of technological development. This applies especially to cooperative agreements whose nature will vary according to which stage of the research process has been reached. Cooperative agreements that relate to technological developments having one goal or the development of one specific technical object are negotiated within a real price system (Byé and Magnaval, 1995). These agreements, though, must be distinguished from those adopted in the exploratory research stages. In these early stages there is a progressive construction of a common reference platform to determine the nature and extent of the collaboration, followed by the construction of a price reference system during the implementation of the cooperative research activities.

Therefore one can propose the hypothesis that what distinguishes cooperative agreements from each other, whether for exploratory research or for technological developments with industrial applications, is not so much the objective of the cooperation, but the price system itself. In all these types of agreement price is taken into consideration. When a cooperative agreement for exploratory research is initially drawn up, the partners do not have a common reference point in any existing price system. The price system is built progressively as the scientific discovery is transformed into a technical object.

This chapter aims, first, to explore how the price system is built up and acts as a reference for determining the nature of the collaborative agreement as the research progresses from exploratory to technological product development.

The second objective of this chapter is to show how there is progressive integration between the partners in a collaborative agreement, and how this leads to greater cooperation between them. Examples will be drawn from the chemical and biological sciences to illustrate the analysis.

DIFFERENTIATION OF COOPERATIVE RESEARCH AGREEMENTS

Cooperative technological R&D is generally presented as a direct response by economic partners, particularly industrialists, to increased risks and uncertainty that are encountered in markets. When particular forms of cooperative alliances are considered, economic rationality appears to be the wisest choice. The gamble each partner takes lies in weighing the risks run due to the agreement and the benefits expected from cooperation. The gamble can be formalized, giving rise to contracts that contain clauses concerning the sharing of costs, risks and anticipated results. Due to competition and the redistribution of productive activities, the agreement becomes regulated by real situations – those of price, profit, sharing and protection (Byé, 1995).

This type of agreement explicitly refers to a value system built on a real price system. The price of production factors is taken into account. Investments are made in relation to the expected returns. Economic rationality appears to carry the day (Tassone, 1993) and to justify the pertinence of standard theory. The reality is certainly more complex, as the learning procedures currently used for improving and adopting technical objects are not always based on the search for pure economic optima. However, the transposition of the tools and concepts from economic analysis to the field of technical cooperation remains possible only if we admit that a common reference price system is responsible for the attitude of each of the agreement's partners.

Assuming that we can differentiate speculative research activities from later stages of development agreements, we suggest that the *ex ante* price system does not exist at the very beginning of a research cooperation agreement. Thus the behaviour of the partners cannot be reduced simply to the calculation of optimization. The price system is built up gradually, as the agreements proceed and succeed, that is, as the original non-commercial object is transformed into a technological object which may become commercial. These types of agreements refer to less systematic and finalized forms of cooperation. They are more exploratory (Levêque, 1993), and pursue goals whose 'science-oriented' content gives rise to knowledge which cannot really be systematized, or to generic techniques which are difficult to appropriate at the beginning. These characteristics mean that access to such agreements is limited to those partners able to accept the inherent constraints: the capacity to make irrecoverable investments without the obligation to produce results, and the capacity to transform and share information without continually claiming to own it. These characteristics greatly reduce the pertinence of the methods and concepts of standard economics, which are supposed to shed light on procedural rationality on the basis of real value systems.

VOLUME OF COOPERATIVE RESEARCH AGREEMENTS

Between 15 and 25 per cent of all agreements are partnerships, according to several authors (Hagendorn and Shakenraad, 1990; Gambardella and Orsenigo, 1993); the number of non-finalized cooperative research agreements varies depending on the maturity of the sector and the period concerned (Faulkner and Senker, 1994; Gaffard et al., 1993). A very small percentage is reported in the food or the iron and steel industries, with more in the pharmaceuticals and the information technology industries. Their number also varies depending on the economic growth regime and/or the particular history of the sectors to which they are related (Byé, 1995), with noticeably fewer agreements being made during periods of strong economic activity. There is an increase in collaborative agreements during periods when ambient economic uncertainty justifies the reintroduction of scientific activities that can offer opportunities for growth, and will support industrial restructuring.

Industrial sectors marked by technical and organizational inertia resulting from their long history, for example, the food and clothing industries and semi-processed goods, have fewer agreements. Conversely, the new science-based sectors and activities, such as pharmaceuticals, new materials, the computer software industry or scientific and medical instrumentation, make cooperative agreements more frequently.

Lastly, there are not many agreements in societies where the range of products or processes is well established, but they increase where industrial redeployment or new social requirements – for food, health, environment or information – become apparent and contribute to the definition of new needs and new markets. Their number also increases at particular moments in history, when societies reorient the functions allotted to the productive systems without knowing the value systems or markets that such reorientations will involve.

Cooperative research agreements develop in a context that is outside the market. They are primarily the product of an anticipatory approach. To the partners, these characteristics justify the willingness to avoid reference to a price system fixed *a priori* (Callon 1994). On the other hand, they explain and justify the role played by public policies in the expansion of these agreements. The *ex ante* absence of a price system does not mean that such a system will not materialize, but that it will be built up progressively with eventual public support as the cooperation becomes clearer and generates tangible results.

CONSTRUCTION OF THE REFERENCE PRICE SYSTEM

Each price system relates to different organizations and agreements: industrial alliances that are focused on production techniques refer to a real price system defined by the rules of competition; a partially regulated price system can be determined for agreements concerning technologies in the process of development; a virtual price system can be forecasted for agreements bearing on non-finalized research.

Thus the more clearly the price system is defined, the more formalized will be the agreement. Conversely, the less advanced the construction of the price system, the greater the flexibility in the content of the agreement; or inversely, the less it is limited by the obligation to produce results or keep to precise time limits, the more it will escape from a sphere of prices induced by competitive factors. The transition from one price system to another bears witness to the modification of the agreement.

The progressive construction of a reference price system specific to the cooperative research agreement takes place, however, within a sphere limited by the values attributed *ex post* by each partner. It is possible that these values do not correspond to the production factors mobilized by the agreement (labour, investment, semi-processed products), on one hand, or to the values anticipated *ex ante* on the other. But the same differences as previously stated – in profits, valorization of assets, opening of markets – result from scientific activities. The price system is, however, developed slowly, based on the initial budget allocated to the development of the research agreement by the partners or by third parties, generally the authorities. The dimension of the sphere initially defined by the partners is modified by the introduction of new standards, for example, rules for the protection of the invention or regulations related to scientific matters or to new social functions. During the course of this redefinition, government intervention contributes to the modification of the effective or anticipated values of the assets mobilized within the agreement. This intervention generally widens the scope of a scientific cooperation agreement.

AN INITIALLY LIMITED PRICE SYSTEM

The budget initially allocated to the implementation of the cooperation agreement is the pivotal point around which the price system is built. This allocation implies the formulation of priorities by the partners. It is often an implicit evaluation of the means mobilized by each of them for carrying out the programme. Frequently this evaluation differs from one partner to the other, and there is a tactical tendency to underestimate the contribution of the other partner in order to overestimate one's own, but in this field anything goes. Reference is not always made to real market prices, preference being given to measuring the contribution of each partner in terms of usage and services (making available equipment, personnel, services, division of tasks, customary clauses, training or apprenticeship). The initial price system is, however, limited by two value systems: those attributed *ex post* to the moveable assets, but especially to the fixed assets which each of the partners allocates to the implementation of the research programme; and those anticipated *ex ante* as a result of cooperative research activities.

In the beginning the agreement validates the activities and results already obtained by each partner. Thus it implicitly confers a value on the different production factors mobilized. Moreover, simply formulating the agreement contributes to increasing the economic value of existing, but non-commercial products or processes. This can be seen in certain types of know-how or professional qualifications. The scientific description of an empirical practice, for example, allows the reinforcement of appropriation regimes. This results in an increase in its commercial value. As Raugel (1993) points out for scientific agreements in the biotechnology field, the capacity to identify molecular and genetic structures resulting from fundamental research is a key element in cooperative research agreements. It accelerates the introduction of a commercial dimension in a sphere where it initially had no place. The agreement then validates *ex ante* the anticipated results.

The same imprecisions and disparities remain. There is the difficulty in estimating a virtual market. As evident strategic elements are also present, reference is implicitly made to market prices. For example, in the application of biotechnology, and in the food or pharmaceuticals industries, current evaluations vary from one to one hundred, depending upon the experts consulted (Byé and Tournier, 1992). Here, as with the production factors, the simple conclusion – even the simple announcement – of an agreement exerts, by anticipation, an effect on the prices of the new products or processes that might eventually result from the research agreement. In the domain of human genetics the prospects for application of gene therapy to vaccines or to medical tests seem to require an *ex ante* privatization of known, but non-described gene sequences (Pracontal, 1994). By these means, virtual values or prices are given to them. Similarly, in the domain of plant genetics the appropriation of these common goods is made possible by the development of generic sciences, and they precede the potential uses. *Ex ante* and *ex post* values constitute the limits, the commercial reference points between which the price system will be built.

PROGRESSIVE ALIGNMENT WITH MARKET PRICES

The fact remains that even if implicit reference to these values – which materialize, for example, during the early appropriation of expertise or the protection of intermediate results – is made very early on in the practice of scientific cooperation agreements, the references to explicit prices are introduced only progressively. This bears witness to two phenomena: the construction of a platform of scientific and technical references among the partners, on one hand, and the transformation of the scientific object into a technical object, on the other. These movements are not linear. They can be delayed, accelerated or inflected by the intervention of the partners and the authorities (see the section on the scientific sphere and price systems below).

The values initially allocated to the implementation of the agreement will evolve over time. At the commercial level, the production factors mobilized by the agreement will acquire their own values. These will progressively change, which will distinguish them from the values allocated at the beginning in relation to existing markets. The market for biological diagnostics, considered originally in terms of the prices of generic reagents and chemical additives, acquires, for example, its specificity and its autonomy concerning prices, first, as the instrumentation market needing such reagents develops, and subsequently as the market for medical diagnosis develops. Aligned with the remuneration of engineers or technicians in large economic sectors, the salaries of specialists in genetic engineering are defined in the same way: first as the specialization becomes known only among research organizations; then by society as a whole. Identical developments can be noted for equipment – instrumentation plays an important role in structuring the price system – or for financing systems. Thus the price system is built progressively according to the results obtained. It confers a value on each of the assets mobilized. It is first produced by the initial agreements, then the research agreements themselves, and finally the institutions that implement them.

But this price system which is built by close reference to the values currently ruling competitive markets is exposed to important deformations. For example, this phenomenon means that all start-up industries, as they grow, anticipate a buyout of their assets by industrial or financial groups for a price which is at least equal to, if not greater than, that allocated for the constitution of its original capital. This implicit and current reference to the stock market, a source of speculation, introduces an important bias in the references to market price systems: assets will be overvalued in order to compensate for the risks taken at the beginning by the promoters of the agreement. In their analysis of agreements between biotechnology firms, Barbanti, Gambardella and Orsenigo (1992) underline the fact that the agreements are being concluded earlier. This is to avoid making reference to a particular technological or commercial development which could compromise the agreement itself by prematurely introducing commercial values. Operating originally under specific price systems, the agreements induce, by proximity and over a period of time, a new price system, leading to reconciliation of the excessively high and low prices of each partner.

THE SCIENTIFIC SPHERE AND PRICE SYSTEMS

The introduction of references to market prices profoundly transforms the content, the functioning and the forms of the agreements (Barley, Freeman and Hybels, 1991). Their use confers a special role on all the partners, particularly on the authorities, which can regulate or modify these references. Any regulation will play an essential role in the forms of cooperation, and beyond that, even when cooperative research agreements already exist.

The Opposing Interventions of the Authorities

Governments participate in the determination of the limits between which the price systems will be implemented. They do this by being in charge of the public budgets allocated to financing scientific agreements and by being responsible for introducing rules for the validation and valorization of results. They also contribute, by reinforcing appropriation procedures, to the elimination of non-commercial rules and behaviour. Thus they limit the sphere in which scientific cooperation agreements develop.

The first type of intervention is periodically contradicted by a second type of intervention which consists in redefining the range of social needs. This reintroduces references into the agreements that lie outside the market. By assuming this role, public authorities open new prospects for development in scientific cooperation agreements.

Through their regulatory and economic initiatives (Rip and Nederhof, 1986), public authorities contribute to accelerating the transformation of non-targeted research results into technical objects (Chakrabarti and Weisenfeld, 1989). Exclusivity concerning information, and limitations concerning publication, secrets and patents thus tend to interfere with the original operating rules of the agreement (Cassier, 1992; Guignard, 1992). Even before the early evaluation of research results has been completed, appropriation has already been established. Safeguard clauses are often imposed by the competitive sector, which profoundly modify the spirit of the agreement. Thus the scientific sphere abandons some of its essential advantages, such as the free circulation of information, which are a source of knowledge enrichment, and also a way to validate generated results.

By periodically widening the fields of knowledge to take account of the concern of the authorities about public goods such as health care, safety, communication of information, or rational management of the environment, governments loosen the stranglehold of competition and of prices. In this way, they can reactivate fields where non-targeted agreements develop, or reinforce the search for generic references (OTA 1984; Pisano et al. 1988), to reduce the constraints exercised by market price systems. In other words, the direct or indirect intervention of governments in price systems generates either an increase or a reduction of the number of cooperative research agreements. Such intervention also plays an essential role in the forms of organization of interactions between partners involved in such agreements.

Maintaining Systems outside the Market: the Role of the Partners

The absence, at the beginning, of references to market prices encourages, in Aoki's (1988) words, the establishment of a fluid, flexible, *ad hoc* link between the partners. This increases the efficacy of cooperation over time (Cassier, 1992). The absence of references to prices allows progressive forms of organization to develop that are designed to modify the contents of the agreements to be adopted. Sequential and decentralized, these types of organization can encourage a scientific synergy within a context open to different approaches and histories. They are in contrast to other more functional forms of organization that are constrained by market variables that seek to converge on a well-defined object in a specific length of time, and are the results of different practices and cultures (Tidd, 1993; Hakanson, 1993).

Of course, it would be natural to consider that the first type of organization precedes the second, and that there are sequences of logical transition. In fact, these types of organization combine among themselves according to the impact exercised by market variables on each production factor, on one hand, and on the commercial applications of research activities, on the other. Thus, the more the price of production factors mobilized in the scientific agreement possesses a recognized market value, the more clearly the prospects of commercial outlines are defined, and the more the terms of the agreements have to be formalized, even put on a contractual basis. Inversely, the less the real or anticipated price system is known, the less need for a formal indication of operating procedures and responsibility sharing.

The agreement's partners determine their behaviour by placing greater or lesser importance on the existing price system. They adopt behavioural patterns of openness to scientific exchange by minimizing references to prices. Usually this is done so that private firms can make irrecoverable investments in the agreement, rather than to improve its immediate competitiveness or to widen its own scientific horizons by observing other methods and approaches.

The use of prices will attempt to create a hierarchical structure designed to protect a firm's own in-house research, and a matrix structure designed to enhance the partner's input.

A behavioural pattern of openness can be developed for public partners, this time by maximizing references to market prices in order to introduce new themes through the agreement, or to improve their social credibility as partners by being engaged in research with industrial recognition. In this way governments and non-profit organizations (Pracontal, 1994) in particular can obtain large budgetary allocations whose final use remains relatively free.

The progressive transformation of the contents of the agreements·and the procedures which regulate them continues at the same pace as the modification of the price systems. This transformation depends on maintaining flexible and porous barriers that would normally limit the boundaries of the agreement. The porosity of these barriers enables the partners to profit from the flow of information resulting from the diversity of practices and networks. The degree of porosity of these barriers cannot be dictated, but develops as the intentions and interests of the collaborators are defined, and as the uses and objectives of the research are collectivized (Hâusler, Hohn and Lütz, 1994).

CONCLUSION

The models of innovation evolving from networking and the linkages between science, technology and the market, have led to confusion of research activities with their technological development and applications. The scientific sphere has its specificity and builds its objectives progressively, but this reduces as the pressure exercised by the price systems increases. However, this pressure is neither homogeneous nor continuous. It varies according to the period and the fields of activity. It also varies depending on the behavioural patterns of the partners who form the research consortium, and especially on their culture in the face of risks and uncertainty.

Public authorities, either as partners in the agreements through budgetary support, or through their involvement as public research organizations, act as regulators of appropriation mechanisms for the protection and the transfer of results. Thus they exercise a major role in the transformation of scientific objects into technical objects. They also play an important role by periodically redefining social needs which constitute new territories for setting up research cooperation agreements.

As agreements of this kind are external to the firm, they play an increasing role (2–3 per cent increase/year) in OECD countries. The distinction between research and development might help us to understand private and public interactions.

REFERENCES

Aoki, M. (1991), *Economie Japonaise: Information, motivations, marchandage*, Paris: Economica.

Bach, L., Ledoux, M., Magnaval, R. and Pero, H. (1994), 'The economic effect of public/private co-operative research', *Futures*, **26**(8), 846–951.

Barbanti, P., Gambardella, A. and Orsenigo, L. (1992), 'The evolution of the forms of collaboration in biotechnology', paper presented at the colloquium: 'Les accords de coopération pour la recherche–développement en biotechnologie', Serd/Inra, Grenoble, October.

Barley, S., Freeman, J. and Hybels, R. (1991), 'Strategic alliances in commercial biotechnology', Tenth Ecos Colloquium, Vienna, Austria.

Byé, P. (1995), 'Managing R.D. Technology trajectories relationships: a sectorial approach', Ninth World Productivity Congress, Istanbul, June.

Byé, P. and Magnaval, R. (1995), 'Recherche coopérative: concurrence ou collaboration', *Biofutur*, February, 33–6.

Byé, P. and Tournier, J. (1992), 'Evaluation du programme mobilisateur français "Essor des biotechnologies"', Rapport du Comité National d'Évaluation de la Recherche, Paris.

Callon, M. (1994), 'La recherche académique est-elle rentable?', *Libération*, 27 October.

Cassier, M. (1992), 'Contrats et coopération de recherche entre université et industrie: le cas du Laboratoire de Technologie Enzymatique de l'Université de Compiègne', communication presented at the colloquium: 'Les accords de coopération pour la recherche–développement en biotechnologie', Grenoble, October.

Chakrabarti, A. and Weisenfeld, U. (1989), 'Marketing and R.&D. strategies for biotechnology firms in the U.S.A.', *Technology Analysis and Strategic Management*, **1**(4), 357–66.

Faulkner, W. and Senker, J. (1994), 'Making sense of diversity: public – private sector research linkage in three technologies', *Research Policy*, **23**(6), November, 673–96.

Gaffard, J.L., Bruno, S., Longhi, C. and Quéré, M. (1993), 'Cohérence et diversité des systèmes d'innovation en Europe. Rapport de synthèse', European Commission Programme, MONITOR/FAST, *Science, Technology and Community Cohesion*, **19**.

Gambardella, A. and Orsenigo, L. (1993), 'The evolution of collaborative relationships among firms in biotechnology', European Commission Programme MONITOR/FAST, *Science, Technology and Community Cohesion*, **23–24**.

Guignard, Ph. (1992), 'Analyse et présentation de l'accord de recherche Eureka sur les semences artificielles', paper presented at the colloquium: 'Les accords de coopération pour la recherche–développement en biotechnologie', Grenoble, October.

Hagendorn, J., and Shakenraad, J. (1990), 'Interfirm partnership and cooperative strategies in core technologies', in Freeman, C. and Soete, L. (eds), *New explorations in the economics of technological change*, London: Pinter Publishers.

Hakanson, L. (1993), 'Managing cooperative research and development: partner selection and contract design', *R&D Management*, **23**(4), 273–85.

Hâusler, J., Hohn, H.W. and Lütz, S. (1994), 'Contingencies of innovative networks: a case study of successful interfirm R/D collaboration', *Research Policy*, **23**, 47–66.

Levêque, F., Bonazzi, C. and Quental, C. (1993), 'Dynamics of cooperation and industrial R&D: First insights into the black box', paper presented to ASEAT Conference: 'Technology Collaboration: Networks Institution and States', Manchester, UK.

OTA (Office of Technological Assessment) (1984), *Commercial biotechnology: an international analysis*, Washington, DC: US Congress.

Pisano, G.P., Shan, W. and Teece, D.J. (1988), 'Joint ventures and collaboration in the biotechnology industry', in Mowery, D.C. (ed.), *Industrial collaborative ventures in U.S. Manufacturing*, Cambridge, MA: Ballinger.

Pracontal, M. de (1994), 'Génétique: la ruée vers l'or', *Nouvel Observateur*, June, 90–93.

Rip, A. and Nederhof, A.J. (1986), 'Between dirigism and laissez faire – Effects of implementing the science policy priority for biotechnology in the Netherlands', *Research Policy*, **15**, 253–68.

Tassone, L. (1993), 'La rationalité économique des accords de coopération en R&D – Ecole d'Eté "Economie des Institutions"', mimeo, September.

Tidd, J. (1993), 'Technological innovation, organization linkages and strategic degrees of freedom', *Technology Analysis and Strategic Management*, **5** (3), 273–93.

4. International technology development structures in multinational firms

Vittorio Chiesa

INTRODUCTION

The internationalization of R&D is a recent phenomenon. In the past, multinational firms have tended to keep their technology development activities in the home country or concentrated in a few locations. In the last decade we have witnessed an increasing dispersion of R&D laboratories in foreign countries and the birth of global R&D, that is, the management of laboratories located in different countries. Statistical data show the growing relevance of international R&D. The amount of the R&D budget that firms spend abroad has increased and in several countries has become a significant percentage of total R&D expenditure: 17 per cent in German industrial firms (Brockhoff and von Boehmer, 1992), 23 per cent in Swedish multinationals (Hakanson and Nobel, 1989) (data refer to the late 1980s). The figure for US companies, according to a National Science Foundation (NSF) survey, is lower, at about 10 per cent. It is even lower in the case of Japanese companies, at less than 5 per cent. Nevertheless, in each country foreign R&D expenditure has grown more rapidly than domestic. The NSF survey shows that R&D investments abroad by US companies grew by 33 per cent in late 1980s, while in the same period domestic investment grew by only 6 per cent. When analysing the first Fortune 500 companies, Pearce and Singh (1992) found that, between 1970 and 1990, 65 per cent of the new laboratories were located abroad. This trend also involves the Japanese firms: in the 1980s, only three of the 26 new labs have been located in the home country.

The aim in this chapter is to understand the motivation for companies to globalize their R&D. It is based on the empirical results of a study of six multinational companies operating in the telecommunications industry, in particular the switching equipment manufacturing business. Studying companies operating in the same business helps one to understand whether there are factors that force them to globalize R&D activities at both industry and firm level.

GLOBAL R&D: BACKGROUND RESEARCH

The main factors which have traditionally been identified as reasons explaining the need for decentralizing R&D activities can be grouped into two broad categories: those of demand and those of supply (Granstrand et al., 1992).

On the demand side, the relevant factors behind decentralization decisions are those of technology transfer between headquarters and subsidiaries, the need to access foreign markets, the need to improve a firm's capability to respond to specific requirements of local markets, and the need to increase the proximity of product development activities to key customers (Hirschey and Caves, 1981; Granstrand et al., 1992).

On the supply side, the relevant factors are the access to new or emerging technologies, the recruitment of qualified technical personnel, and the access to entrepreneurial and/or technical talents. Where these last have been concentrated in geographical pockets of scientific and technological knowledge, firms have had to decentralize their R&D units to tap into foreign scientific infrastructures (Hewitt, 1980; Pearce, 1989; Hamel and Prahalad, 1993).

Several other factors have been suggested as reasons for decentralizing R&D, such as political factors and image. Political factors are related to the fact that local governments place pressures on companies to increase the local technological content of production. In some instances, companies are forced to localize technical activities to facilitate interactions with governmental bodies. In other cases, globalizing R&D helps enhance a firm's competitive image.

Earlier empirical studies have shown that centralization determinants have strongly prevailed and firms have had a low propensity to decentralize their R&D activity.[1] Very few companies have dispersed their R&D units to be able to access foreign scientific, technical or educational environments. Even when a division of labour in R&D has occurred, it has seldom taken place between home country laboratories and foreign R&D units. Most global R&D units play a supporting role within the innovation processes of multinational firms. Motivations to decentralize a unit have essentially been to provide local firm functions with technical support, to adapt products developed in the home country to the requirements of local demand (Pearce, 1989; Casson, 1991), to support competition in foreign countries, and reasons connected with politics or image. In conclusion, we can state that, in the past, foreign R&D units have played a peripheral role within the overall R&D process of multinational companies.[2]

In the last two decades, globalization of firms' activities has been increasing. As part of the process of globalization we have witnessed an increasing internationalization of R&D activities and the growing relevance of foreign R&D within the overall process of innovation in multinational companies.

Pearce (1989) found that 'overseas R&D far from being residual or peripheral activity, now covers a heterogeneous range of activities designed to fulfill variously clearly perceived objectives', and that 'R&D is taking place among the key internationalised functions'. Increasingly, there are cases of division of labour between centralized and overseas R&D, and foreign laboratories make a distinctive contribution to programmes centrally coordinated.

Many reasons have been put forward to explain the growing importance of foreign R&D. First, the nature of the technological innovation process has changed, and this affects organizational and location factors within research operations. For example, a division of labour is taking place on a worldwide basis in knowledge production:

> New technologies and the specialised talent that produces them will continue to develop locally in 'pockets of innovation' around the world. Nurturing those technologies, uprooting them, and cross-fertilising them for commercialisation and global distribution will continue to be major challenges in technology management'. (Perrino and Tipping, 1989)

In other words, the increasing specialization of skills and capabilities required to innovate in certain technological fields has meant that these specialized resources are increasingly found concentrated only in certain regions of the world. If some firm needs to access these resources, it has to be where they are found, irrespective where this is (Sakakibara and Westney, 1992). Accessing technological sources can be done in a variety of ways (alliances, agreements, licensing in, and so on). Decentralizing R&D units enables companies to learn more effectively and to internalize knowledge absorbed from external sources more quickly. Locating a unit abroad creates absorptive capacity locally, and defines the value of knowledge which is available at a given site.[3]

Second, time-to-market is increasingly important as source of competitive advantage. Competing on time implies that to be locally responsive and to access local pockets of knowledge, firms have to be in foreign countries. Accelerating the process of learning and knowledge absorption from external sources allows time to be saved. Again, tapping geographically dispersed knowledge sources can be undertaken in a variety of ways: scanning technology, strategic alliances, joint ventures, cross-licensing. Managers are increasingly realizing that this process can be most effectively undertaken by local technology development units. These then act as insiders within the local technology system and thus speed up the learning process (Sakakibara and Westney, 1992; De Meyer, 1993).

Third, the intra-organizational linkages required during the technological innovation process mean that R&D units need to interact with other functions of the firm that are subject to the internationalization process (Prahalad and

Doz, 1987; Pavitt, 1990 and 1991). R&D is thus located outside the home country to increase its proximity to firms' functions which have been and are increasingly internationalized.

De Meyer (1993) has summarized these points in one proposition. In his study on international R&D in 14 multinationals, he has suggested that decentralization of R&D activities is undertaken to enhance and accelerate the process of technical learning and that this explains why

> companies go through the pain of creating an international network. Learning about customer needs, monitoring the hot spots of the field to quickly learn about most recent developments, and having access to resources (engineers, scientists) which can process this information quickly is the objective of the internationalisation process.

This also explains why firms increasingly commit themselves to integrate their R&D activities worldwide:

> The outcome of the learning process for an organization is knowledge that is distributed across the organization ... If one applies this to the technical learning process, it appears that exposure to sources of knowledge in different countries is important but that, to be effective, one has to create mechanisms on an international scale to diffuse, validate and integrate the new knowledge across the whole network of laboratories'.

This suggests that firms tend to take a global view of their operations, and that R&D processes are shaped to be globally effective.

Other studies suggest that companies are now paying more attention to managing and coordinating their dispersed R&D capabilities and efforts than in the past. Hakanson and Zander (1988), studying four Swedish multinationals, conclude that firms are moving towards an 'integrated network model', characterized by tight and complex controls between parent company and subsidiaries, and a higher subsidiary involvement in the formulation and implementation of innovation strategies. Other research shows that successful companies are those able to develop and manage different ways of conceiving and generating new products, processes and administrative systems. This requires them to capitalize on the resources of the various subsidiaries, to integrate the resources and capabilities of the different units, and to exploit the uniqueness of the resources and the learning process that takes place at each unit to enable innovations to be exploited worldwide (Bartlett and Ghoshal, 1989).

Organizationally, companies are challenged to go beyond the traditional models of innovation processes. Models of central innovation are where centralized resources of the home country are used to generate an innovation afterwards exploited worldwide; local innovation is where national subsidiaries use their own resources and capabilities to create innovations responding to the local needs. It has been suggested that the innovation processes in the transnational solution tend to fall into two broad categories: locally exploited and globally linked:

> The first capitalises on the resources and entrepreneurship of individual national subsidiaries but leverages them to create innovation for exploitation on a world-wide basis. The second links the resources and capabilities of diverse worldwide units in the company, at both headquarters and subsidiary level, to create and implement innovations on a joint basis. (Bartlett and Ghoshal, 1989).

Successful companies are those able to allocate different roles to the various units of the company, exploit the learning process which takes place at each location, and to create an organization able to exploit the differentiation among units.

R&D is now deployed in foreign countries more frequently than in the past, but foreign R&D units are changing their role within the overall process of technological innovation of multinational firms. They take part in the R&D process by contributing to programmes centrally coordinated and produce innovations that are marketed across different countries.

We can therefore conclude that the process of R&D globalization has changed quite strongly in the last few years in the following ways:

- there is a greater propensity to decentralize technical activities abroad (Pearce, 1989; Westney, 1990; De Meyer, 1993);
- the strategic relevance of foreign technical activities has increased (Pearce and Singh, 1992; De Meyer, 1993);
- the process of technological innovation within multinational firms has increasingly involved foreign units (Bartlett and Ghoshal, 1989; De Meyer, 1992).

These trends apply to firms in different industries, especially those which are technology-intensive. Most empirical studies in this area have been conducted on the basis of cross-industry analysis (De Meyer, 1992; Pearce and Singh, 1992; Brockhoff and von Boehmer, 1992; Hakanson and Nobel, 1989). However, the discussion about the factors that cause firms to globalize with their R&D raises several questions. In the past, causes of globalization have been related to industry factors, such as market differentiation (which requires firms to go abroad with technical capacities to match the local demand requirements) and the existence of geographical areas where specific technological resources are concentrated and need to be accessed. More recent contributions have emphasized the role of learning as a key to explain the globalization of R&D. Decentralizing R&D units is viewed as an alternative way to access external sources of knowledge when compared with other forms of external acquisition. Accessing external sources of knowledge through a pure market transaction or a certain form of agreement reduces the cost of technology development and is less costly than developing technical knowledge in-house. It does not, however, ensure that knowledge is appropriately absorbed, assimilated and internalized, and ultimately applied to commercial ends. To do this, firms need to have a wholly owned structure accessing the external technological environment and growing the internal resources.

This suggests that firms, although operating in the same business, may be subject to different internationalization pressures. The importance of a certain technology or type of knowledge may vary from firm to firm according to their specific characteristics. When R&D is central to a firm's learning process, and given that learning is firm-specific, it can be argued that the process of R&D globalization is also driven by firm-specific factors, such as strategy, technological competences and group diversification.

To test the hypothesis that firm-specific factors are at least equally important as industry factors in explaining the globalization of a firm's R&D, an empirical study was conducted on a sample of six firms operating in the telecommunications industry, in particular the switching equipment manufacturing business.

THE EMPIRICAL STUDY

The six multinational firms chosen for the study were Alcatel, AT&T, Ericsson, NEC, Northern Telecom and Siemens. Data were collected through direct interviews with R&D managers, industry experts and consultants, and through company publications (such as annual reports and company brochures) and specialized journals. Table 4.1 summarizes the data on the profile of the sample companies.

The focus of the research was the switching equipment business. This represents a segment within the telecommunications industry. Table 4.2 shows the activities of the sample companies by segment. It can be seen that AT&T and Northern Telecom are vertically integrated downstream into telecommunications services while Siemens and NEC are vertically integrated upstream into semiconductors and basic electronic technologies. Ericsson and Alcatel concentrate on the businesses of telecommunications systems and related products such as cables and transmission components.

Table 4.3 shows the data on the R&D activities of the sample companies carried out in foreign countries. It can be seen that the propensity to go abroad with R&D varies strongly from firm to firm. This raises the question

Table 4.1   Sample company description (1993)

Company	Turnover (M $)	Employees (number)	Market share (%)	Turnover from foreign activities (%)
AT&T	67 156	308 911	20.5	10
Alcatel	27 599	196 500	18.9	75
Northern Telecom	8 148	60 293	17.9	47
Ericsson	8 083	69 597	11.4	87
Siemens	50 381	391 000	8.5	30
NEC	33 176	147 910	6.0	n.a.

Note: n.a. = not available

Sources: *Fortune*, Dataquest.

Table 4.2   Business lines of the sample companies

	AT&T	Alcatel	Ericsson	Northern Telecom	Siemens	NEC
Telecommunications services	X			X		
Telecommunications systems (switching equipments)	X	X	X	X	X	X
Transmission systems		X	X	X		
Cables		X	X	X		
Semiconductors and electronics					X	X

Source: Dataquest, Frost & Sullivan.

of why firms operating in the same business areas globalize their R&D so differently. The types of R&D units located abroad also vary strongly from firm to firm. The foreign R&D activities can be classified according to the content of technological activities into: research for new switching technologies and production techniques, design of new switching equipment, trial-and-error phase to adjust the new product, engineering and manufacturing ramp-up, and feature proliferation (which mostly relies on the development

Table 4.3   R&D data of the sample companies

Company	R&D expenses (% of turnover)	R&D personnel	Foreign R&D personnel	No. of foreign laboratories	No. of countries involved
AT&T	4.9	23 000	230	1	1
Alcatel	11.9	18 000	10 800	16	14
Northern Telecom	11.6	7 200	2 376	9	6
Ericsson	15.4	8 600	2 580	18	18
Siemens	10.8	15 000	4 950	4	4
NEC	6.5	n.a.	120	3	2

Note: n.a. = not available

Source: Dataquest, *Business Week*.

of software packages). The first activity can be classified as research, while the other activities are part of the development phase.

A third category consists of adaptive units, small operations which adapt products developed elsewhere to local demand characteristics and also provide technical service to other firm functions and to local customers. In addition to the three major R&D tasks (technical support, product development and research), must be added the category of technology scanning units (aimed to monitor the technological progress and/or market evolution in foreign countries). Although these units do not carry out actual technical activities, they are integrated in the global R&D structure of the firm and have to be considered a part of it; the findings make reference to this type of unit. It does not seem useful to provide a table giving the number of units for each type as it is actually difficult to make a distinction between R&D units according to their technical activities. Several units could not be defined clearly as doing pure research or pure development. Moreover, several foreign technical units carry out technological activities for different business lines. It is therefore difficult to separate the type of activity done in the switching equipment business. However, reference will be made to the classification proposed in order to comment on and discuss the international R&D structure of the sample firms.

Significant data on the number of researchers of the five largest laboratories in each firm are shown in Table 4.4.

Finally, the localization of foreign technical activities by geographical area is shown in Table 4.5.

Table 4.4   Size of the largest foreign R&D laboratories (number of researchers)

Company	Laboratory 1	Laboratory 2	Laboratory 3	Laboratory 4	Laboratory 5
AT&T	230	n.s.	n.s.	n.s.	n.s.
Alcatel	3718	1992	1380	889	839
Northern Telecom	1550	250	250	n.a.	n.a.
Ericsson	500	500	416	n.a.	n.a.
Siemens	3300	650	500	500	n.s.
NEC	50	30	n.a.	n.s.	n.s.

Note: n.s. = not significant; n.a. = not available

Source: elaboration on annual report data, Frost & Sullivan, Northern Business Information, A.D. Little.

Table 4.5   Geographical presence of the R&D activities of the sample companies

Company	Europe	America	Far East	Australia
AT&T	*	*		
Alcatel	*	*		'
Northern Telecom	*	*		
Ericsson	*	*	*	*
Siemens	*	*		
NEC	*	*	*	

THE EMPIRICAL FINDINGS

The findings show that with the internationalization of the R&D activities firms behave differently. Three clusters can be identified. The first comprises two North American firms, which show a low propensity to go abroad with their R&D units. Their business is mainly in the home country or in the North American area (only 10 per cent of the turnover of AT&T comes from foreign activities; in the case of Northern Telecom the figure is 47 per cent, but if the

US market is considered as part of the domestic market the figure is 19 per cent).

In terms of R&D, AT&T has only one laboratory abroad (in Holland) and adapts products to the European markets. Northern Telecom has many more laboratories abroad. One is quite large (1500 people) and is located in the USA. The others are smaller (less than 250 people) and are mainly of the adaptive type. They are located in both North America (the USA and Mexico) and Europe. Thus these two firms tend to keep their R&D centralized in the home country or in the North American area, and to disperse small adaptive units abroad.

In the case of AT&T, the penetration into foreign markets is pursued through agreements and alliances with local companies, such as Olivetti, Philips, Telefonica, Italtel, Cable and Wireless in Europe, and Ricoh, Mitsubishi and NEC in Japan. Electronic technologies acquired externally until a few years ago are now developed internally, a consequence of the acquisition of NCR, which has relevant competences in computing.

The tendency in Northern Telecom is to foster foreign R&D activities. The firm has recognized that the adaptations which have been developed at certain subsidiaries could be marketed across different countries. Each geographical area may raise particular technical problems. This is because the communication infrastructure is country-specific, and users are accustomed to certain features not used or diffused elsewhere. As innovation stimuli often result in country-specific developments, the country laboratories are forced to develop specific technological skills. In a global context, this means that the dispersed units may provide ideas, skills and capabilities that need to be integrated globally to benefit from them. In other words, as needs are country-specific, local laboratories need to be locally responsive; on the other hand, local laboratories' efforts have to be coordinated to exploit their developments on a global basis. This forces firms to increase foreign R&D activities. A relevant case of this kind is that of the Mexican subsidiary which developed product adaptations that had been commercialized in other countries. Given that the telecommunications infrastructure does not allow the technical solutions developed in the USA and Canada to be used in other countries, specific developments have to be undertaken by the subsidiary to overcome technical barriers. The technical results achieved have produced new technical solutions for products to be marketed in both Canada and the USA.

The second cluster comprises Siemens and NEC, which show a greater propensity to go abroad. Their foreign R&D is both adaptive and pure research. On the one hand, this seems to be motivated by the need to adapt products to local needs; on the other hand, it seems driven by the need to access technical resources concentrated in foreign centres of excellence. However, the two cases are different. NEC shows a lower propensity to go abroad with its research. It is only recently that it has started to decentralize its research units, and so locate small research centres close to centres of excellence in Europe (especially the UK) and the USA. The aim is to learn how to do basic research rather than do basic research itself. The research activities carried out in these units are in bioelectronics, artificial intelligence, development of new techniques for software development and engineering, and neural computing. These are areas where telecommunications companies are exploring potential applications in their industry with a long-term perspective.

Siemens has decentralized research laboratories to a larger extent than NEC. It has established a large laboratory of 3300 people in the USA for silicon technologies, chip design and electronic technologies research. Its organizational structure tends to exploit technical capabilities dispersed at the various subsidiaries in Europe and North America. In each technological field or business line, it has a world competence centre which is globally responsible for research programmes and coordinates works carried out in several other locations. This enables it to exploit research group capabilities located in different countries which have a strong technical background in several specific fields. At the same time, the company can coordinate, at a global level, research activities in each technical area. For example, the Italian subsidiary is the world competence centre in transmission systems based on microwave technologies and stations for cellular phoning.

For this structure to work it is necessary to create forms of interdependence among units. These then are competence centres in certain technological fields, and operate as contributors in other areas. This creates a reciprocal interdependence which ensures that units contribute actively in programmes managed by the other units. Keeping each unit committed in different technological fields facilitates the exploitation of development activities based on the integration of these different technologies.

The third cluster is that of Ericsson and Alcatel, which have a large amount of their R&D dispersed abroad in Europe, the USA, the Far East and Australia. Their global R&D structure comprises a number of laboratories that operate as local units, that is, they develop new products for the local market. The structure is centrally coordinated to avoid duplication of activities and operates globally to exploit the R&D efforts conducted at the various sites. This leads to the integration and coordination of the R&D work carried out at different locations, and establishes mechanisms to facilitate joint development activities among the different subsidiaries. Temporary international teams are created with an exchange of technical personnel among units. This approach enables the acquisition of market knowledge at the various units and the exchange of knowledge within the group to take place.

Given that firms are pursuing a strategy based on the capability to offer customized products to their users, market knowledge is fundamental to sustaining this type of competition. Moreover, it is increasingly necessary to bring product development activities nearer to users themselves. Therefore, the need to locate product development activities abroad, close to key customers, and the need to create a structure which avoids duplication and ensures the exchange of technical results among units, have to be matched.

Although these international R&D structures are similar, and support the integration of the activities dispersed, they are actually slightly different. The integration of the activities on a global basis is more advanced at Ericsson than at Alcatel. Differences between the two structures mirror the different processes behind their creation. The international expansion of Alcatel has taken place mainly through acquisitions (the European activities of ITT, Telettra and Rockwell), whereas Ericsson has had a global attitude since its foundation. In the case of Alcatel, the integrated global structure is the result of a long-term strategy aimed at rationalizing the technological capabilities dispersed.

Because of the small size of the home country market, Ericsson has always had a strong propensity to go abroad. International expansion has taken place mainly through internal growth. This historical heritage has created a managerial attitude that is globally oriented rather than locally oriented, and a culture strongly based on cross-border integration and global coordination of efforts.

For both Alcatel and Ericsson the strong orientation to market-driven development means that few research activities are carried out in-house. In the case of Ericsson, research activities are carried out in cooperation with academic and research institutions. In the case of Alcatel with SGS-Thomson, basic technologies are acquired in the market, or through alliances with suppliers.

FACTORS AFFECTING THE FIRM'S GLOBAL R&D

To summarize, there are multiple factors which encourage telecommunications companies to go abroad. They can be grouped into three major categories: market adaptation, technological knowledge supply, and market knowledge supply.

Market Adaptation

The first factor which forces firms to decentralize their R&D activities is the need to adapt their products to local markets. These needs are technical reasons (the specific characteristics of the telecommunications infrastructure of the various countries and the particular features the customers are used to), the pressures of local government to expand technical activities at subsidiaries, and the need to take part in the processes of standardization of that country or region. Each firm must have decentralized adaptive units or local technological capabilities in order to respond to local market requirements. Moreover, the proliferation of local features requires market differentiation. This in turn means that firms have to disperse technical activities so as to be locally present and responsive. From a technological perspective, competences in software development, on which the features of a switching equipment depend, will be crucial for future competition. This is one reason why Northern Telecom goes abroad more readily than AT&T. It is considered to be the world leader in software engineering and to adapt its products to local demand requirements more easily.

Technical Knowledge Supply

Technology supply is another reason why companies go abroad with wholly owned R&D labs. Siemens and NEC more readily decentralize R&D units so as to carry out research activities close to world technological centres of excellence. Their specific aims vary from unit to unit and from firm to firm. Siemens has a much stronger tradition in managing international operations, and some of its foreign units play a key role within the overall R&D structure of the firm. Having several foreign locations enables the firm to create the conditions that facilitate the exploitation of synergies arising from the convergence and the integration of computing, semiconductors and telecommunication technologies. NEC's international R&D seems to be at an embryonic stage. Nevertheless, the aim is to gain knowledge not available in the home country in both technical and managerial (how to manage and conduct a research unit) terms.

Market Knowledge Supply

Technological capabilities that are decentralized also bring the product development process nearer to key customers and lead-users. This provides a stronger market orientation and quicker technical problem solving. Alcatel and Ericsson have widely dispersed their technological capabilities for this reason.

Although each firm is subject to these pressures, the way they behave is very different. The propensity to decentralize R&D units and adopt an international R&D structure varies from firm to firm. There are a number of firm-specific factors which influence global R&D decisions. These can be grouped into three main categories: firms' competences, degree of vertical integration, and the firm's history, international expansion and administrative heritage.

Firms' competences

The firm's distinctive competences seem strongly to affect the type of foreign R&D. For this purpose, two clusters of companies can be identified. There are four companies that are strongly market-oriented and aim to build competences on their capabilities to enable them to develop customized equipment. These are AT&T, Alcatel, Northern Telecom and Ericsson. The key factor for them is to link product development activities with customer needs, and then to gain market knowledge to be embodied into new products. In terms of R&D locations, this means going abroad with technical capabilities, increasing the proximity to key customers and relevant users. The other two firms, Siemens and NEC, are much more technology-oriented. Their competences are based on their technological capabilities to exploit the convergence of electronic and telecommunications technologies. This has two major consequences. First, telecommunications R&D is carried out in units that also carry out R&D in the electronics field. The communication and interaction among research groups allow them to exploit the synergies from doing research in both these fields. Second, they tend to develop basic technologies of their own, and to go abroad to access technological knowledge and to learn from external technological centres of excellence. Establishing wholly owned units abroad close to these centres of excellence allows them to internalize and process more quickly the knowledge gained from external sources. The acquisition of NCR by AT&T could suggest that they tend to enlarge their competences in the basic technologies used in telecommunications. Other market-oriented firms acquire electronic technologies from external suppliers through markets or temporary alliances.

Competences play a central role in determining the type of R&D or the content of R&D decentralized. Firms decentralize their R&D units in those activities which contribute to their competence-building process. These activities are considered crucial for sustaining long-term competition: access to external sources is a key to acquiring knowledge, but on the other hand it is also crucial to ensure that this knowledge is gained, internalized and processed quickly. This can only be done by decentralizing R&D units. Market-oriented firms tend to decentralize development labs to increase the proximity of their units to local sources of market knowledge, whereas technology-oriented firms tend to decentralize technical development activities to gain technological knowledge. This increases the proximity of their units to technical knowledge sources and facilitates the exploitation of technological convergence of different technologies at different locations. Firms that do not focus their competence building process on the capability to exploit synergies between telecommunications and electronics technologies seem to prefer other forms of technology acquisition (alliances or market transactions).

Degree of vertical integration
Another factor that affects the internationalization of R&D is the degree of vertical integration. This seems strongly to affect the propensity to decentralize R&D units and locate R&D abroad. Firms (that focus their competences on the capability to develop customized equipment) show different behaviours according to their degree of vertical integration. Firms that are vertically integrated into services are not forced to go abroad to gain market knowledge from their equipment users. Market knowledge is to a certain extent captive. This helps us to understand why Northern Telecom and AT&T do not decentralize technical units to gain market knowledge:[4] their home country demand is the most complex and technologically sophisticated. The greater propensity of Alcatel and Ericsson to decentralize their R&D can be explained by the need to gain market knowledge from external sources (typically key customers and lead users such as common carriers and public networks). Given that their home country markets are small and do not provide enough market knowledge, and their major markets may show both technical and regulatory aspects which are country-specific, a lab is needed to interact with the local system.

Firm's history, international expansion and administrative heritage
Another factor that influences the decentralization of R&D is the firm's history and administrative heritage. The decentralization of technological capabilities is the result of the propensity of a firm to disperse its activities worldwide and the firm's international expansion. Ericsson has always had a strong propensity to go abroad because its home country market is small. This historical heritage affects the dispersion of activities in two ways. On the one hand, the propensity to disperse the firm's efforts is greater; on the other hand, it is more likely that such a firm has a cross-border mentality and a managerial attitude to global orientation that enables it more easily to go abroad with new units.

The dispersion of technological activities is also the consequence of the international expansion of the firm. This takes place through the establishment of greenfield units and acquisition processes. Direct placement of a new unit abroad is the result of a firm's decision, but acquisition can be undertaken either for technical reasons, that is, to acquire the technical competences of the acquired firm, or for non-technical reasons. Thus, it may be that firms find themselves managing technical activities abroad that are the accidental consequences of acquisition processes and these duplicate each other. Firms may then be forced to rationalize their international R&D structure. This process takes time and the role of a unit may be changed both in terms of technological and geographical scope. Alcatel, for example, after the acquisition of ITT European operations, Telettra and Telefonica, has started a rationalization process aimed to create forms of specialization between its various technical units and so avoid duplications. This is a long-term process and will lead to a more efficient utilization of the firm's dispersed technical resources. In conclusion, the configuration of an international R&D structure at a given time is also the result of the firm's history, international expansion and administrative heritage.

The historical propensity to go abroad and the managerial attitude seem also to influence the international R&D structure. Firms with a stronger tradition in managing international operations and a more diffused global mentality tend to put up structures in which there is a strong integration among dispersed activities. This confirms the trend that firms are paying more attention to their coordination of foreign operations and to an integrated management of dispersed activities.

CONCLUDING REMARKS

The chapter started from the point that learning is the key issue to explain why firms go abroad with their R&D facilities. Decentralization of R&D units is an alternative way to access technological knowledge sources. It is more effective in terms of time and enhancement of technological capabilities than either ventures or agreements of different kinds. On the other hand, it can be more costly. R&D units that are decentralized to enhance learning in those knowledge areas also represent the base for developing a firm's distinctive competence. They form knowledge areas where it is important to reduce the time to absorb knowledge and enable the knowledge gained from outside sources to be integrated into the firm's knowledge base.

This strongly affects the propensity to go abroad and determines the type of R&D to be decentralized. In other words, apart from the traditional determinants of international R&D, such as market differentiation and technology supply factors, the processes of R&D internationalization can only be understood when firm-specific factors are also taken into account. This study shows that firm-specific factors strongly affect the way a firm accesses the sources of knowledge relevant to the innovation process, and ultimately the process of dispersion of its technological capabilities.

In this study, three main factors have been identified: the firm's distinctive competences, the degree of vertical integration and the firm's history and administrative heritage. Competences identify the knowledge base relevant to sustain competition over the long term and the key knowledge areas that are central to the process of competence building. In turn, the vertical integration affects the availability of sources of knowledge internal to the firm. Firms operating in the same business but with different vertical integration show a propensity to go abroad and look for other types of knowledge outside. Finally, the firm's history and historical heritage affect the degree of dispersion of firms' locations. The international attitude and the cultural orientation towards a global mentality influence the internationalization of the firm's activities.

NOTES

1. Reasons explaining the traditional low propensity to decentralize R&D activities are multiple and helpful to a better understanding of the tendency both to concentrate R&D in a limited number of units and to localize such activities in the home country. Historically, secrecy about technical information and knowledge has been considered as a reason for keeping R&D centralized in the home country (Terpstra, 1977; Rugman, 1981). A factor forcing centralization of R&D activities is the increase in costs of coordination and control associated with globalization, due to greater difficulties in communication (De Meyer and Mizushima, 1989). Another argument is related to the presence of economies of scale in R&D and to the difficulties in achieving the needed critical mass in research activities in decentralized units. Another explanation has been provided by the international product life cycle model (Vernon, 1966). All this shows that it is firm-specific technological advantages that tend to emerge from home market conditions. R&D activities are then kept centralized and located in the home country.
2. This approach to R&D globalization is the consequence of the view of R&D as an ivory tower, which has strongly prevailed in the 1960s and 1970s. The R&D function has been considered separated from the rest of the structure, a sort of black box which produces innovative ideas, and has tended to be kept in the home country (Roussel et al., 1991).
3. The concept of absorptive capacity has been introduced by Cohen and Levinthal (1990). They argue that the ability of a firm to recognize the value of new, external information, assimilate it and apply it to commercial results is critical to its innovative capabilities. This capability is labelled the firm's absorptive capacity and is largely a function of the firm's level of prior related knowledge.
4. Obviously, the low propensity to go abroad is due to a variety of reasons: first, the turnover of AT&T and Northern Telecom abroad is a small percentage of the total; second, they are located in the most developed area in this field in terms of market sophistication and complexity; and third, they are vertically integrated into services. Their penetration into foreign market tends to be export-based or, at most, through alliances.

REFERENCES

Bartlett, C.A. and Ghoshal, S. (1989), *Managing Across Borders. The Transnational Solution*, Boston, MA: Harvard Business School Press.

Brockhoff, K. and von Boehmer, A. (1992), 'Global R&D Activities of German Industrial Firms', Working Paper, Institute for Research in Innovation Management, Kiel.

Casson, M. (1991), *Global Research Strategy and International Competitiveness*, Cambridge, MA: Basil Blackwell.

Cohen, W.M. and Levinthal, D.A. (1990), 'Absorptive Capacity: A New Perspective on Learning and Innovation', *Administrative Science Quarterly*, **35**, 128–52.

De Meyer, A. (1992), 'Management of International R&D Operations', in Granstrand, O., Hakanson, L. and Sjolander, S. (eds), *Technology Management and International Business – Internationalization of R&D and Technology*, Chichester, UK: Wiley.

De Meyer, A. (1993), 'Internationalisation of R&D', ORSA/TIMS Conference on Transportation and Logistics, Chicago, May.

De Meyer, A. and Mizushima, A. (1989), 'Global R&D Management', *R&D Management*, **19** (2), 135–46.

Granstrand, O., Hakanson, A. and Sjolander, S. (1992), *Technology Management and International Business – Internationalization of R&D and Technology*, Chichester, UK: Wiley.

Hakanson, L. and Nobel, R. (1989), 'Overseas Research and Development in Swedish Multinationals', Academy of International Business Meeting, Singapore, December.

Hakanson, L. and Zander, U. (1988), 'International Management of R&D: The Swedish Experience', *R&D Management*, **18** (3), 217–26.

Hamel, G. and Prahalad, K. (1993), 'Strategy as stretch and leverage', *Harvard Business Review*, **71** (2), 75–84.

Hewitt, G. (1980), 'Research and Development Performed Abroad by U.S. Manufacturing Multinationals', *Kyklos*, **33**, 308–26.

Hirschey, R.C. and Caves, R.E. (1981), 'Research and Transfer of Technology by Multinational Enterprises', *Oxford Bulletin of Economics and Statistics*, **43**, 115–30.

Pavitt, K. (1990), 'What we Know about Strategic Management of Technology', *California Management Review*, **32** (3), 41–50.

Pavitt, K. (1991), 'Key Characteristics of the Large Innovating Firm', *British Journal of Management*, **2**.

Pearce, R.D. (1989), *The Internationalization of Research of Development by Multinational Enterprises*, University of Reading of European and International Studies, London: Macmillan Press.

Pearce, R.D. and Singh, S. (1992), *Globalizing Research and Development*, London: Macmillan Press.

Perrino, A.C. and Tipping, J.W. (1989), 'Global Management of Technology', *Research and Technology Management*, **32** (3).

Prahalad, C.K. and Doz, Y.L. (1987), *The Multinational Mission: Balancing Local Demand and Global Vision*, New York: The Free Press.

Roussel, P.A., Saad, K.N. and Erikson, T.J. (1991), *Third Generation R&D: Managing the Link to Corporate Strategy*, Boston: Harvard Business School Press.

Rugman, A.M. (1981), 'Research and Development by Multinational and Domestic Firms in Canada', *Canadian Public Policy*, **7** (4), 604–16.

Sakakibara, K. and Westney, E. (1992), 'Japan's Management of Global Innovation: Technology Management Crossing Borders', in Rosenberg, N., Landau, R. and Mowery, D. (eds), *Technology and the Wealth of Nations*, Stanford, CA: Stanford University Press.

Terpstra, V. (1977), 'International Product Policy: The Role of Foreign R&D', *Columbia Journal of Business*, **12** (4), 24–32.

Vernon, R. (1966), 'International Investment and International Trade in the Product Cycle', *Quarterly Journal of Economics*, **88**, 190–207.

Westney, D.E. (1990), 'Internal and External Linkages in the MNC: The Case of R&D Subsidiaries in Japan', in Bartlett, C.A., Doz, Y. and Hedlund, G. (eds), *Managing the Global Firm*, New York: Routledge.

5. Management of technology in multiproduct firms

Jens-Frøslev Christensen

INTRODUCTION

The basic purpose of this chapter is to re-examine the 'Chandlerian' strategy–structure theme from the perspective of accumulating, organizing and exploiting innovative/technological competences in multiproduct and multi-technology corporations.

After this introduction, the chapter is divided into five main sections. The first proposes a framework for a resource-based analysis of competences for technological innovation, for the technology base of the firm or corporation, and the coherence of the technology base. The second section discusses general tendencies in the strategy–structure development of the large diversified corporation and their (negative) implications for the coherence of the technology base. Next, the chapter discusses the strategy–structure implications of placing technology-base coherence high on the corporate strategy agenda. It then moves on to consider strengthening the corporate coherence of the technology base. A final section concludes.

The concept of technology base is defined as a portfolio of innovative/technological competences. A framework for analysing the coherence of the technology base is proposed that includes two general dimensions, an internal/external dimension and a static/reproductive versus dynamic/explorative dimension. While 'external coherence' refers to the fit between internal competences and the requirements of the environment (the competition and the market), 'internal coherence' refers to the internal relations between competences and the potential for economies of scope and dynamic synergy. While 'reproductive coherence' refers to the ability to exploit existing competences for efficient operation and new combinations, 'explorative coherence' refers to the ability to explore new territories and build new competences.

In the third section the Chandler–Williamson argument for the multi-divisional structure is revisited. Three general tendencies have followed in the wake of the development of the large multidivisional corporation: diversification, increasing division of labour, and decentralization. The implication of these tendencies for the structure and profile of the technology base is discussed. It is argued that these overall tendencies have promoted an inherent movement towards fragmentation of the technology base, more short-termism and risk-aversion in R&D investments, but also a stronger market orientation in innovative efforts. However, it is argued that these implications primarily hold for the 'pure' Williamsonian M-form trajectory that stresses economies of internal financial markets, while other M-form variants provide a different picture.

The fourth section discusses the organizational implications of strengthening the management of the corporate technology base. The chapter certainly has no naïve pretension to settle this highly complex issue. Its ambition is to penetrate somewhat deeper into a matter that is critical to the way we conceive management of technology in diversified corporations.

FRAMEWORK FOR ANALYSIS OF COMPETENCES

Innovative Competences

Innovative and technological competences (henceforth, innovative competences[1]) are required to produce technological innovation. They can be classified in two different ways: according to their constituent technical fields ('technologies') and scientific disciplines, and according to their functional role in the innovation process. The former approach represents the conventional 'technology mapping' approach. This approach, however, does not by itself provide any insights into the innovative potential to the firm of the technological assets identified. Elsewhere Christensen (1995) has proposed a more differentiated 'innovative asset' framework that distinguishes four generic categories of innovative competences:

- scientific research competences comprising competences in basic research, and applied/industrial research;
- process-innovative competences for 'hardware' innovation, systemic development of production, logistics and quality control, and plant layouts;
- product-innovative application competences, subdivided into competences in technical and functional application; and
- aesthetic design competences.

Thus, innovative competences may be characterized by specifying both the technologies or scientific disciplines and the innovative functions involved.[2]

Innovative competences may be more or less generic versus integrative. Mostly, the innovative competences of firms are better characterized by idiosyncratic interdisciplinary constellations than by an additive constellation of generic fields or disciplines. This is due to the fact that technologies in use tend to be interdependent rather than discrete (Dubarle, 1994; Kodoma, 1992; OECD, 1992; Rosenberg, 1992). Most industrial innovation requires the combination of two or more innovative competence categories in terms of innovative functions (that is, product- and process-innovative competences) and two or more competence categories in terms of technical fields (that is, mechanical and electronic engineering). The capacity to accumulate these competences and exploit the interfaces between them may constitute the basis of sustainable competitive advantage (as well as severe lock-in dilemmas). These interfaces may involve different teams and departments within the firm or between divisions and firms. In terms of transaction cost economics we may speak of inter-asset specificity or co-specialization between different innovative and technological competences (Christensen, 1995, 1996b), and between innovative competences and complementary assets (Teece, 1986).

Innovative competences can moreover reflect more or less reproductive versus explorative learning processes. If they are reproductive, they promote *experiential learning* processes that are strongly path-dependent, and therefore serve to push innovation along existing technological trajectories in the form of incremental innovation. Innovative explorative competences are based on *experimental learning* that reflects more intensive and risk-taking search processes that tend to promote more radical innovation and the building of new competences.[3]

The Technology Base and its Strategic Coherence

The total portfolio of innovative competences constitutes the technology base of the firm, and while the analysis at the level of individual competences and inter-competence couplings is relevant when focus is directed at innovation processes, analysis at the level of the technology base as a whole is relevant to the overall strategy of the firm or corporation.

Recently, the conception of coherence has been applied to the firm or corporate level to signify the relatedness among the businesses in multiproduct corporations (Teece et al., 1994): 'A firm exhibits coherence when its lines of business are related, in the sense that there are certain technological and market characteristics common to each' (p. 4). From a resource-based perspective, coherence should be analysed at the level of resources and competences, and not at the level of products or businesses. How then should we analyse the strategic coherence of the technology base? Below we suggest an analysis along two dimensions: an external/internal dimension and a reproductive/dynamic dimension.

The external internal dimension
The technology base may be analysed both in terms of its 'external coherence' and its 'internal coherence'. The issue of external coherence has been more generally discussed than internal coherence. This is true both with respect to the strategic management literature and the more specialized literature on technology management and strategy that has focused much attention on the 'coherence' or 'fit' between firm capabilities and strategies on the one hand and the competitive environment on the other.

External coherence The external coherence of the technology base refers to its actual and potential competitive significance and comparative strength, or in other words: How does the technology base fit the requirements from both competitors and customers? The role of a firm's innovative competences in providing and sustaining competitive advantage first of all depends on its relative importance for competition at the level of product markets and technology regimes, and the firm's innovative and technology position *vis-à-vis* competitors (Welch and Nayak, 1992). A strong external coherence means that the firm possesses or has the capacity (and luck) to build superior innovative competences that are the most decisive for competition in the targeted product markets, and that provide the firm with favourable options for technology-related diversification in the longer term. While analysing the technology base of the firm is a very introverted task for the firm, analysing external coherence, that is, its potential competitive significance and its most promising course of direction, involves a much broader focus on industry trends, technological opportunities, competitor moves, customer priorities, regulatory measures, and so on.

An important dimension of the external coherence problem concerns the conditions for appropriability, that is, the ability to monopolize innovative assets and prevent decisive knowledge from diffusing to potential rivals. The ease with which critical innovative knowledge may diffuse to external parties depends on the characteristics of the knowledge in question and the measures taken to prevent imitation. Winter (1987) has proposed a relevant typology of knowledge dimensions that can provide a basis for appraising the ease of knowledge diffusion. Thus the more tacit, the less observable in use, the more complex, and the more systemic the knowledge is, the more difficult is the transference of that knowledge from one firm to another. The firm may also pursue various measures to prevent knowledge diffusion or prolong the possible lead time (such as patent protection, secrecy measures, building switching costs through sales and service efforts, or continuously creating lead time by offensive R&D). As convincingly argued by Teece (1986), complementary assets that are tightly knit to the innovative assets and the products and processes they give rise to may form an important second line of defence.

Internal coherence   The internal coherence of the technology base focuses attention on internal interdependences between innovative competences of the firm. The internal coherence of the technology base may apply to two sub-levels of analysis: coherence between the elements of the technology base ('local coherence'), and coherence between the technology base and the broader firm or corporate context ('contextual coherence').

The local coherence perspective focuses on the degree of integration and interrelatedness within the technology base between the different technological and innovative competences. A strong local coherence reflects a technology base comprising a varied portfolio of innovative competences. It is characterized by the exploitation and exploration of a high level of inter-competence specificity and synergy in innovative efforts. The local coherence is not a reflection of the diversity of the technology base (that is, the more diverse, the less coherent). To exhibit coherence in a highly diverse technology base in a diversified corporation is much more demanding than exhibiting coherence in a specialized firm with a narrow technology base.[4] Thus local technology-base coherence only makes sense in a diverse multi-technology context and reflects the capacity to generate economies of scope and dynamic synergies – or in other terms – economies of co-specialized competences within the technology base.[5] This involves couplings between technological competences in different fields, or between different innovative competences, for example, between product- and process-innovative competences (cf. Christensen, 1995).

The contextual coherence concept focuses attention on the correspondence between the technology base and the broader firm or corporate context (the complementary assets, the operational and infrastructural firm context, business and corporate level strategy and culture). This coherence is more problematic and complex in large diversified corporations than in small firms. A 'bad fit' may be characterized by 'balkanized rivalry' over resources and mutual mistrust between the 'innovative asset agents' and the 'operational asset agents' or the top management. A 'good fit' is not necessarily marked by harmonious relations and agreement between parties. But these tensions and conflicts are dealt with in ways that promote a synergy and a common sense of contributing to the same general goal.

Part of the contextual coherence problem can be analysed in terms of couplings between innovative competences and complementary assets (see Teece, 1986; Christensen, 1996b).

The reproductive dynamic dimension

Technology-base coherence should also be specified according to its reproductive (or static efficiency) versus dynamic or explorative nature.

Reproductive (or 'static') coherence refers to a technology base that is primarily based on reproductive or incrementally oriented innovative competences. The technology base is focused at the existing portfolio of product or business lines. Interdependences focus on exploitation of economies of scope (asset and competence sharing or transference) and experiential learning along existing technological trajectories. Dynamic or explorative coherence refers to a technology base with a strong core of dynamic innovative competences that are well suited for radical or systemic innovations or for building new competences and aligning them with existing competences. Interdependences are here more directed at experimental, synergistic learning in which stretch and leverage dynamics (Hamel and Prahalad, 1993) provide new technological as well as market opportunities.

Reproductive coherence is conducive to a market-oriented, incremental technological development and operational efficiency that may provide a competitive edge in the shorter to medium term. However, in the longer term the strong focus on tight interdependences and exploitation of existing competences in existing product markets may lock firms into trajectories that gradually come to diverge from those dominating the industry. Firms that exert explorative coherence possess the leverage capacities and incentives for more radical technological and product-market change that may provide the firm both with first-mover positions and a capacity to manage technological discontinuities. On the other hand, such firms may have difficulties in operational efficiency and incremental innovation.

Sustainable competitive advantage can only be achieved if the management of the corporate technology base not only strives for external and internal coherence in general, but also focuses attention on the highly complex task of balancing the trade-off between the reproductive and dynamic or explorative dimensions of the technology base. The proper balance is likely to be changing over time, often with cyclical characteristics. Thus, after a period of extensive and risky investments and innovative efforts in which the balance favours the dynamic side, there will come a period of consolidation and exploitation where the reproductive side takes the lead. However, neither the reproductive nor the explorative side should become heavily dominating for longer periods of time.

The long-term evolution of large industrial corporations (such as IBM, Rank Xerox, Philips and General Motors) indicates that exploratively coherent corporations often emerge into a position of reproductive coherence, and this may happen without any distinct economic warning signals in due time for managerial action. However, once reproductive coherence has turned into a full-scale lock-in crisis, this may trigger a (long) period of reflection (diagnosis, potential solutions), experimentation and trial and error, and power struggles within the corporation, the outcome of which may be a new coherence that provides both a new momentum for the corporation and a dynamic fit with the long-term industry trajectory.

STRATEGY–STRUCTURE REVISITED

Since the work of Chandler (1962) the relationship between the strategy and the organizational structure of diversified large corporations has been the subject of systematic research. The recently emerging theory of dynamic firm capabilities and core competences (Hamel and Heene, 1994; Nelson, 1991; Prahalad and Hamel, 1990; Teece and Pisano, 1994) has made it urgent to re-examine this relationship from the perspective of accumulating, organizing and exploiting core competences, including central parts of the technology base.

The Generic M-form Dynamics and the Technology Base

Following Chandler (1962) and Williamson (1975) it has become conventional wisdom that the decentralized multidivisional (M-form) structure – as compared to the functional structure – provides the best way of dealing with administrative and operational problems of managing the multiproduct corporation. According to Williamson (1975), M-form organization is more likely to favour goal pursuit and least-cost behaviour in line with neoclassical maximization behaviour than are functionally organized corporations.

Three general tendencies have characterized the development of the large corporation: diversification, increasing division of labour, and decentralization. We shall not dwell here on the overall aspects of these tendencies, but instead focus on the way they are reflected in the management and coherence of the corporate technology base.

Diversification has been the subject of systematic research by economists and strategy researchers for many years. Mostly this research has focused on product or business diversification, while the dynamics of technology diversification, that is, the firm's expansion of its innovative and technological asset base, has attracted much less research interest (among the exceptions, see Pavitt et al., 1989; Granstrand et al., 1990; Oskarsson, 1993). The trend for technology diversification seems to have been even more pronounced – at least within technology-intensive firms – than product diversification (Pavitt et al., 1989). This tendency for increasing diversity of the technology base has been a central factor stimulating the rising academic and managerial attention to technology management and strategy in recent years.

Technological diversification implies increasing diversity of the technology base, but this does not necessarily imply decreasing coherence. If technological diversification is exclusively linked to product strategies at divisional levels, and no corporate or interdivisional coordination is taking place, the corporate technology base will tend to become increasingly fragmented (or non-coherent).

Increasing division of labour has led to further compartmentalization, professionalization, specialization, cultural segregation and political rivalry between various parts of the technology base. There is no longer one R&D department that comprises the total corporate portfolio of innovative and technological assets. Rather, different parts of the technology base are spread all over the corporation, from central science laboratories to product development, engineering and design departments (or individuals/groups) in product divisions, subsidiaries or joint ventures. Unless met by countervailing coordination and integration measures, this division of labour dynamic promotes a fragmented competence building at the level of the specialized competence categories, and a lack of inter-competence specificity and coherence at the level of the total technology base. This may contribute to the undermining of existing core capabilities and make it difficult to build synergies between different assets (Prahalad and Hamel, 1990).

The tendency for decentralization has in part been a necessary outcome of increasing complexity (and thus increasing difficulty in centralized planning) due to (a) the process of diversification, and (b) increasing division of labour. But decentralization is also a consequence of the organizational principles (formulated by Williamson, 1975) for controlling the efficiency of divisions, and achieving efficient allocation of capital resources: first, the separation of strategic and operating functions; second, the implementation of functional autonomy of divisions; and third, the establishing of a top–down financial control of divisional profit performance.

Decentralization in the form of divisionalization has also involved decentralization of the management of R&D resources in large diversified corporations (Coombs and Richards, 1991). Loescher (1984) argues that the tendency for tight, top-down financial control may lead to risk avoidance by divisional managers. Hill (1985) hypothesizes that M-form efficiency focus is linked to short-termism and low R&D commitment, that is, 'static efficiency' (or reproductive competences) at the expense of long-term effectiveness (or dynamic or explorative competences). But divisionalization of innovative investments also leads to stronger market orientation and a focus on incremental innovation. In short, the decentralization dynamics tend to promote both short-termism in innovative efforts and a strong, but risk-averse, market orientation.

Taken together, the three tendencies provide incentives for changes in innovative efforts and innovative competence profiles. There may be a general pressure to downgrade total R&D or innovative investments. Hoskisson and Hitt (1988) provide moderate (although not statistically significant) support for the hypothesis that M-form firms invest relatively less in R&D than functionally organized firms. However, rather than an overall downgrading of R&D, the decentralized M-form may induce incentives for changes in the innovative asset profile that will tend to, first, fragment or weaken the internal coherence of the technology base (implying failure to explore and exploit cross-divisional synergies, as well as risk of duplication of innovative efforts); and second, favour short-termism and incrementalism in innovative efforts such as line extensions and suppress more radical innovation, thus moving the balance between reproductive and explorative competences in favour of the former. This move toward incrementalism may moreover favour process, product and design innovative competences over science-based competences (especially those linked to basic research). Such a changing balance of the innovative competence profile may underlie the tendencies to reduce the role and autonomy of central science laboratories and to induce a stronger 'market orientation', that is, guiding and funding from divisional levels (see for example Barpal, 1990).

In sum, when the dominant dynamics of the corporation are based on strategies and trajectories at divisional level rather than strategies and visions at corporate level, the outcome is likely to be increasing interdivisional and corporate-wide fragmentation of the technology base despite possibly increasing intradivisional coherence. To use the terminology suggested earlier, the internal coherence of the technology base is weakened, while the external coherence may be strengthened (at least at the short term). At the same time the constituent competences and the (high or low level of) coherence tend to become dominated more by reproductive than by explorative features.

Variants within the M-form and the Role of the Technology Base

Today most diversified firms are multidivisionals (Hill and Pickering, 1986). However, as Hill and Hoskisson (1987) have pointed out, M-form structures are not homogeneous, and many M-form firms depart in substantial ways from the ideal form suggested by Williamson.

Hill and Hoskisson (1987) identify three main strategies that firms use to become multiproduct companies: vertical integration, related diversification and unrelated diversification. Each of these strategies is associated with a specific type of economic objective. Vertical integration strategies seek to exploit 'vertical economies' that arise from scale or integration economies, from increases in control over resources or outlets, or from elimination of the transaction costs of using the market. Related diversification strategies seek to benefit from 'synergistic economies' (or synergies between assets and competences, or economies of scope). Finally, unrelated diversification strategies seek to exploit financial economies (by reducing risk, applying portfolio management, and overcoming external capital market failures).

To each of these three strategies corresponds a set of planning and control arrangements within the basic M-form framework (Hill and Hoskisson, 1987, p. 333). They argue that the 'pure' Williamsonian M-form[6] is consistent with a strategy of unrelated diversification in order to realize financial economies, but not consistent with either vertical integration or related diversification strategies. Both of these latter strategies require a degree of central coordination, interdivisional cooperation and/or asset and competence sharing. Moreover, they maintain that it is difficult for a firm to go for both financial economies on the one hand, and synergistic or vertical economies on the other:

> The requisite control systems are incompatible. Thus, one disadvantage of attempting to realize financial economies is that the firm may have to forgo gains from synergistic and vertical economies. The converse also holds: One disadvantage of attempting to realize vertical or synergistic economy is the loss of potential financial economies. On the other hand, similarities between the systems necessary to realize vertical and synergistic economies suggest that these are more compatible. Hence, the firm may be able to realize both. (Hill and Hoskisson, 1987, p. 335)

If we now return to the technology-base perspective, it is obvious that while the 'pure' M-form (to realize a strategy of financial economies) will tend to 'balkanize' the corporate technology base along the lines discussed in the previous section, the 'synergistic' M-form structures (to realize vertical or synergistic economies) are in accordance with an overall corporate coherence perspective (as suggested by Teece et al., 1994), and possibly also with a technology-base coherence perspective (to the extent that technology-base synergies come to the attention of the corporate strategy agenda). This is indicated by the findings of a strong bimodal distribution of corporate technological staff in Pitts's (1977) study of 21 large companies. The corporate technological staff was either very small, corresponding to the financial economies strategy and the 'pure' M-form, or relatively large, corresponding to synergistic economies strategy, including a focus on corporate technology base coherence.

Based on rich case studies of 16 diversified UK corporations, Goold and Campbell (1987) find three major types of management styles used by senior management at corporate headquarters: strategic planning, strategic control and financial control. These management styles are defined in terms of two dimensions of the centre's influence, planning influence and control influence. The planning styles influence concerns the centre's contribution to the strategy process in the business units. The influence of the control style concerns the centre's way of reacting to results achieved. Strategic planning corporations have a high level of central planning influence, while the centre's control influence is flexible and focused more on strategic targets than on annual budgets. Strategic control corporations exert a more moderate level of planning influence, while control measures are stricter and cover both financial and strategic targets. Finally, financial control companies have a low level of central planning influence, while the centre focuses on tight financial control.

In a recent paper Chandler (1994) reviews his own and Goold and Campbell's work on the functions of headquarters in multibusiness companies. Like Goold and Campbell, he finds that strategic planning and strategic control companies are generally smaller and less diversified than financial control companies. While the former tend to operate in relatively high-technology industries, have relatively large R&D departments, and exploit interbusiness and interdivisional opportunities, financial control companies tend to operate in service industries and in industries involving relatively inexpensive production facilities and small R&D expenditures. Moreover, financial control companies show a low level of interbusiness and interdivisional interdependences. Thus it is likely that strategic planning companies (and to a lesser degree strategic control companies) will tend to be more coherent both in general terms and in terms of the technology base than financial control companies.

STRENGTHENING THE CORPORATE COHERENCE OF THE TECHNOLOGY BASE

Strengthening the corporate coherence of the technology base should not, of course, be the only strategic concern for corporate management in diversified corporations. But it should certainly be of central concern to the corporation that seeks synergistic and vertical economies. It is, however, likely that the problems of short-termism in innovative efforts and balkanization of the corporate technology base are not exclusively associated with the 'pure' M-form, but are also present or inherently creeping into the more 'synergistic' M-form corporations as they diversify into still new business areas and the technology base grows more complex.

The appropriate response to these problems is not simply a rejection of the M-form structure as a general organizational arrangement, and a 'back to centralism' in corporate management of the technology base, which could be one interpretation of the ideas of Prahalad and Hamel (1990). That would impose dramatic bureaucratic costs, and undermine the advantages that the decentralized M-form has demonstrated, such as a stronger market orientation in technological development and innovative efforts, less bureaucracy and fewer vertical levels involved in decisions concerning the allocation of R&D resources between alternative projects, and greater motivation and creative spirit as a consequence of a situation in which local operations and initiatives are not constantly disturbed or overruled from higher levels.

Nor would it be easy to transform the decentralized product divisions into core technology divisions. As maintained by Contractor and Narayanan (1990), 'it is difficult to think in terms of technology as a profit centre or as a unit of measure since its boundaries are often fuzzy and spill over into several product areas' (p. 306).

To deal with the issue of corporate coherence of the technology base implies that the 'pure' decentralized M-form has to be counterbalanced by some elements of central coordination and interdivisional cooperation, and generally by loosening the rigidity of organizational structures and creating elements of flexibility and variety in exploring opportunities. Pavitt (1991) argues that an essential dimension of successful large firms' managerial competence is the ability to combine the differentiated technological competences into effective units for identifying and developing innovations.

We may identify four basic trade-off axes that should be relaxed relative to the conventional prescriptions underlying the M-form (Ghoshal and Mintzberg, 1994; Hill, 1994):

1. The vertical trade-off between central control of investments and resource allocation versus decentralized initiative.
2. The horizontal trade-off between differentiation and autonomy of the individual divisions, on the one hand, and integration or synergy between divisions, on the other.
3. The trade-off in corporate control of divisional economic performance between purely financial measures and more subjective and complex measures.
4. The trade-off in incentive schemes for divisional managers between incentives to increase intradivisional efficiency and performance versus interdivisional cooperation.

The Vertical Trade-off

The vertical trade-off would have to be subject of considerations in which both product-market perspectives (as perceived from product divisions) and technological and innovative competence perspectives (as perceived from a corporate coherence perspective) should be counterbalanced. Compared to the 'pure' M-form model, this would generally tend to mean more involve-

ment from a corporate centre. This does not necessarily imply a centralization of R&D in corporate laboratories, although early studies (Berg, 1973;
Pitts, 1977) indicate that an interdivisional synergy and sharing with respect
to technological assets can be achieved by centralized R&D. Centralized
R&D may also play a role in countervailing the tendency toward compromis-
ing exploration and risky R&D investments in favour of exploitation (and
short-termism). Thus, some degree of centralized control over and impetus
for strategic and operating investments and resource mobilization is required
to assure a corporate coherence of the technology base that balances the
trade-off between reproductive and explorative efforts (or between exploitation and exploration).

The Horizontal Trade-off

The horizontal trade-off between differentiation/autonomy of divisions versus integration/synergy between divisions would have to be moved away
from the extreme differentiation/autonomy position of the 'pure' M-form, in
which the product-market perspective possesses hegemony, towards a dynamic balance including stronger elements of integrative or synergetic measures. This would involve some elements of interdivisional exchange of
personnel and experience, for example, coordination groups and committees
that cut across the interest of individual businesses and divisions; rotation
programmes among divisions for the younger personnel; cross-divisional
project teams for diffusing core competences and for loosing the bonds that
might tie an individual to one business (Prahalad and Hamel, 1990, p. 91); or
implementing the 'merchandiser' concept (Collinson, 1993) as developed by
Sony. 'Merchandisers' are individuals with a cross-divisional perspective.
They are freed from routine tasks and given the authority to act as internal
entrepreneurs.

The complexity and stability of such integrating mechanisms can vary,
depending on the degree of interdependence and the uncertainty and durability of the relations (Hill, 1994).

In their study of 24 diversified companies with significant R&D performance, Coombs and Richards (1993) found that

> some companies are creating small units at the centre of the corporate structure
> (which may or may not be within the R&D function), the purposes of which
> include the following:
>
> - examining the structure of the overall technology;
> - ensuring that a technological competence in one business is known to and
>   available to other potential user businesses in the group;

- identifying technical competencies which straddle businesses, in order to take steps to strengthen them through 'horizontal' organizational links and through small special budgets;
- considering the overall technology portfolio and injecting an appreciation of this portfolio into the broader strategic management processes of the company. (p. 390)

Thus, such a corporate centre of strategic technology management could be a vital vehicle in promoting a coherent technology base along the vertical and horizontal trade-off dimensions.

The Performance Control and Incentive Structure

However, increasing cooperation and synergy between divisions create problems of performance measuring: 'Specifically, when divisions lack complete autonomy with regard to operating and strategic decisions, objective rate-of-return criteria, which might be used to assess divisional performance, do not constitute an unambiguous signal of divisional efficiency' (Hill, 1994, p. 309). This means that divisional rate-of-return measures should have reduced emphasis in corporate control and resource allocation decisions, while other criteria that may require more complex information should have increased emphasis. Such criteria could be directly linked to the technology base (for example indicators of the ability to innovate, or to build high-level competences in strategic technologies or innovative sub-functions) or they could be linked to extended performance measures (such as the total performance of divisions that are involved in especially intensive interaction).

This issue has been examined in some detail by Goold and Campbell (1987). They see the control issue in terms of three interlinked processes: the process of setting of (and agreeing) objectives, monitoring of results and applying pressures and incentives. By examining how different companies execute these processes Goold and Campbell define three different control styles: flexible strategic control, tight strategic control and tight financial control. Flexible strategic control involves both financial targets (such as return on sales) and strategic targets (such as market share). However, enforcement is flexible, implying that the centre may accept that there sometimes can be good reasons why targets are not met. Tight strategic control also comprises both financial and strategic targets. Enforcement is, however, relatively strict. In tight financial control, objectives are set primarily in terms of annual financial performance. Enforcement is strict, and performance below budget will affect career prospects for unit managers (Goold and Campbell, 1987, pp. 40–41).

Incentive schemes for divisional management should be consistent with the overall corporate strategy. While the conventional M-form prescriptions include incentives and rewards for the economic performance of the individual division, the coherence and synergy-oriented corporation should (also) emphasize interdivisional cooperation (for example, if profit bonuses for divisional managers are linked to corporate rather than divisional profitability) (Hill, 1994).

The general point in this argument is, however, not to move corporate organization and management from the one extreme position of the trade-off axes, decentralized autonomy and purely financial control of individual divisions, to the other extreme position, implying centralized, over-bureaucratic and tightly integrated structures. Rather, the balance is dynamic and the object of constant adjustment and restructuring in which the product-market and the technology-base (and ultimately, core competence) perspective, the reproductive and the explorative competence perspective, are constantly subject to review and adjustment.

CONCLUSION

It is my conjecture that the strategy–structure literature has not so far appropriately assimilated the insights from the resource-based (or competence-based) studies of the firm. This chapter has taken one step in this direction with respect to the role of the technology base in the corporate strategy–structure development.

I have focused particularly on the issue of corporate coherence of the technology base. I believe that while the promotion of external coherence of the technology base (or its relevance in terms of market and competitor dynamics) requires substantial divisional autonomy and decentralized initiative, the promotion of internal coherence of the technology base requires substantial involvement at the corporate level. A strong internal (local) coherence reflects a technology base comprising a varied portfolio of technologies and innovative assets characterized by: the exploitation of a high level of interaction and synergy between the constituent innovative and technological competence fields; both reproductive and explorative learning and searching dynamics, and the capacity to balance between the two; and technology diversification that explicitly addresses the need to remain coherent or build coherence by integrating the newly acquired assets into the technology base.

If the external and internal coherence of the technology base becomes a corporate strategic objective, then a corporate centre must take (at least part of the) responsibility for promoting synergy, balancing exploitation and exploration (and perhaps primarily take responsibility for the long-term explorative perspective in innovative efforts), and assuring that the logic of technology diversification is subject to strategic analysis in terms of technology-base coherence, and not exclusively the reflection of the business strategy of the company (or, worse, the product strategies of the individual divisions).

NOTES

1. In Christensen (1996a) I make the conceptual distinction between capability and competence: a capability signifies lower-order functional or technical capacities to mobilize resources for productive activities; a competence signifies a higher-order managerial capacity of the firm to mobilize, harmonize and develop resources and capabilities to create value and competitive advantage. In this chapter, however, the distinction is not critical, and I systematically use the term competence to refer to both technical and managerial capacities.
2. Of course, innovative competences necessarily contain strong elements of organizational skills and not only technical skills. Likewise, there are both internal learning dynamics as well as external learning, or absorptive capacities, involved. However, I shall not focus on these issues here (see Christensen 1996a).
3. This distinction between experiential and experimental learning is similar to the distinction between exploitation and exploration as proposed by March (1991) and Levinthal and March (1993).
4. Coombs and Richards (1993) provide some illustrative evidence on the complexity of promoting strategic technology-base coherence in large diversified companies.
5. Teece et al. (1994) similarily define corporate coherence in a multiproduct sense.
6. Williamson (1975) argued that M-form firms are (should be) characterized by: (1) separation of strategic and operating functions; (2) functional autonomy of divisions; (3) reallocation of resources generated by divisions on the basis of relative yields rather than returning them to their source division; (4) use of corporate incentives to promote profit seeking behaviour; and (5) employment of a specialized 'corporate' staff to audit the affairs of the divisions.

REFERENCES

Barg, N.A. (1973), 'Corporate Role in Diversified Companies', in Taylor, B. and Macmillan, K. (eds), *Business Policy: Teaching and Research*, New York: John Wiley & Sons.
Barpal, I.R. (1990), 'Business-Driven Technology for a Technology-Based Firm', *Research Technology Management*, 4 (July–August), 27–30.
Chandler, A.D. (1962), *Strategy and Structure*, Cambridge, MA.: MIT Press.
Chandler, A.D. (1994), 'The Functions of the HQ Unit in the Multibusiness Firm', in Rumelt, R.P., Schendel, D.E. and Teece, D.J. (eds), *Fundamental Issues in Strategy. A Research Agenda*, Boston, MA.: Harvard Business School Press.
Christensen, J.F. (1995), 'Asset profiles for technological innovation', *Research Policy*, 24, 727–45.
Christensen, J.F. (1996a), 'Analysing the Technology Base of the Firm. A Multidimensional resource and competence perspective', in Foss, N. and Knudsen, C. (eds), *Towards a Competence Theory of the Firm*, London: Routledge.
Christensen, J.F (1996b), 'Innovative Assets and Inter-Asset Linkages – A Resource-Based Approach to Innovation', *Economics of Innovation and New Technology*, 4, 193–209.

Collinson, S. (1993), 'Managing Product Innovation at Sony: The Development of the Data Discman', *Technology Analysis & Strategic Management*, **3**, 285–306.
Contractor, F.J. and Narayanan, V.K. (1990), 'Technology development in the multinational firm: a framework for planning and strategy', *R&D Management*, **20** (4), 305–22.
Coombs, R. and Richards, A. (1991), 'Technologies, Products and Firms' Strategies. Part 1 – A Framework for Analysis', *Technology Analysis & Strategic Management*, **3** (1), 77–86. 'Part 2 – Analysis of Three Cases' **3** (2), 157–75.
Coombs, R. and Richards, A. (1993), 'Strategic Control of Technology in Diversified Companies with Decentralized R&D', *Technology Analysis & Strategic Management*, **5** (4), 385–96.
Dubarle, P. (1994), 'The Coalescence of Technology', *The OECD Observer*, no. 185.
Ghoshal, S. and Mintzberg, H. (1994), 'Diversification and Diversifact', *California Management Review*, **37** (1), 8–27.
Goold, M. and Campbell, A. (1987), *Strategies and Styles. The Role of the Centre in Managing Diversified Corporations*, Oxford: Basil Blackwell.
Granstrand, O., Oskarsson, C., Sjöberg, N. and Sjölander, S. (1990), 'Business strategies for new technologies', in Deiaco, E. Hörnell, E. and Vickery, G. (eds), *Technology and Investment. Critical issues for the 1990s*, London: Pinter Publishers.
Hamel, G. and Heene, A. (eds) (1994), *Competence-Based Competition*, New York: John Wiley & Sons.
Hamel, G. and Prahalad, C.K. (1993), 'Strategy as Stretch and Leverage', *Harvard Business Review*, March-April.
Hill, C.W.L. (1985), 'Oliver Williamson and the M-Form firm: a critical review', *Journal of Economic Issues*, **19**, 731–56.
Hill, C.W.L. (1994), 'Diversification and Economic Performance: Bringing Structure and Corporate Management Back into the Picture', in Rumelt, R.P., Schendel, D.E. and Teece, D.J. (eds), *Fundamental Issues in Strategy. A Research Agenda*, Boston, MA.: Harvard Business School Press.
Hill, C.W.L. and Hoskisson, R.E. (1987), 'Strategy and Structure in the Multiproduct Firm', *Academy of Management Review*, **12** (2), 331–41.
Hill, C.W.L. and Pickering, J.F. (1986), 'Divisionalization, decentralization and performance of large UK companies', *Journal of Management Studies*, **23**, 26–50.
Hoskisson, R.E. and Hitt, M.A. (1988), 'Strategic Control Systems and Relative R&D Investment in Large Multiproduct Firms', *Strategic Management Journal*, **9**, 605–21.
Kodoma, F. (1992), 'Technology Fusion and The New R&D', *Harvard Business Review*, July–August, 70–78.
Levinthal, D.A. and March, J.G. (1993), 'The Myopia of Learning', *Strategic Management Journal*, **14**, 95–112.
Loescher, S.M. (1984), 'Bureaucratic measurement, shuttling stock shares, and shortened time horizon: implications for economic growth', *Quarterly Review of Economics and Business*, **24**, 1–23.
March, J.G. (1991), 'Exploration and exploitation in organizational learning', *Organization Science*, **2**, 71–87.
Nelson, R. (1991), 'Why Firms Differ, and How Does it Matter?', *Strategic Management Journal*, **12**, 61–74.
OECD (1992), *Technology and the Economy. The Key Relationships*, Paris: OECD.
Oskarsson, C. (1993), *Technology Diversification – The Phenomenon, its Causes and*

Effects, Göteborg: Chalmers University of Technology, Department of Industrial Management and Economics.

Pavitt, K. (1991), 'Key Characteristics of the Large Innovating Firm', *British Journal of Management*, **2**, 41–50.

Pavitt, K., Robson, M. and Townsend, J. (1989), 'Technological accumulation, diversification and organization in UK companies 1945–1983', *Management Science*, **35** (1), 81–99.

Pitts, R. (1977), 'Strategies and structures for diversification', *Academy of Management Journal*, **20**, 197–208.

Prahalad, C.K. and Hamel, G. (1990), 'The Core Competence of the Corporation', *Harvard Business Review*, May–June, 79–91.

Rosenberg, N. (1992), 'Science and Technology in the Twentieth Century', in Dosi, G., Gianetti, R. and Toninelli, P.A. (eds), *Technology and the Enterprise in a Historical Perspective*, Oxford: The Clarendon Press.

Teece, D.J. (1986), 'Profiting from technological innovation: Implications for integration, collaboration, licensing and public policy', *Research Policy*, **15**, 285–305.

Teece, D. and Pisano, G. (1994), 'The Dynamic Capabilities of Firms: An Introduction', *Industrial and Corporate Change*, **3** (3), 537–56.

Teece, D.J., Rumelt, R., Dosi, G. and Winter, S. (1994), 'Understanding corporate coherence. Theory and evidence', *Journal of Economic Behavior and Organization*, **23**, 1–30.

Welch, J.A. and Nayak, P.R. (1992), 'Strategic sourcing: a progressive approach to the make-or-buy decision', *Academy of Management Executives*, **6** (1), 23–31.

Williamson, D.E. (1975), *Markets and Hierarchies*, New York: The Free Press.

Winter, S.G. (1987), 'Knowledge and Competence as Strategic Assets', in Teece, D.J. (ed.), *The Competitive Challenge: Strategies for Industrial Innovation and Renewal*, New York: Harper & Row.

6. Reorganizing for knowledge integration and constituency building: product development at Sony and Philips

Simon Collinson and Alfredo Molina

INTRODUCTION

Some of the hype surrounding the rise of multimedia is now beginning to give way to real investment by companies, usable products for consumers, and tangible changes in the ways people and organizations communicate. But the combination of industry sectors and emerging markets that make up the multimedia 'milieu' are still filled with a great deal of uncertainty as to the emerging pattern of uses, users, technical platforms and standards, dominant suppliers, and intra- and inter-sector alliances. All of this has critical implications for companies involved in developing new products in the multimedia field.

This chapter discusses how two leading consumer electronics firms, Sony and Philips, are coping with these uncertainties. In particular, it looks at how they have reorganized their management of the product development process in response to the convergence of some core technologies and changes in their traditional markets. In the past they have relied on consumer products, such as televisions, audio systems, VCRs and camcorders, where hardware was the main focus of innovation and product development was incremental, based on improvements to key components and took place within distinct product groups. They are now having to manage the development of products whose market success depends on fundamentally new combinations of technologies in which software development is at least as important as hardware development. We compare and contrast how these two firms, one Japanese, one European, have responded to the industry changes affecting them both.

The chapter is based on two matched case studies of product development projects, the development of Photo-CD in Philips and the Data Discman in Sony, to provide a 'window' into the management practices of each firm (the initial research was funded by the ESRC[1]). The project case studies both examine CD-ROM-based interactive systems, one of the fastest-growing areas of multimedia, and one that clearly illustrates the need for reorganization within firms and cross-sector cooperation between firms. In particular, how did Philips and Sony integrate technical and market expertise from different internal divisions and from software developers into the hardware development process? How did they then establish a 'critical mass' amongst co-developers to establish their respective hardware platforms? Moreover, how did the organizational and alliance-building mechanisms used by each of these firms differ in their form and resultant efficiency and effectiveness?

Past studies show that successfully innovative firms tend to be those that have evolved organizational mechanisms that promote interaction and cooperation between specialist functional divisions (R&D, production, design, marketing and so on) and between specialist technical divisions, such as product groups, inside and outside the firm. For the bulk of innovative activity, far more than tends to be acknowledged in most studies of innovation, new products and processes arise from novel *combinations* of existing technologies and the knowledge and expertise that have already evolved around them, rather than from truly new or original ideas. Crucial influences are the dynamic capabilities and core competences underlying competitive advantages within firms and inter-firm alliances (Teece, Pisano and Shuen, 1990; Teece and Pisano, 1994).

We propose, more specifically, that particular corporate structures and organizational mechanisms must be consciously developed to promote particular 'sociotechnical alignments' and facilitate 'knowledge integration' between specialist divisions inside the firm and between allied companies across different industry sectors if individual projects are to succeed.

At the heart of the product development process project team members have to bring together specialist knowledge and expertise to focus on the creation of a new product that is technically sound (functional), cost-effective (affordable) and fulfils a real (or perceived, or 'latent') demand from users. The effectiveness and efficiency of this 'knowledge integration' process, and therefore the entire product development function, is dependent on the management mechanisms and organizational context which facilitate or constrain it.

The 'sociotechnical constituencies' methodology that we use allows us to map out the various sources of knowledge and expertise, as well as the broad range of other influences over the product development process, and identify what role each played. It highlights the social and organizational elements, as well as the purely technical factors, that shape the innovation process. It also helps us to identify the alliances, alignments and particular areas of knowledge integration that were critical to the success (or failure) of the projects and then examine the management mechanisms and organizational structures that helped (or hindered) their emergence.

We illustrate the validity of the 'sociotechnical constituencies' approach and the concept of knowledge integration for examining the product development process by comparing project management practices in two firms. We apply both to the Sony–Philips comparison and also focus specifically on some of the management mechanisms within Sony that appear to facilitate constituency building and knowledge integration at the project level.

We first review briefly the case studies of Sony and Philips, their respective approaches to managing the product development process, and their current responses to the emerging threats and opportunities posed by multimedia. We also provide some background details on the Photo-CD and Data Discman projects. Then we summarize the concept of knowledge integration and the sociotechnical constituencies methodology, in terms of their application to the product development process. Examples from the case studies are used to illustrate each aspect of the methodology and this provides further insights into the management of new product development by the two firms. We then examine some specific management mechanisms in Sony that appear to facilitate the alignment process and promote knowledge integration for project success. We conclude with a discussion of the benefits to be gained from using the approach as described.

SONY AND PHILIPS COMPARED

Philips and Sony are the second and third largest consumer electronics firms in the world, after Matsushita. Both firms have undergone a recent period of restructuring following mixed performances in the face of turbulent markets. Philips suffered heavy losses between 1987 and 1992 before picking up in subsequent years after a series of reorganizations under Jan Timmer. Sony, half as old as its European rival, overtook Philips in terms of net sales in 1993, but has also had problems with newer products and management changes.

Restructuring in both companies in recent years has focused on promoting the development of new businesses on the back of existing core activities. In particular, both have talked about boosting software activities as a business area that needs to be further developed and better integrated with the rest of their traditional hardware activities. Timmer is explicitly looking to gain 30 to 40 per cent of Philips's revenues from software, services and multimedia by the year 2000, compared to the current 20 per cent.

In Philips the strategic aims of the reorganization process have been spelled out in 'Operation Centurion', established by Timmer in 1991. The 'Philips Way' philosophy is central to this, prompting employees to 'delight customers' and 'encourage entrepreneurial behaviour at all levels'. There are obvious similarities with Sony's recent changes, particularly its restructuring exercise in 1994. Reduced layers of management and greater organizational flexibility in response to market change are all part of the restructuring objectives. These fulfil the company's aim to be more market-driven, with further coordination between marketing and manufacturing.

A main impetus prompting the restructuring of both these firms, and an issue at the heart of the development projects, compared later, is the emergence of multimedia market opportunities and the need for these firms to adapt existing capabilities to meet them. In particular, the process of combining disparate technologies into single products raises the difficulty of integrating specialist knowledge and expertise which is divided into distinct product groups. Product development and production activities at Sony and Philips (and most other consumer electronics firms) have in the past been organized into product divisions that relate to distinct technologies (including audio, television and VCR groups). These were geared towards incremental product development along fairly predictable ('path-dependent') trajectories within their own groups. In both companies, as will be seen in the case studies, the process of knowledge integration has been hindered by institutional inertia and territorialism, promoted by the separate divisional cultures that have evolved within product groups.

Despite the restructuring described above, these problems still remain. Different sociotechnical constituencies still exist as echoes of the old regimes and these groups are divided by their different 'visions' of multimedia, key products, technologies and applications, and compete for control over corporate product development strategy.

Similar kinds of problem are mirrored at the inter-firm and inter-sector levels. Companies from various hardware and software industry sectors, including telecommunications, computers, consumer electronics, publishing, entertainment and the media, have been engaged in a shifting range of alliances to establish standards platforms and to co-develop and co-market delivery systems and applications. Some have successfully built sociotechnical constituencies to back certain strategies; others have not. Again, the specific problems involved with inter-firm cooperation can clearly be observed at the project level, where alliances with outside specialists and co-developers are established to create saleable product packages.

For Sony and Philips, and most hardware manufacturers entering the multimedia arena, the challenge has been to bridge the gap with software producers. This has been achieved through permanent takeovers and buyouts, and temporary joint ventures and alliances. Sony's difficult association with Columbia Pictures contrasts with Philips's longer-running link (almost full ownership) with Polygram, but each has had a series of successes and failures in recent years, trying to balance software and hardware interests.

These difficulties, and the different ways in which Sony and Philips have coped with them in managing the product development process, will be examined further at the project level as we describe the two case studies. First we provide some details about the products and the projects at the core of what we call respectively the Data Discman and Photo-CD constituencies. This is followed by a detailed discussion of the process of knowledge integration and the sociotechnical constituencies involved.

PRODUCT DEVELOPMENT PROJECTS COMPARED

Both firms have sought to develop CD-ROM-based multimedia products. The project team in Sony created the Data Discman, also called an 'electronic book player', which allows the user to search and retrieve information in the form of text, graphics and sound, from an 8 cm (200 MB) CD-ROM, with in-built LCD screen.

The development project, based in 'General Audio' or 'GA' Group, followed a bottom-up route in the company, beginning with a committed, informal group of engineers and a manager with sufficient funds 'siphoned' from existing budgets to create a prototype. As is the case for most innovative and cost-effective product developments, the Data Discman was created predominantly by combining a range of existing technologies, with no original 'research' and a focus on design and development.

Some of the more novel aspects of the product were: adaptations of the CD-ROM drive mechanism of the CD-Audio Discman, from which the Data Discman evolved (involving expertise from the Components Development Group and the Recording Media Group); the creation of the information-retrieval software ('search engine'), written in the Zilog Z-80 processor's read-only memory; a new standard for 'laying down' data on the 8 cm discs and a new authoring system for applications publishers. All this required close interaction with a broader range of expertise across other companies compared to the development of the hardware (further details of this case study are in Collinson, 1993).

Philips's Photo-CD project involved the development of several related products for scanning and digitizing photographs taken using normal celluloid-based cameras and storing them on 'WORM' ('write once read many' times) CD-ROMs for displaying on TVs. The basic consumer product was a Photo-CD 'Viewer' or 'Player' for reading the prerecorded CD-ROMs, using technology developed for the CD-Interactive (CD-I) family of products by Philips. But for consumers to record their photographs on to CD-ROMs a Photo-CD 'Recorder' or 'Writer' (the CDD 521 and the more recent CDD 522) was also developed to be used by professional photo-labs who would provide CD-ROM recording services. A range of additional services, software applications and peripheral products was developed around these two main devices.

The products were jointly developed and marketed by Philips and Kodak and began selling in mid-1992. The Philips project was organized in a more linear, less concurrent fashion than the Data Discman, with the work being passed between divisions rather than being handled by one project team. It was also very much initiated and managed from the top down, with senior managers organizing the joint venture and passing down detailed project activities, in contrast to the Discman project. The IMS (Interactive Media Systems) division was responsible for much of the pre-development work and for coordinating the project.

CONCEPTS AND FRAMEWORKS FOR COMPARATIVE ANALYSIS OF TECHNOLOGICAL DEVELOPMENT

Knowledge Integration for New Product Development

A wide body of literature deals with the various aspects of how firms organize to innovate and manage to develop and exploit new product and process technologies. A common thread that runs through them is that successful innovators tend to be the firms that have evolved organizational mechanisms to facilitate the knowledge integration process. In the specific case of new product development, knowledge integration is simply the process of bringing together all relevant knowledge (information and expertise) to bear, at the project level, on the design and development of the product. Relevant knowledge includes specialist technical knowledge relating to the many product components and knowledge relating to the various corporate functions such as marketing, manufacturing, R&D and finance. It also includes less obvious areas of knowledge such as managerial experience and an understanding among participants of the social and political context in which decision making and resource allocation takes place (such as power relations, territorial boundaries, 'rules of the game') (Fleck and Tierney, 1991).

Harnessing the collective knowledge of the firm (in the sense described by Metcalfe and Gibbons, 1989) when it is fragmented in specialist divisions around the firm is difficult, but critical to successful product development. Knowledge integration is problematic in the same way that knowledge transfer has been described as difficult, because knowledge itself is tacit, specialist and embedded in the psychology of the individual and in the sociocultural and even 'political' context of host organizations (Polanyi, 1966; Vincenti, 1990; Nonaka, 1992).

The evidence that knowledge integration is important to project success and that particularly innovative companies are those that have established mechanisms to facilitate the knowledge integration process comes from various fields of innovation and management studies.

Innovation and management studies

A range of long-accepted empirical studies has confirmed that firms which are structured to increase functional integration, enhance cross-divisional collaboration and facilitate efficient communications tend to be more innovative (Rothwell, 1987; Dodgson, 1991). Numerous studies have built up a detailed picture of the 'successfully innovative firm' (Pavitt, 1984; Baron, 1990). Significant 'promoters' of innovation identified in such studies are often mechanisms that directly enhance knowledge integration within the firm. 'Good communications, both within the firm and with outside agents'; 'a general attitude toward innovation as a "corporate-wide task"'; the 'promotion of key cross-divisional individuals: the "product champion" and the "business innovator"' are all cited (Myers and Marquis, 1969; Ramanathan, 1990).

Business consultants, on the whole better known to practising managers than academic researchers, cite similar factors as targets for those aiming to improve their management of innovation. Tom Peters, for example, calls for increasingly 'fast, flexible and flat' organizational structures and the nurturing of cross-functional business units and development teams that are empowered, structured for efficient internal communication, and far more involved with their specific customers (Peters, 1992). In the same vein Lawler III (1992) urges the development of 'high-involvement' organizations and Gary Hamel of London Business School talks of the integration and exploitation of 'core competencies' (Hamel and Prahalad in Lorenz, 1992).

Similarly, within the wide-ranging literature on the product development process, a number of studies have included the concept of knowledge integration in models of technological innovation, though not particularly effectively (Forrest, 1991, provides a useful review). One of the better known is Twiss's 'Activity Stage Model', which shows how key inputs are 'scientific and technological knowledge' on the one hand and 'knowledge of market needs' on the other, representing the well-known forces of 'technology-push' and 'market-pull' (Twiss, 1980). More recent work is appearing with richer empirical evidence and useful international comparisons (Deschamps and Nayak, 1995).

There has been a strong revival emphasizing 'concurrent engineering' (or 'phase overlapping'), which involves carrying out the specialist functions of product development, such as design, engineering, marketing and production, simultaneously rather than consecutively. This is the most obvious evidence of the importance of knowledge integration in the product development process. It allows for a more effective synergy between the different specialists whose ideas and requirements need to be assimilated and incorporated before development costs are 'locked in' at the design stage, and reduces the number of late revisions necessary before the product is brought to market (Boston Consulting Group, 1992; Reinertsen and Smith, 1992).

Japanese company studies
A growing set of studies specifically compares Japanese and Western corporations in terms of their efficiency and effectiveness in managing product innovation. Most writers try to identify how and why Japanese firms are more successful in managing the product development process and therefore by far the most work has been done in the particular sectors and firms where the Japanese are undeniably superior. Contrary to the beliefs of some observers, Japanese supremacy in product development does not extend across all industrial sectors and all firms.

The most detailed comparative studies involving Japanese manufacturers have been carried out in the auto sector, shown by the comprehensive work done by Womack, Jones and Roos (1990). Clark and Fujimoto (1991) focus at the project level within individual firms from the USA, Japan and Europe, looking at performance, productivity, lead time and design quality, and relating these to differences in product strategy. Sakakibara and Aoshima (1988) have examined product strategy at the project and firm levels, particularly in terms of product fit with similar models. Imai, Nonaka and Takeuchi (1985) looked at relationships between organization and development performance, comparing a key project at Honda with successes in other industrial sectors. Other useful research has been carried out by Cusumano and Nobeoka (1992) and new insights as to Japanese–Western differences appear in Clark and Wheelwright (1995).

The findings from these studies (for others see Collinson, 1994) provide us with a list of 'general' factors said to contribute to the success of product development initiatives in Japanese firms. In the sectors covered, notably the automobile sector and, here, the consumer electronics industry, more readily available data on market share, quality and cost of Japanese products attest to these strengths.

For example, the rapid speed of concept-to-market project timescale in many Japanese firms stems from their ability to overlap the various development phases (parallel, concurrent or simultaneous engineering rather than 'relay-race' development) and from their close relations with components suppliers, which helps accelerate prototype development. Their ability to match product to market results from having close links with customers (feedback via distribution systems) and strong internal communication channels between R&D divisions, product development teams, marketing and market research departments. Many Japanese firms also have the ability quickly and successfully to introduce incremental product innovations by focusing on customer-led improvements and upgrades. Again, close relations between components suppliers, product development teams and manufacturing divisions help in this objective.

Overall, efficient interdepartmental communications centred on flexible, multifunctional teams facilitate non-routine project-based activities. These are in keeping with the general management style of many Japanese firms, characterized by: effective communications (decentralized, horizontal information flows); less separation of corporate functions, the lifetime employment tradition, plus job rotation and a strong emphasis on training (supporting the development of cross-divisional experience and personal network building across divisions); a strong group ethic, loyalty and motivation combined with competitiveness; a strict 'formal' hierarchy (seniority system) combined with strong underlying 'informal' networks; and a general 'long-termism', a focus (until very recently) on growth and employment stability rather than profits and shareholder dividends. Again, factors that facilitate the knowledge-integration process underlie a great many of these strengths.

A significant recent shift in this literature is towards both the dynamic capabilities approach and a consideration of 'integrative capabilities' among firms (Ianisti and Clark, 1994). Work by Bowonder and Miyake (1993), using the examples of Hitachi and Nippon Steel, identifies a range of 'integrative mechanisms' within Japanese firms that bring managerial functions, technical competences and information systems closer together to promote innovation. They discuss the following 'mechanisms' specifically: organizational intelligence, technology fusion, concurrent engineering, horizontal information flow structures, corporate networking, technology forecasting and organizational learning.

A new era of multimedia product development
Managing the process of knowledge integration for all areas of corporate activity has always been a central, underlying determinant of company performance, and particularly of success in new product development. Technical, economic and social changes in general mean that the ability to manage this process well has taken on a new significance (Hamel, 1995).

For the wide range of companies involved in the emerging multimedia industry, however, knowledge integration has taken on an even greater significance. Because multimedia products incorporate a broader range of technologies, developed in the past in separate divisions of individual companies and separate companies in different industry sectors (computer hardware, software, consumer electronics, telecommunications, media and so on), the range of specialist knowledge underpinning the technical inputs for a single product is much broader and more widely dispersed. This places an emphasis on the accumulation of technological capabilities (Miyazaki, 1994) and on the combination of separate specialisms within development projects (Frumau, 1992, discusses this in the context of Philips's R&D 'portfolio').

Software, as mentioned, is an increasingly important, integral component of multimedia products, and Sony and Philips have both had a variety of problems integrating hardware and software knowledge and expertise in a balanced way. Furthermore, the uncertainties surrounding emerging multimedia markets and the mismatch between these markets and existing market research, marketing and distribution channels in 'single-sector' firms has increased the need for new mechanisms to develop and integrate market-related knowledge as part of the product development process.

These changes, as well as the rapid advances in new technologies, the confusing array of new applications product possibilities and user expectations, and the profusion of inter-firm and inter-sector alliances, have all placed new pressures on internal project management in firms like Sony and Philips. Reorganization within firms and the associated (hotly contested) reallocation of resources is happening in response to these large-scale changes. Above all, there is a premium placed on the ability of firms to facilitate knowledge integration.

A central question is whether the competitive advantages developed by Japanese firms will be eroded by the changes taking place in consumer electronics, or whether they will in fact help them adapt to the new conditions and increase their lead over European companies.

To answer these questions, it is useful to position the process of knowledge integration within the holistic perspective afforded by the sociotechnical constituencies framework. This enables us to identify systematically some of the key factors influencing the eventual market performance of both products.

Sociotechnical Constituencies

Sociotechnical constituencies may be defined as dynamic ensembles of technical constituents (tools, machines, and so on) and social constituents (people and their values, interest groups, and the like), which interact and shape each other in the course of the creation, production and diffusion (including implementation) of specific technologies.[2]

The development of consumer products such as the Data Discman and the Photo-CD Viewer can be treated as constituency-building processes consisting of broad fronts of sub-processes, involving a variety of specific and interrelated technical, organizational and commercial factors. The combination of these sub-processes exhibits a wide scope for configuration; it also manifests itself through various levels of operation: from intra-company to cross-industry standard-setting initiatives.

An advantage of the constituencies approach is the focus it provides for comparative analysis. It puts the understanding of *technological processes* at the centre of the analysis (see Figure 6.1).[3] The approach emphasizes the idea of interrelation and interaction, including knowledge integration, in technological development. In the present case, the constituency-building action involves both intra- and inter-institutional processes with the goal of creating new products and establishing these as leaders in the global arena. The type of interactions between different sets of social constituents is critical to the

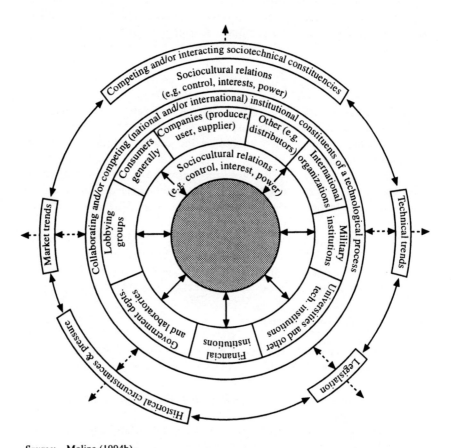

Source: Molina (1994b)

Figure 6.1a   Possible intra- and inter-organizational sociotechnical constituency

performance of sociotechnical constituencies, whether these be individual engineers and managers, or companies or multisector consortia. In the case of Sony's Data Discman and Philips's Photo-CD, an indication of who the key constituents were and why they were involved will become clearer as we apply the framework to the case studies.

The example of Figure 6.1[4] highlights certain essential features of all sociotechnical constituencies. The two-way arrows indicate that influence may be bidirectional: from the inner circle of technology (**T**) towards the outer circles and vice versa. The second circle indicates that technology is conditioned by the opportunities and constraints imposed by the physical

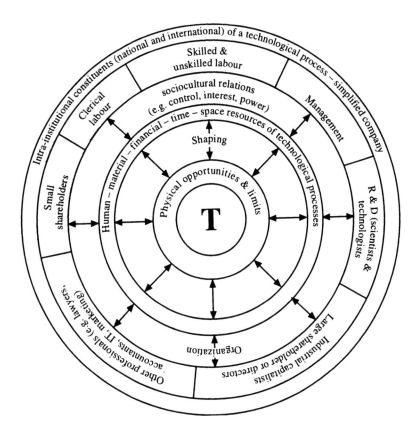

Figure 6.1b

world and its own nature and state of the art at any given time. A major objective of the product development process is to extend these limits to improve the functionality and cost-efficiency of the final product. The third circle indicates that technologies generally result from the integration of time and space, and human, material and financial resources. These are context-specific and change continuously as the sociotechnical constituency evolves.

The development process may involve new knowledge or the integration of existing knowledge at the project level. A major aspect of our approach is to recognize that this knowledge does not exist in isolation; it is 'embedded' as an intrinsic part of the (different) sociopolitical and economic context(s) of the organization(s).

The fourth circle of Figure 6.1, in the projects we examined, was the domain of senior managers, who translate strategic corporate objectives from the top into projects and processes further down the hierarchy. This selection mechanism guides the allocation of resources and gives managers control over the development process, and again is effected through the interaction of different intra-institutional social constituents. The fifth circle extends this reasoning to the more aggregate inter-institutional dimension.

The main constituents, outside Sony and Philips, involved in the Data Discman and Photo-CD projects include the subcontractors and co-developers, as well as final customers, who are all part of the sociotechnical constituency. Competing hardware manufacturers with alternative standards platforms, and software producers with complementary products and technologies (particularly important in the Sony study) also characterize this level of the model.

As we move to the outermost circle, Figure 6.1 highlights the fact that the development of a given technology is not simply the result of an insular, intra-constituency process. It is influenced, for example, by legislation and regulation, and by technical and market standards and trends which are themselves the result of interaction between sociotechnical constituencies (that is, an inter-constituency process).

Finally, it must be noted that despite their perception of benefit, social constituents participating in a constituency do not invariably have a clear idea of what their specific interests are in relation to a given technology. Nor does the development of this technology invariably follow the intended path or yield the results expected by the constituents. Uncertainty and unpredictability are inherent in the technological process, particularly where constituents are trying to break completely new ground. This uncertainty factor is likely to figure prominently in new multimedia technologies, especially as they come to involve the development and integration of a broad front of innovations.

Thus this 'map' of the relevant constituents, identifying how they fit into the evolving combination of factors influencing the product development process, is one application of our approach. Beyond this it is important to understand how these constituents come together to promote a specific product or technology. This can be defined as the process of sociotechnical 'alignment'.

INTRA- AND INTER-INSTITUTIONAL CONSTITUENCY BUILDING AS PROCESSES OF SOCIOTECHNICAL ALIGNMENT

The emergence of both the Data Discman and the Photo-CD Viewer can be treated as the intra- and inter-institutional construction of mass market product constituencies through processes of sociotechnical alignment. Sociotechnical alignment is what constituents engage in (however consciously, successfully, partially or imperfectly) when they are promoting the development of specific technologies. It can be defined as the process of creation, adoption, accommodation (adaptation) and close or loose interaction (interrelation) of technical and social factors and actors which underlies the emergence and development of an identifiable constituency. Alignment should neither be seen as a jigsaw-like accommodation of static available pieces nor as complete and permanent, once achieved. 'Misalignment', for example, expresses a situation of tension and disharmony, and 're-alignment' refers to changes or reaccommodations in the life of a constituency. Also, alignment is not necessarily consensual. 'Authoritarian' forms in which alignment is enforced by one party over another also occur.

In alignment, the flow of influences is multidirectional and the interrelations involved are not only among people and institutions but, simultaneously, among people/institutions and technical elements. Thus, when two or more people or institutions join to pursue a common goal, we may talk of alignment between people or institutions; when developers shape technologies in accordance with potential users' specifications, we may talk of aligning technology to people; when people have to learn new skills to be able to use a technology, we may talk of aligning people to technology; lastly, when technologies are shaped in accordance with the features of other technologies such as standards, we talk of aligning technology to technology. In practice, all these elements imply forms of knowledge integration and are likely to be present in the development of a constituency at one time or another.

The 'Diamond of Alignment'

The concept of the 'diamond of alignment' has been used to illustrate the multiple dimensions of alignment involved in the generation of large-scale inter-institutional initiatives as well as in the company implementation of a

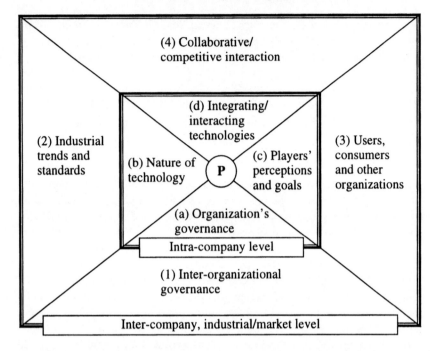

Figure 6.2   The diamond of intra- and inter-organizational alignment

new technology (Molina, 1994b). The cases of the Data Discman and Photo-CD implement the 'diamond' to compare innovation processes from their companies' origins to market diffusion.

In Figure 6.2 the centre of the diamond is the evolving technology of the constituency. At all times, specific products, solutions and applications are not separate from the constituency. Rather, they must be seen as evolving technical crystallizations of the state of development of the constituency. The market performance of innovations such as Data Discman and Photo-CD is likely to be closely associated with effective and consistent alignment in several dimensions. The next section provides illustrations from the Sony and Philips case studies alongside an explanation of each element in Figure 6.2. First we examine the 'intra-company' level (dimensions a, b, c, d), then we shall look at the inter-company level (dimensions 1, 2, 3, 4). At any time the generation of product **P** remains the focus of the alignment process.

Intra-company level

(a) Organization's governance   Effective constituency building will exhibit identifiable alignment of the evolving product or technology with the govern-

ance[5] and strategic priorities of the organization and, hence, relevant decision making and management structure. This means, on the one hand, that the market or objective addressed by the technology is perceived as highly significant to the organization's performance; on the other hand, it means a simultaneous perception that the potential technical and market solution is sufficiently viable so as to merit allocation of resources. It should be noted that the flow of influence is not merely unidirectional, and emerging constituencies may challenge the organization's governance as they develop, sometimes leading to adaptations, modifications and new boundaries in functional structure and power relations.

In both case studies there are examples of the importance of this alignment. In Sony's Data Discman case, in particular, the project team was forced to realign itself with the broader product development and sales strategy of the company. Indeed, before it could be given official standing as a company project, a working prototype had to form part of a presentation to Sony's President and CEO, Norio Ohga. With responsibility for product development strategy and marketing across the entire company, he decided that the 8 cm CD-ROMs would need to be housed in a casing to distinguish them from music CD-ROMs and justify the higher price to the customer (product differentiation). The result was a realignment of the constituency since a wholesale redesigning of the Data Discman to incorporate a disk caddy-loading mechanism was required.

Later in this chapter we shall examine some of the management mechanisms in Sony that promote a balance between (1) creativity and flexibility of resource (human and capital) allocation for 'bottom-up' entrepreneurial development activities, and (2) 'filtering' and checking mechanisms to ensure that only technically and commercially viable projects that fit with the company's overall market strategy evolve beyond the initial project stages.

(b) Nature of technology   There are two related aspects to this dimension: alignment of constituency-building strategies with the particular characteristics of the product (that is, the nature of the technology), and alignment of these strategies with the realizable use-value of the product at any given time (that is, matching expectation and feasibility).

First, the nature and state of development (maturity) of a given technology (see second circle in Figure 6.1) is almost certain to condition the strategic limits and opportunities for its constituency-building process. It is a simple fact that the nature of telecommunications networks is different from that of biscuits or drugs, and a single 'universal' approach will not do. For our cases, the following intrinsic characteristics have critical strategic value: pioneering emerging technologies; technologies with indirect network externalities; and architectural technologies.

Pioneering emerging technology stresses first-to-market and hence high uncertainty and risk due to lack of precedents. Market-stimulation strategies aimed at aligning users with the technology and vice versa are essential.

This is illustrated by the problems that Philips has had with the CD-I family of products in general. It is still not established as a mass market consumer product and appears to be losing out to the PC plus CD-ROM combination in its main target market, the home. The biggest question mark surrounding CD-I and the Photo-CD concept is whether or not consumers really want to interact with their TVs. When one attempts to forecast the adoption of new technologies it provides one of the best illustrations of how technology itself is so often less important than the social and economic context of its application (amongst many, see Cawson et al., 1995).

In Sony's case a clear link between project team members and local consumer electronics retailers and dealers in Tokyo helped overcome some of the uncertainties surrounding the uptake of the 'electronic book' concept in general and the Data Discman in particular. Interaction with retailers made it clear at an early stage in the project that the software applications that would run on the Data Discman would be its key selling point, rather than the novelty of the technology itself. A wide variety of software to appeal to the existing hobbies and interests of the general consumer (golf games, language tutors, interactive reference books and so on) was eventually packaged with the hardware and led marketing efforts for the Discman line.

Indirect network externality stresses the dependence of the use-value of one product on the existence of another (for example, computers are useless without software and vice versa). The immediate strategic implication is a need to engage software developers early in the constituency.

The hardware–software co-dependency in the Data Discman case also illustrates this aspect of alignment. Co-development of both components was necessary for the final packaged product. In the Philips project, the close interdependence of all the hardware and software components of the full Photo-CD system is also evident. For consumers to buy Viewers they must have access to professional photo-shops equipped with the Writers to transfer their photographs on to CD-ROMs. For professional photo-processing shops to invest in Writers they must have, or anticipate having in the near future, a ready market for these specialist services. Sales of both components failed to reach the levels needed to support a mass consumer market.

From the outset, Kodak and Philips took different routes in spreading the Photo-CD standard, and it became a point of contention between them. Philips wanted to distribute the processing software as widely as possible and license the rights to use the Photo-CD standard to anyone interested, thereby hoping to sell more hardware. Kodak pursued a strategy of exclusivity, wanting to retain its hold over professional photo-shop customers and remain the only provider of the recording service. Because they had divided up the patents and ownership rights early on in the project, and Kodak retained ownership of much of the applications software, the strategies were incompatible.

Architectural technology stresses simultaneous change and continuity in technological development and constituency building (for example, computers may undergo dramatic changes in performance while offering software compatibility and accumulation which make it possible to migrate the constituency from hardware generation to generation). The implication is the buttressing and migratory competitive effect of accumulated software, which reinforces the effect of network externalities.

Again, the example given earlier of the evolving CD-ROM standards books applies here. In both products embedded processing software and chip hardware represent evolving generations of specific technologies. Another example is Philips's CDM9, the CD mechanism for focusing and moving the laser for optical pick-up, which is the latest in an ever-improving line of specific components. At the same time, every new improved product in the family is able to make use of the accumulating pool of applications software.

Second, and critically related to the first aspect, is a clear alignment between the capabilities of the constituency and the technical demands intrinsic to the realization of the use-value of the product (that is, target functionality and cost). The literature of technology development is full of examples of failure to deliver the promise (misalignment between the promise – expectation – and what was eventually possible to bring to the market). To avoid 'failure', the constituency must simply have the technical capacity to deliver the goods within the resources available at any given time. Capacity and resources, however, are dynamic, mutually influencing factors, and part of the capacity to deliver may imply an ability to expand the resources available.

On the whole the resources and technical expertise were available to create both the Photo-CD and Data Discman to meet their design parameters and both products came up to original expectations. This is not to say these were technically straightforward projects, with no mistakes or trial-and-error improvement; only that the final products did what they were initially expected to do. This arguably did not occur, for example, in the case of Apple's Newton, where its telecommunications capabilities were not developed and the final product did not meet with hyped-up market expectations.

(c) Players' perceptions and goals   This refers to the identifiable alignment of perceptions and goals between the constituency's original developers and potential or target constituents (and also alignment among the latter) in the intra-company process. The aim is for them to become members, even developers, of the constituency. This implies three possible directions of align-

ment, most likely in combinations: alignment between originators and other parties contributing relevant inputs such as management authority, funding and expertise; alignment of the technology with players' interests and contributions (social shaping); and alignment of players with characteristics, functionality and use of the technology (for example, training of marketing personnel).

Within Sony and Philips this aspect of alignment refers to the internal participants in the two projects, including the originators of the product ideas, plus the whole range of technical, financial, marketing and manufacturing expertise from various divisions. Gaining backing and support formally and informally for a product idea is necessary to gain the resources, finance and expertise required for the project to evolve from concept to the final mass-produced product.

Project teams tend to be the focus of alignment and knowledge integration but interdivisional coordination and cooperation are essential for project success. There are many examples of misalignment, forced alignment, non-alignment and so on from the projects examined, some of which were described earlier.

Integrating/interacting technologies   Commonly, a new constituency's technology or product will emerge in an intra-company environment populated by other technologies and constituencies. Some will be required to realize the emerging product (for example, production technology); others may have a similar, even competing, claim for resources. Alignment or management of misalignment of the constituency's technology with other interacting technologies (hence constituencies) in the creation, production and diffusion system of the company is a critical strategic issue. This can give rise to a situation of 'obligatory complementarity', in which the product technology requires others in order to realize its contribution (for example, product and production process). In this case, interaction and solutions demand strong expertise-based alignment, giving rise to a process of knowledge integration. In some senses this case applies to all of the hardware and many of the software components of our two products, which rely on each other for the overall product to work. It also applies to the production technology necessary in both companies to manufacture the products.

Alternatively, the situation may become 'antagonistic competitive', in which the product and other technologies are disputing the same role and resources in the organization and the acceptance of one may imply total displacement of the other. The essence of this case is high degree of conflict and no knowledge integration is possible.

Even within companies a surprisingly common occurrence is for two or more divisions to be developing competing products or technologies in separate domains (it is sometimes even orchestrated to boost internal competition). At the start of the Sony project conflict over the hosting of the Data Discman initiative between the MSX computer unit and the General Audio (GA) Group restricted alignment and cross-divisional knowledge integration, despite top–down enforcement of cooperation. The Discman's project team in the GA group actually trained an 'insider' in the software programming language 'C', rather than bringing in expertise from elsewhere in the firm, to develop the embedded search engine.

Inter-company level

(1) Inter-organizational governance   As the alignment process goes beyond the boundaries of the originator company, interactions and knowledge integration around the creation, production and diffusion of the product may involve institutions of the same type (for example, several companies) or institutions of different types (companies, universities, or governments), nationally or internationally. In all instances, arrangements for inter-organizational governance are necessary to express, facilitate and guide the alignment between different organizations. It is crucial for product strategies to acknowledge the existence and quality of these arrangements, either to align with them or to create or modify them to satisfy the needs of the constituency-building process. Lack of attention to inter-organizational governance may be the source of much misalignment and conflict.

This was conspicuously illustrated by the relationship between Philips and its joint-venture partner Kodak. They had significant problems, partly leading to their failure fully to establish the Photo-CD standard across the emerging digital-imaging industry. These two very different firms, in different industry sectors, consumer electronics and photography (or 'imaging'), were poorly aligned. Although they had a shared vision of the desired final product, they had different ideas on how to involve co-developers and users and how to promote the product concept to a mass market. Moreover, they had different management methods and organizational practices for overcoming the various development problems that emerged in the course of the project, and at times conflict threatened to overcome consensus. Legal wranglings that continued throughout the duration of the project attest to these difficulties.

A prominent example of effective inter-organizational governance is given by Sony's arrangement for its 'Electronic Book Committee' (EBC), which quickly grew to over 100 members (see below) supporting the Data Discman format. Here the basis of the agreement was that publishers would not be paid by Sony to produce software applications for the Data Discman, but rather they bought from Sony the rights to publish this software to the Sony specifications. Being convinced of the large market potential of the product and, more importantly, that the electronic-book standard advocated by Sony would become the dominant format, publishers agreed. Under the auspices of the EBC, Sony also licensed out the right to manufacture Data Discman hardware to other manufacturers at very low rates, as part of the rationale of standard setting and consensus building.

(2) Industrial trends and standards   Effective constituency building will also seek to promote alignment between the product of the emerging constituency and widely recognized technical and market trends and standards in the target industrial area. Included in this alignment is a good understanding of the evolution, present strategies, and likely future actions of actual and potential competing constituencies. The balance of standard following and standard setting is likely to vary with organizational 'muscle' and with the nature of the technology.

Both Sony and Philips are at the heart of a highly successful institutional framework for governing the ongoing evolution of CD-ROM standards, which includes a wide range of hardware and software producers.[6] Each project team had to take both existing standards and the ongoing evolution of new CD-ROM versions into account in its development activities. This was to ensure at least partial backward compatibility and to help build alignment around the proposed standards for the Photo-CD and Data Discman products. These were, however, truly pioneering technologies and both Sony's and Philips's products came to market to set standards.[7]

(3) Users, consumers and other organizations   Critical to the growth of the constituency is an alignment between the intra-company constituents and outside parties who are potential or target constituents (for example, suppliers, co-developers and individual consumers). The aim again is for them to become members of the product constituency. Given the broader context, however, this alignment does not necessarily mean all parties working together across the board. Often, competing companies are involved and misalignments at certain levels are an unavoidable part of the constituency's make-up. In practice, players will be aligned on the broad perception that the product is worth the investment, although they may differ on the ways to achieve certain specific aims.

Convincing or coercing co-developers to invest in a particular standard is especially difficult in a time of rapid change when a large variety of technologies are competing for mass markets. To make sure the Data Discman would be supported by a range of software applications, Sony established the 'Electronic Book Committee' (EBC) in Tokyo in October 1989, about nine months before the Data Discman was first marketed at the Osaka International Exposition. This acted as a forum for aligning software and other hardware manufacturers (of the 28 initial members Sanyo and Matsushita were the only hardware developers). The EBC grew to have 90 members by 1992 and 116 by 1994 and supports around 130 Japanese titles in the Discman format.

To join the EBC software publishers, distributors and other ancillary co-product or service providers had to be convinced that Sony had the power and commitment to establish their technical standard as *the* dominant format before they would commit resources and investment to a particular standard. It was therefore in Sony's interests to collaborate with other competitor hardware manufacturers to limit the development of alternative technologies. Likewise it was in the interests of the other hardware manufacturers, particularly when they were 'latecomers' or technology 'followers' in a specific product area, to make sure they aligned their hardware to the format chosen by the majority of software publishers (Collinson, 1993).

The largely successful alignment promotion by the Data Discman contrasted strongly with the Kodak–Philips's less effective attempt to align photo labs and consumers with their own 'software' (photographs).

(4) Collaborative/competitive interaction   This alignment simply extends the concepts described in (d) to the inter-organizational, industrial/market dimension. In effect, beyond the confines of the company a new constituency's product will also emerge in an environment populated by other technologies and constituencies. Again, some will be required to realize the emerging product (for example, tools, production technologies); others may be competing for similar markets. The success of the overall constituency-building process will depend critically on the effectiveness of the alignment, or management of misalignment, with these interacting technologies. Within the wider industrial/market dimension, the same possible situations are implied, including 'obligatory complementarity', 'antagonistic competitive', and 'non-antagonistic competitive'.

This category refers to the entire, complex range of products and technologies that support or compete with our two case study products. As discussed, the main single competitor for both products is the PC plus CD-ROM combination (variations include 3DO's Interactive Multiplayer, Tandy's Video Information System and systems from Nintendo, Sega and Apple). Due to the success of the alternative PC-CD-ROM configuration, there has been an observable shift in the marketing and product placement strategies of both Sony and Philips.

Initially Photo-CD and Data Discman, with their connections only to TVs and the built-in LCD screen, could be characterized as being 'antagonistic competitive' *vis-à-vis* the bundled PC-CD-ROM combination. However, a strategic change has taken place regarding PCs, with both products now including built-in connections to them (that is, a situation of 'non-obligatory complementarity'). This is characteristic of the convergence taking place across the emerging multimedia industry, with the PC- and TV-related products now competing directly across the board.

Considering all the dimensions of alignment, it is clear that the process of constituency building and sociotechnical alignment implied in product innovations will vary greatly in terms of complexity and conflicts depending on the nature of the technology and its initial relationship to the various dimensions in the 'diamond' of alignment. In this process, knowledge-based misalignments play a critical part.

The key point for newly emerging multimedia products, such as both of our examples, is that different organizational players will often be highly uncertain about what they want or can expect from them. This poses challenging problems in the process of constituency building and there is a premium on the ability of companies to manage it effectively. In the next section we examine in detail how Sony dealt with this challenge.

PROMOTING ALIGNMENT AND KNOWLEDGE INTEGRATION AT SONY

Both Sony and Philips experienced problems in their product development projects. Specific additional difficulties arose because of the nature of the product, and both companies had to respond by:

- facilitating the integration of specialist technical knowledge and expertise internally across previous divisional boundaries to create the final product;
- gaining access to complementary areas of knowledge and technical expertise by building alliances with other firms in other sectors;
- establishing new information channels between the product developers and emerging user communities and anticipated markets (and redesigning marketing strategies); and
- building co-developer and co-marketing alliances with other firms to establish industry standards to capture emerging markets.

As discussed earlier, these additional problems, related to multimedia product development, place an added premium on the abilities of the individual firm or project team to integrate fragmented knowledge and build sociotechnical constituencies. From our cases we can identify a number of organizational structures and management mechanisms that facilitate or constrain the firms' ability to overcome these problems and achieve their development objectives. We shall describe two such mechanisms in Sony that directly contributed to the success of the Data Discman project and appear partly to underlie Sony's ability to promote alignment among internal and external constituents and specifically foster the process of knowledge integration. These advantages go some way to explaining Sony's renowned strength in new product development.

Sony Management Mechanisms

The 'merchandiser' concept
The special role of the merchandiser was developed by Akio Morita in the early 1980s, specifically to overcome a perceived lack of individuals with a cross-divisional perspective in Sony. This was necessary to exploit better the variety of potential technological synergies across product groups. The aim, moreover, was to harness the motivation, drive and inventiveness of younger employees toward commercially viable projects by freeing them from routine tasks. In a number of ways the role directly meets the needs for knowledge integration and constituents' alignment.

The merchandiser's role was: to identify product development opportunities within and across product divisions; to organize and motivate product development team members; to coordinate links between the project team and other functional divisions or outside subcontractors; to identify key markets for the product, and willing distributors; and to recruit support for the project from upper management. To carry out these tasks, merchandisers had a degree of freedom from routine tasks, fewer ties to specific divisions, and some flexibility to act as internal 'entrepreneur'.

Two merchandisers worked on the Discman project and only 20 existed in the whole company at that time. In contrast to most 'product champions', merchandisers often have no specialist technical skills themselves. Their role as project coordinator depends more on having a cross-divisional perspective of the firm, its compartmentalized specializations and thus potential collaborations.

Also, in contrast to most product champions, merchandisers tend to be young and, although 'ideally' they have the power to coordinate a project and put together engineers and experts from a variety of divisions, in practice they lack authority. As a result they are forced to get the backing of a senior manager to make any project 'politically' accepted, financed and staffed. They are forced to build alignments across the organization and this acts as a 'filtering' mechanism (or internal market) whereby more experienced line managers block less practical initiatives before resources are committed.

The unique 'subculture' of the product group

The General Audio (GA) Group was the product group within which the project team was housed. The project team, some members of which came initially from outside the GA Group, closely associated themselves with the strong divisional culture of the GA Group. This gave them a number of advantages, including a cohesive team spirit and an element of competitiveness *vis-à-vis* the other groups.

The following tenets or principles, handed down by the head of the GA Group (an original member of the project team that developed the famous Sony Walkman), are seen to be central to the group's uniqueness. Indeed, they can be seen as providing the basic framework for the group's own governance:

1. Believe everything can be *half* the size initially thought of.
2. Decide what size the product should be, even before considering what it should consist of.
3. The target must be clear and simple.
4. Agree to the target and motivate yourself for success before considering the detailed substance of the project or product.
5. 'Difficult' means 'possible'; 'impossible' should be excluded from the equation.
6. Before *explaining* (or attempting to explain) the idea, *make* the product.
7. Brainstorm in your hotel; do not end your discussions or return to work before your target is reached.
8. The most promising ideas or products must be kept secret from your boss; you must make the product before telling him.
9. If you want assistance, ask the busiest people; they are the ones who will have all the best ideas.

Many of the more renowned, innovative characteristics of Sony are reflected in this 'creed' of the GA Group, including the push for product miniaturization (1) and the problem-solving, market orientation (rather than following the 'linear model') (3) and (6). In particular (4), (7) and (8) urge team building and alignment, and suggest that developers should maintain a degree of flexibility and autonomy from the routine management hierarchy. Sharing this credo, product developers are encouraged to feel and act differently and this promotes a coherent GA Group culture that facilitates communication, cooperation, knowledge integration, and effective overall alignment.

The merchandiser role and the strong allegiance to the subculture of a specific product group were two influential organizational factors that enhanced the efficiency and effectiveness of the Data Discman development project. The merchandisers were responsible for internal coordination, between both functional specialists (marketing, manufacturing and so on) and technical specialists in different divisions. They also engaged in external constituency building by taking the prototype to retailers to gain market feedback on the product concept, identify a target market and develop a marketing strategy. The same strategy was used from an early stage in the project to build the necessary alignment and ensure joint design, development and marketing with software producers. As part of this process the merchandisers were central to the creation of the EBC.

A central objective is to strike a balance between motivating team participants through 'ownership' of a project and developing a sense of loyalty and 'belonging' and a degree of interdepartmental competition (as deliberately nurtured by the GA Group subculturel) on the one hand, and, on the other, exploiting the specialist capabilities of different product groups and functional divisions by integrating existing knowledge across the firm (a problem for all firms, both internally and within inter-firm alliances). The merchandiser's objective (not always met) is to overcome interdivisional rivalry and territorial competitiveness in order to exploit existing synergies rather than duplicating knowledge and expertise in different parts of the firm. The merchandisers' efforts were particularly effective in the context of the concurrent engineering or 'phase overlapping' style of project management which contrasted with Philips's more linear pattern of development.

To work effectively to these ends, the activities of the merchandisers and the subculture of the GA Group both relied on a range of organizational elements that were listed earlier as characteristic of Japanese firms in general. The practice of job rotation, dense interdivisional communications, close relations with suppliers and sub-component manufacturers, the strong group ethic and a strict formal hierarchy combined with strong informal networks all underlie their operation (and reduce their transferability to other companies). Other, Sony-specific factors, such as the high degree of organizational flexibility in terms of resource allocation (human and capital) in particular divisions (enabling informal, bottom–up development of product ideas) and the constant movement of young R&D staff from research units to product divisions,[8] also play a part and appear to contribute to Sony's competitive advantage in product innovation. Their contribution at the project level was highlighted by our focus on the processes of alignment and knowledge integration in the Data Discman case study.

CONCLUSIONS

This chapter began by describing the companies, products and projects at the core of the Data Discman and Photo-CD constituencies. It then combined two conceptual strands to analyse how their development was organized, and identified a number of ways in which Sony appears to facilitate alignment and knowledge integration for project success.

This served to illustrate the relevance of the combined approach, focusing on knowledge integration as central to the process of sociotechnical alignment underlying product development; emphasize the significance of effectively managing knowledge integration for successful constituency building in the new era of multimedia; and highlight specific management mechanisms at Sony that appear to underlie its innovativeness, using the Data Discman example.

The sociotechnical constituencies approach in particular allowed us to identify the multiple alignment dimensions which have an influence (positive or negative) on the product development process, giving us an insight into the factors shaping the final product (social and technical factors combined). By applying this model to the development projects examined in Philips and Sony we identified how the internal and external constituents became aligned, where there were problems, and how these two firms coped with them. This led us to a revealing analysis of some of the key structures and management mechanisms making up the organizational context within which alignment was engineered in both Sony and Philips.

The product at the centre of the sociotechnical constituency we have been analysing represents a combination of technologies that support various features intended to fulfil (perceived) consumer requirements. In the case of emerging multimedia technologies, uncertainty is endemic. There is never complete agreement from the outset as to the product specifics. Which features should be incorporated? What features come highest on customers' lists of priorities? What (technically) can we create, at what price? How can we best combine the necessary functions – for technical efficiency and user-friendliness? What complementary technologies or products are essential to sell our product? Should we create these as well, or create outside alliances? and so on.

Intra- and inter-organizationally the development process is one of conflict and negotiation between competing and collaborating interests with their own ideas of the optimal final outcome. The inner box of the 'diamond of alignment' pointed specifically to the fact that the process takes place in the context of the firm, with layers of procedures, regulations and cultural 'norms' that govern decision-making behavour, strategic choices and the allocation of human and financial resources. Specialist knowledge and power are divisionalized and hierarchical, and various competing and complementary perceptions and goals have, at least temporarily, to be aligned for knowledge and technologies to be integrated into a new product.

Similar factors can be identified beyond the boundaries of the firm (in the outer box of the diamond). Other companies and organizations, with their own perceptions, goals and modes of governance, compete or collaborate in the development process, also shaping the final product. Technical trends and standards influence the nature of the technology and the format of the product, and all must generate positive alignment with the demands of users and customers.

For the particular cases of Data Discman and Photo-CD, Sony's organization in many ways contrasted with the less flexible, bureaucratic mechanisms in operation at Philips. In Sony the main objective, the development of usable technologies and saleable products, took priority over aspects of structure or organization and directly guided resource allocation. In Philips structure and organization seemed to take priority and the project was developed *despite* the organization, not because of it. However, both firms showed evidence of good and bad management practices and the final conclusions are not intended to paint a static, stereotypical picture of Sony 'good', Philips 'bad' at product development.

This is particularly valid in the light of recent major restructuring efforts in Philips. While the Photo-CD exhibited the classic problem of poor communication and knowledge integration between the R&D, applied development (commercialization) and marketing functions at Philips, there are now growing indications that recent restructuring, in response to steep declines in sales and profits, has at least partly overcome these problems.

This relates to a broader question underlying our Sony–Philips study: namely, whether the competitive advantages developed by Japanese firms like Sony will be eroded by the changes taking place in the consumer electronics industry, or whether they will in fact help them adapt to the new conditions and increase their lead over European companies.

It certainly appears that Japanese prowess in the area of incremental product development and in manufacturing will not be the decisive factor in helping overcome the problems associated with the current stage of multimedia product development. Moreover, their strong reliance on domestic Japanese markets as testing grounds for new products could be a critical weakness. Other characteristics, however, such as close developer–market links (for example, via the merchandiser), strong links with component suppliers as co-developers, and the internal management mechanisms that promote cross-divisional knowledge integration in Japanese firms will continue to be an advantage.

How the changes in the industry will eventually affect these competing firms still hinges to a great extent on their evolving ability to incorporate software development more firmly alongside hardware development in the product development process. In some cases this means a considerable shift in strategy, moving from hardware- to software-led market research, product development and marketing. It also means boosting internal software capabilities and creating closer alliances with software companies both to meet and 'shape' new markets more effectively than they have done up to now. In the end it may be that both firms eventually lose out to expanding computer hardware and software companies (so that the USA comes to dominate a global multimedia industry).

It is too early yet to forecast absolute winners and losers at this stage in the evolution of the multimedia industry. However, as this chapter shows, the main problem for companies everywhere is that their structure, the experience of their employees, and the competences of senior decision makers stem from the past, but their success and even their survival lies in a very different future.

NOTES

1. The support of the Economic and Social Research Council is gratefully acknowledged. The research was funded by ESRC award number R000234659.
2. See, for instance, Molina (1989, 1990, 1992, 1993a, 1993b, 1993c, 1994a). The sociotechnical constituencies approach relates to other theoretical work, for instance, networks and systems approaches found in literature from different disciplines. However, it is not the purpose of this chapter to discuss this relationship. This kind of discussion is found in Molina (1993a, 1993b).
3. The central circle **T** in Figure 6.1 illustrates the fact that the central concern of sociotechnical constituencies is with the analysis of technological processes. This does not mean that the technology is external to the constituency. Figure 6.1 should be taken as an effort to visualize on paper the richness and complexity of an integrated micro/macro environment.
4. Not all sociotechnical constituencies will have the same mix of intra- and inter-institutional constituents as the one exemplified in Figure 6.1. For instance, some of them may be just national; some may not have any military constituent at all, and so on. The variety can be infinite.
5. Williamson (1979) uses the term 'governance structure' to refer to 'the institutional matrix or framework within which transactions are negotiated and executed' (p. 239). Governance is used here in the similar sense of the organization's framework guiding or influencing individual and collective interactions and associated resource allocations.
6. From the original Red Book (for CD-audio, 1980) and the Yellow Book (CD-ROM, 1985 and CD-ROM-XA, 1988), both driven by Sony and Philips, came the Green Book for the CD-I standard (1988), established properly by an alliance between Philips and Matsushita in 1991. Since then a range of new technical developments (mainly in the area of digital compression) and a host of new players (PC manufacturers, computer software companies and media firms) have greatly reduced the coherence of this standards constituency.
7. Acceptance of this standard by consumers is dependent on a wide range of factors beyond the simple product-related advantages of technical superiority or quality. As the Betamax–VHS conflict between Sony and arch-rival Matsushita showed in the early 1980s (Baba and Imai, 1990), establishing a dominant standard in the market is often influenced more by the level of support won from software developers and system distributors than by the hardware features of the product itself (the lesser known case of Philips V2000 video recorder provides an even better illustration: Metze, 1993). Backing the losing format means a great deal of wasted investment in R&D, production and distribution, for software and hardware developers alike.
8. Sony's Central Research Laboratories in Yokohama are filled with young recruits who are moved out and into other areas of the company (even manufacturing divisions) after a

relatively short period of time (around five years), usually with a technology or product idea which they will develop in the product groups. Although this system can impede 'institutional memory', with the danger that there will be a certain amount of 'reinventing of the wheel', the advantage is that the best and brightest are strongly motivated to work on projects that have applied product development potential, which they can take into the development phase with beneficial career prospects for themselves. There are no significant career tracks in the research laboratories themselves, which leaves noticeably few older researchers in the laboratories (according to Robert White, professor of Electrical Engineering at Stanford, who took the Sony Sabbatical Chair at the Central Research Labs in 1994).

REFERENCES

Baba, Y. and Imai, K. (1990), 'Systemic Innovation and Cross-border Networks: The Case of the Evolution of the VCR Systems', paper prepared for the 'Schumpeter Society Conference on Entrepreneurship, Technological Innovation and Economic Growth: International Perspectives', Virginia, June.

Baron, P.J. (1990), 'Factors Influencing Innovation', *Technovation*, **10** (6), 379–87.

Boston Consulting Group (1992), *Competing Against Time*, Maxwell Communications Corporation Free Press.

Bowonder, B. and Miyake, T. (1993), 'Japanese Innovations in Advanced Technologies: An Analysis of Functional Integration', *International Journal of Technology Management*, Special Issue on New Technological Foundations of Strategic Management, **8** (1/2), 135–56.

Cawson, A. et al. (1995), *The Shape of Things to Consume: Delivering Information Technology into the Home*, Aldershot, UK: Avebury.

Clark, K.B. and Fujimoto, T. (1991), *Product Development Performance: Strategy, Organization, and Management in the World Auto Industry*, Boston, MA: Harvard Business School Press.

Clark, K.B. and Wheelwright, S. (eds) (1995), *The Product Development Challenge*, Boston, MA: Harvard Business School Press.

Collinson, S.C. (1993), 'Managing Product Innovation at Sony: the Development of the Data Discman', *Technology Analysis and Strategic Management*, **5** (3), 285–306.

Collinson, S.C. (1994), 'New Multimedia Product Development at Sony: Organising for Innovation and Market Success', *JETS Working Paper*, no. 10, University of Edinburgh.

Cusumano, M.A. and Nobeoka, K. (1992), 'Strategy, Structure and Performance in Product Development: Observations from the Auto Industry', *Research Policy*, **21**, 265–93.

Deschamps, J.-P. and Nayak, P.R. (1995), *Product Juggernauts*, Boston, MA: Harvard Business School Press.

Dodgson, M.J. (1991), 'Technology Learning, Technology Strategy and Competitive Pressures', *British Journal of Management*, **2**, 133–49.

Fleck, J. and Tierney, M. (1991), 'The Management of Expertise: Knowledge, Power and the Economics of Expert Labour', *Edinburgh PICT Working Paper* 29, Research Centre for the Social Sciences, University of Edinburgh.

Forrest, J.E. (1991), 'Models of the Process of Technological Innovation', *Technology Analysis and Strategic Management*, **3** (4), 439–53.

Frumau, C.C.F. (1992), 'Choices in R&D and Business Portfolio in the Electronics Industry: What the Bibliometric Data Show', *Research Policy*, **21**, 97–124.

Hamel, G. (1992), quoted in Lorenz, C. (1992). These ideas were later developed in Hamel, G. and Prahalad, C.K. (1994), *Competing into the Future*, Boston, MA: Harvard Business School Press.

Hamel, G. (1995), 'The Prize That Lies in Foreseeing the Future', *Financial Times*, 3 June (edited foreword to *FT Handbook*, FT Pitman, 1995).

Ianisti, M. and Clark, K.B. (1994), 'Integration and Dynamic Capability: Evidence from Product Development in Automobiles and Mainframe Computers', *Industrial and Corporate Change* (Special Issue on Dynamic Capabilities), **3** (3), 557–607.

Imai, K., Nonaka, I. and Takeuchi, H. (1985), 'Managing the New Product Development Process: How Japanese Companies Learn and Unlearn', in: Clark, K.B. et al. (eds), *The Uneasy Alliance*, Boston, MA: Harvard Business School Press.

Lawler III, E.E. (1992), *The Ultimate Advantage: Creating the High-Involvement Organization*, London: Maxwell Macmillan.

Lorenz, C. (1992), 'Into the Great Wide Open', *Financial Times*, 2 November, London.

Metcalfe, S. and Gibbons, M. (1989), 'Technology, Variety and Organization: A Systematic Perspective on the Competitive Process', in Rosenbloom, R. and Bergman, R. (eds), *Research on Technological Innovation, Management and Policy*, Vol. 4, Greenwich, Conn. and London: JAI Press.

Metze, M. (1993), *Short Circuit: The Decline of a Once Great Company*, London: Minerva Press.

Miyazaki, K. (1994), 'Search, Learning and Accumulation of Technological Competences; The Case of Optoelectronics', *Industrial and Corporate Change* (Special Issue on Dynamic Capabilities), **3** (3), 631–54.

Molina, A.H. (1989), *The Transputer Constituency: Building Up UK/European Capabilities in Information Technology*, Research Centre for the Social Sciences, Edinburgh: The University of Edinburgh.

Molina, A.H. (1990), 'Transputers and Transputer-Based Parallel Computers: Sociotechnical Constituencies and the Build Up of British-European Capabilities in Information Technology', *Research Policy*, **19**, 309–33.

Molina, A.H. (1992), 'Integrating the Creation, Production and Diffusion of Technology in the Design of Large-Scale and Targetted European IT Programmes', *Technology Analysis and Strategic Management*, **4** (3), 299–309.

Molina, A.H. (1993a), 'In Search of Insights into the Generation of Techno-economic trends: Micro and Macro-constituencies in the micro-processor industry', *Research Policy*, **22** (5/6), 479–506.

Molina, A.H. (1993b), *Networks, Communities, Systems and Sociotechnical Constituencies: Analysing Failure in a European Technological Initiative*, Edinburgh PICT Working Paper No. 46, RCSS, Edinburgh: University of Edinburgh.

Molina, A.H. (1993c), *The Formal-Methods Constituency: Diffusion of an Emerging Technology into a High-Volume Industrial Environment*, Research Centre for the Social Sciences, Edinburgh: The University of Edinburgh.

Molina, A.H. (1994a), 'Understanding Economic Trends: Micro- and Macro-Constituencies in the Microprocessor Industry, the Emergence of a Large-Scale European Initiative in Technology', *Science and Public Policy*, February (1994), 31–41.

Molina, A.H. (1994b), 'Technology diffusion and RTD programme development: What can be learnt from the analysis of sociotechnical constituencies?', *DGXII*

Occasional Paper XII, 378–94, Brussels: Commission of the European Community/DGXII-A/5.

Myers, S. and Marquis, D.G. (1969), *Successful Industrial Innovation*, New York: National Science Foundation, 69:17.

Nonaka, I. (1992), 'Managing Innovation as an Organizational Knowledge Creation Process', paper prepared as chapter for the *Handbook of Technology Management*.

Pavitt, K. (1984), *Technological Innovation and Strategic Management*, SPRU mimeo, Brighton: University of Sussex.

Peters, T. (1992), *Liberation Management: Necessary Disorganization for the Nanosecond Nineties*, London: Macmillan.

Polanyi, M. (1966), *The Tacit Dimension*, London: Routledge and Kegan Paul.

Ramanathan, K. (1990), 'Management of Technology: Issues of Management Skill and Effectiveness', *International Journal of Technology Management*, 5 (4), 409–22, Oxford: Pergamon Press.

Reinertsen, D. and Smith, P. (1992), *Developing Products in Half the Time*, London: Chapman and Hall/Van Nostrand.

Rothwell, R. (1987), 'The Successfully Innovative Firm', prepared for the *European Conference on the Regional Environment for Innovation and Technology*, Barcelona, Spain, 25–26 February.

Sakakibara, K. and Aoshima, Y. (1988), 'Company Growth and the "Wholeness" of Product Strategy', in Hiroyuki, I., et al. (eds), *Competition and Innovation: Company Growth in the Auto Sector*, Tokyo: Toyo Keizai.

Teece, D. and Pisano, G. (1994), 'The Dynamic Capabilities of Firms: An Introduction', *Industrial and Corporate Change (Special Issue on Dynamic Capabilities)*, 3 (3), Oxford University Press, pp. 537–556.

Teece, D., Pisano, G. and Shuen, A. (1990), 'Firm Capabilities, Resources, and the Concept of Strategy', *CCC Working Paper 90–8*, Center for Research on Management, Berkeley: University of California.

Twiss, B.C. (1980), *Managing Technological Innovation*, 2nd edn, London: Longman.

Vincenti, W. (1990), *What Engineers Know and How They Know It: Analytical Studies from Aeronautical History*, Baltimore, MD: Johns Hopkins University Press.

Womack, J.P., Jones, D.T. and Roos, D. (1990), *The Machine that Changed the World*, New York: Macmillan.

Williamson, O. (1979), 'Transaction-Cost Economics: The Governance of Contractual Relations', *The Journal of Law and Economics*, 22, 233–61.

7. Rapid technological change and shortening business horizons[1]

Peter Swann

INTRODUCTION AND BACKGROUND

As the pace of technological change continues unabated, and product life cycles become shorter, many businesses are having to plan within ever shortening time horizons. A major issue for the management of technology in the future is how to ensure that shortening business horizons do not deter important long term strategic investments in new technologies.

This chapter has three aims. The first is to clarify when shortening business horizons are a consequence of financial short-termism, when a consequence of technological and market realism, and when simply a function of sheer uncertainty. The second is to clarify when these shortening business horizons will lead to under-investment. As we point out, just because a business horizon is short need not mean that it is too short. The third is to assess the potential of two contemporary management philosophies, defining core competences and building strategic visions, as ways of offsetting the problem of under-investment.

Much of the debate about short-termism revolves around the question of whether financial markets and/or managers apply too high a discount rate to risky investment projects – or equivalently demand too short a payback period. In this debate a required discount rate is considered too high and a required payback period too short if they deter socially profitable projects.

But the use of very short payback periods in itself need not imply financial short-termism. There are other circumstances in which it is eminently reasonable for managers to require a short payback period. If product life cycles are very short, then any project which is expected to deliver returns *only* within the next product life cycle will have to pay back the initial investment within that short period – or else it will never pay back. In such cases, it is not financial short-termism but technological and market realism that requires a short payback period.

In the argument which follows we recognize three potential reasons for under-investment. The first is that companies may be obliged to apply too high a discount rate. The second is that companies only look at the payoff of an investment within the current product life cycle, and ignore benefits for subsequent generations of products. The third is that the future beyond a short time horizon is simply too uncertain, and hence companies require payback within that short horizon. While most attention has been directed at under-investment for the first reason, it is arguable that the others are just as important.

We suggest that two popular management philosophies of recent years can provide a framework in which to assess the carry-over benefits of a particular investment from one generation of products to the next. The organization that tries to identify and delimit its core competences can be seen (from an accounting perspective) as defining those intangible assets in which it wishes to invest – though see the section on core competences and strategic vision below. In this setting, individual investment projects are interpreted less in terms of what they deliver in particular product and market settings, and more in terms of what they add to the intangible balance sheet. In a similar way, the strategy of articulating a corporate technological vision can also provide a framework in which to account for the payoffs of particular technology investments beyond the immediate products for which they were intended. Both perspectives may help to reduce under-investment that results from an inability to appreciate the future payoffs from specific investments.

The structure of the rest of the chapter is as follows. First we ask why rapid technological change makes planning difficult and may lead to corporate myopia. Then we revisit the debate about financial and organizational 'short-termism'. Next we address the question of shortening product life cycles, and the implications for the use of short payback periods. We then draw out the implications of these for under-investment and employment. The next section summarizes how two popular recent management philosophies can be interpreted as helping to offset some of the under-investment. Finally we conclude our discussion with some implications.

WHY DOES RAPID TECHNOLOGICAL CHANGE MAKE PLANNING DIFFICULT?

To some, the answer to this question may seem so obvious that it hardly needs to be discussed. To put it simply, it is difficult to plan when things are moving fast and you can't see where you're going.

This simple intuition, however, is unduly pessimistic. The economic and organizational behaviour literature on how organizations cope with rapid change has demonstrated that even large and bureaucratic organizations can cope with change – even rapid change – so long as it is change for which the organization can plan. Nelson and Winter (1982) argue that organizations develop routines which tell them how to adapt to changing circumstances, and by doing so enable themselves to cope with rapid change – so long as it can be anticipated. This is not to deny that rapid technological change may mean that product life cycles become very short, but even that does not necessarily make planning very difficult, as we shall see below.

One of the pioneers of the economics of innovation, Christopher Freeman (1982), stressed the distinction between incremental technological change, which is not unduly disruptive, and radical technological change, which is. It is important to note that incremental need not imply slow change; rapid incremental change (such as the steady improvement in some technology parameters while preserving the basic structure of a technology) is common and is not necessarily disruptive.

In the same way, Tushman and Anderson (1986) used the distinction between competence-enhancing (or competence-preserving) change, which can be handled using existing organizational routines and competences, and competence-destroying change which is not compatible with existing routines and competences. The former may or may not be rapid; that is not the issue. The point is that it is manageable change. The latter is not manageable without a major reorganization, and if that cannot be achieved it may lead to the company's decline or exit from a market (Hannan and Freeman, 1977, 1984). One of the pioneers in the field, Utterback (1994), reviews what companies must try to do to master the dynamics of innovation.

Two case studies in the semiconductor industry bring out these distinctions. Much of the technological change in the semiconductor memory market has been very rapid – with successive generations of chip appearing every three years or so, which offer a fourfold increase in capacity. This change has indeed been rapid, but in a sense it has been incremental, and competence-preserving. Contrast this with the episode in the early 1970s when the microprocessor first appeared, and started to replace standard logic components. This was a much more radical change, and certainly competence-destroying – for some companies. Moreover, it led to substantial disruption in market leadership in the 1970s (Swann and Gill, 1993).

The difficulty that rapid technological change poses for planning is that its direction is unpredictable, rather than that it is rapid. Why is it unpredictable? Again, the answer may seem obvious: because even given a full knowledge of the state of the art in a certain technology, we cannot know which parts will enjoy market success and which will not.

And yet, in some discussions of the marketing of technology, this deep uncertainty does not seem to feature. While the so-called linear model has fallen into discredit – as has been signalled in the writings of the past Chairman of the ESRC, Newby (1993) – some still tell a simple story that scientists first generate science, technologists then turn it into technology, and finally companies turn it into commercial processes and marketed products. In the linear model, technology pushes its way into commercial application: there does not need to be any independent pull from the demand side. It is implausible, however, to expect that technology push can create a new market unless demand is responsive. Equally, unsatisfied demand on its own will not bring forward new technologies unless the technological and scientific base is in place and capable of responding to such demand. The most interesting cases of technologies generating new markets arise where technology pushes and demand pulls, and this is what leads to the other source of uncertainty here. In this setting, technological change as it evolves in a market will be unpredictable even if the basic technology is predictable; this is because the nature of demand is much harder to predict.

This unpredictability may be at least a part of the reason for apparent myopia. If technological change is simply too unpredictable beyond a fairly short horizon, then it may be prudent to ignore returns from a particular project beyond that horizon. This does not imply that the organization doesn't care about the future, nor that investments in one technology will have no payoff in the future development of another, but simply that this is too imponderable to put into a discounted cash flow calculation.

FINANCIAL AND ORGANIZATIONAL SHORT-TERMISM

In some quarters, the epithet short-termism is treated with suspicion. It is seen as a convenient excuse for why an apparently important strategic investment is not undertaken. And yet many in industry claim that vital strategic investments have been cut because financial markets and/or company accountants do not give proper weight to the future importance of these investments. If this is happening, we need to be clear why: is it because financial markets or accountants apply too high a discount rate to the future – and what do we mean by too high? Or is it a result of technological unpredictability or technological and market realism?

In the debate about short-termism, a critical distinction is whether this phenomenon – if indeed it exists – is a property of financial markets or if it is internal to organizations or, indeed, both. We discuss these two in turn.

Financial Market Short-termism

One of the most comprehensive discussions of short-termism is by Marsh (1990). Do stock markets undervalue the long term? More precisely, do share prices put too much weight on short-term profits and dividends and insufficient weight on future profits? Or again, do stock markets discount the future more heavily than is justified by the cost of capital?

Marsh argues that it is difficult to test this directly, but considers that the evidence from a large number of studies of market efficiency is broadly consistent with the view that financial markets are efficient – meaning that they are concerned about and (on average) correctly discount the long-term and the short-term implications of relevant news items and key events. Marsh considers that there is little evidence that financial markets systematically apply a discount rate to future profits that is higher than would be justified by the cost of capital. In a rather different piece of research, Goodacre et al. (1993) conducted an experimental study of analysts' attitude to company accounts in which R&D was treated in different ways. They found that analysts did place a value on R&D expenditures up to the norm for that industry, and were not 'fooled' by accounts which reported higher profits and assets simply by choosing (where legitimate) to capitalize rather than realize R&D expenditures.

In consequence, if short-termism is seen as a problem (and many still think it is – Jacobs, 1991), Marsh argues that the direct cause for this must lie with managers and not shareholders or financiers. He acknowledges that one reason for internal short-termism is that managers may shun long-term investments that depress short-term accounting profits. But then the question is why this is of concern to managers: part of the reason is thought to be that managers are acting under duress from the financial system and fear hostile takeover bids if short-term accounting profits look weak (Cosh et al., 1990). The fear of an unwanted takeover bid will encourage managers to maximize short-term profits and dividends in the hope that this will boost their share price and so keep the predator at bay. Marsh's review of the evidence, however, concludes that this does not necessarily happen.

Recent research by Miles (1993) does not dispatch short-termism so easily. Indeed, Miles finds systematic evidence that future profits are discounted at too high a rate. But if, as Marsh suggests, short-termism is not primarily a result of stock-market inefficiency or adverse effects from duress, then what other factors may be responsible? Two contributory factors are suggested: cross-country differences in the cost of capital; and managerial short-termism.

In comparing the UK and Japan, Odagiri (1981, 1992) has argued that the UK operates at a disadvantage because in effect the City of London is rather too efficient from the point of view of the economy as a whole. In Japan companies have been able to pursue growth-oriented, as opposed to profit-oriented strategies. This is partly a result of lower discount rates, and partly because the hostile takeover is such a rarity there. It is a legitimate and important role of the stock exchange to constrain companies to maximize the present value of their assets, but if there are substantial spillovers to investment activity, then society as a whole would benefit from investment in excess of what profit maximization permits. These spillovers arise if the benefits from strategic investments cannot be fully appropriated by individual companies, but spread out to others who are not funding these investments.

Organizational Short-termism

Turning to managerial short-termism, some argue that it results from the way management reward systems are designed. Managers are rewarded for profitability during their own (possibly short-term) tenure within the organization, and not for the unknown effects of their decisions on future performance. The practice of rewarding managers with share options may partially correct for this, though there are probably better ways of boosting share values than investment in R&D.

In summarizing case study research on the internal and external constraints on investment in technology, Lonie et al. (1993) stress the critical role of the product champion in the company as a way of overcoming organizational myopia. Their case studies found that when the champion was vigorous and charismatic enough, most companies would be able to operate a strategic override – so that projects which would not be financed on normal payback criteria would still be approved by the board.

Another source of internal short-termism may be the failure of managers to realize that the payoff from strategic investments may extend beyond the immediate project for which they were intended. Research by Geroski et al. (1992; 1993) suggests that it is easy to underestimate the effects of innovation on company performance. This study attempted to measure the effects of major innovations on the short- and long-run profitability of a sample of large quoted UK firms. They found two effects: first, that each innovation had a noticeable but fairly modest effect on profitability over the four to six years after the innovation was first produced; and, second, that firms who produced an innovation any time during the late 1960s and early 1970s survived the recession of the early 1980s much more easily than did non-innovative firms. What is more, the size of this second, indirect effect of innovation on profitability was several times larger than the size of the direct effect.

These results suggest that innovations have two effects on the company. First, there is a direct effect which arises because the production of an innovation alters a firm's market position relative to rivals (say by lowering its costs, or affecting its demand). However, there is a second, indirect effect that arises because the act of doing R&D and producing an innovation appears to transform a firm's internal capabilities, making it more alert, flexible and adaptable. It is this second effect which seems to account for the superior performance of innovators during a recession.

If companies take account of only the first effect when deciding whether or not to undertake innovative activity, then they are likely severely to understate the total benefits of innovative activity. Regardless of what discount rate they use, they will almost certainly appear to be acting 'short-sightedly' and not doing enough innovation.

We shall revisit this theme later when we suggest that two recent and popular management philosophies offer a way to account for these longer-term effects of strategic investments.

SHORTER PRODUCT LIFE CYCLES

There is a widespread belief that product life cycles have become progressively shorter in the last ten to twenty years. If companies demand short payback periods, this is not necessarily evidence of financial short-termism. It may simply reflect technological and market realism: if product life cycles are short, then projects must pay back quickly or they will not pay back at all.

There is much, if scattered, evidence for the shortening of product life cycles in the trade press. Some sources refer to product life cycles of a year, others nine months (Haber, 1994) or even four months (Goldberg, 1994). In fact, some recent research casts doubt on this, and concludes that it is not entirely clear whether life cycles have grown shorter or not (Rifkin, 1994).

The reason for the ambiguity here is quite simple. If we treat each model that a manufacturer introduces as a separate product, with a separate product life cycle, regardless of what degree of advance it offers over the previous model, then product life cycles have indubitably shortened. But part of this, at least, is a result of the tendency to proliferate models with ever smaller technological distance between them. It may be that each four months a new hi-fi model is introduced, but the technological difference between it and the preceding model is becoming smaller and smaller. If we try to adjust for this and ask instead whether manufacturers are covering the same technological distance more rapidly now than in the past, then the answer is much less clear. Rifkin (1994) discusses some of the reasons why they may not.

The semiconductor memory market is often held up as an example of very rapid product advance, but here on average there has been a two- to three-year gap between the introduction of one generation of memory chip and the introduction of the next generation. That doesn't sound short at all, relative to some of the numbers quoted above, but remember that the technological distance between one generation and the next has been increased in capacity by a factor of four (Swann and Gill, 1993). For those products where life cycles are much shorter, it appears that the order of magnitude increase in performance/capacity from one generation to the next is a great deal smaller.

The key issue here is how long is the market lifetime of a product or group of products to which the same strategic investments apply. If this market lifetime is the duration of one product life cycle only, then we do have a worsening investment problem. But for the reasons discussed above that need not necessarily be so.

Whether or not life cycles are getting shorter is perhaps less important than the related question of how long is the period over which strategic investments can be expected to pay back. Even if life cycles are short, so long as the strategic investment can be expected to generate payoffs over many generations of products, then this need not force a company to insist on a short payback period. Conversely, if the investment is only relevant to one product generation, then companies will still have to insist on a short payback period even if the life cycle of that single product is reasonably long by modern standards (for example, four years). Ultimately the length of the payback period depends on the product of the average lifetime per model and the number of model generations over which the investment will generate payoffs.

This key but often neglected point is developed in the work of Meyer and Utterback (1993). For them it is the lifetime of a product family rather than a specific model that is critical.

Finally, it is worth pointing out that the length of product life cycles is not some exogenously, or purely technologically determined constant. It depends on the degree and form of technological and product competition. Indeed, we can see the phenomenon of short model life cycles as an attempt by some manufacturers to proliferate over time the number of different models. Seen from this perspective, proliferating models over time is very like proliferating models at any given time (Schmalensee, 1978): both can act to deter small-scale entry by companies who can only sell in one part of the product space (one product niche) or can only sell for a limited period of time. If there is proliferation of slightly differentiated models over time, then only long-term entrants will recoup their costs, since the life cycle for each individual model is so short. Both sorts of product proliferation can be seen as a strategy to raise rivals' costs (Salop and Scheffman, 1983), to deter entry, and hence to increase long-term profitability.

UNDER-INVESTMENT AND EMPLOYMENT

We have seen three generic reasons why firms may have to apply high discount rates (or equivalently require short payback periods) on their investment projects: first, because they have no idea what the investment might yield beyond the reasonably short time horizon in which their markets and technologies are predictable – and so prudently limit their time horizon; second, because they wish to apply, or are required by external financial market pressures to apply, high discount rates or short payback criteria; and third, because they can only envisage an investment yielding any payoff during the lifetime of the relevant product family – which is seen to be short.

We have to remember, though, that just because a required payback period is short this doesn't mean it is *too* short – and, equivalently, that just because a required rate of return is too high doesn't mean that it is *too* high. In the Appendix we set out a simple model in which market realism and short product life cycles mean that companies must apply higher discount rates than they would to other projects.

When is it reasonable to say that these high discount rates are too high – or, equivalently, that the required payback periods are too short? The three answers, corresponding to the three generic reasons in the previous paragraph, are as follows.

1. Suppose that those with reasonable knowledge of the future of a particular market foresee a time horizon of t_2 over which an investment can generate payoffs, and suppose the investor's required payback period is t_1. Then if $t_2 > t_1$, we can say that there is under-investment in this setting, because the investor is requiring a shorter payback period than he would if he were better informed about his own interests.
2. Suppose that financial markets require a rate of return of r_2 when general opinion is that the appropriate social discount rate is r_1. Then if $r_2 > r_1$, we can say that there will be under-investment. Some believe that financial market rates of return should converge on the social discount rate – but that requires strong assumptions about market efficiency (which may be justifiable) and strong assumptions about the distribution of income (which are unlikely to be satisfied).
3. Suppose that a particular strategic investment will generate payoffs over a family of products extending forward to a time horizon of t_2. Suppose that the investor is unaware of this, and assumes that the payoffs will only accrue over a time horizon t_1, and hence requires a payback period of t_1, where $t_2 > t_1$. Once again, we can say that there is under-investment in this setting, because the investor is taking a payback period that is too short for his own interests.

In each case there is under-investment because the required payback period is shorter (or the required rate of return higher) than it should be. In two cases, the reason for the under-investment is ignorance or perhaps even a failing on the part of investors. In the third case, it is because of a disjunction between the requirements of financial markets or managers and wider interests.

Under-investment will often bring with it under-employment. If certain projects that should be undertaken are not, for whichever of the reasons above, then certain types of employment will be lost. If the lost projects are those associated with risky strategic investments – such as R&D – then it is that sort of employment that will be lost. A recent study by Bosworth and Wilson (1993) is interesting in this context. They surveyed 700 companies in the UK about the educational background of the MD, members of the board, and the workforce, and also about their technological activities and their performance. Their research found that the background of the MD, and the structure of the board (including the level of qualifications and discipline) have a positive correlation with the growth, technological prowess, and over-all performance of the company. Moreover, they found that foreign-owned companies based in Britain tend to have a more highly qualified board and workforce than British-owned firms. This could be a symptom of under-investment in the UK. Alternatively it could simply reflect differences in product market orientation between their average British company, and their sample of foreign-owned companies based in the UK.

CORE COMPETENCES AND STRATEGIC VISION

We consider that two popular management philosophies can be interpreted as (among other things) an attempt to offset – if not exactly overcome – the sorts of under-investment mentioned above.

The strategy of defining and specializing in core competences (Prahalad and Hamel, 1990) can be seen as a way of trying to ensure that strategic investments made today will have a longer expected lifetime of playoffs, because the strategy aims to ensure a close fit between today's competences and future competences. In this way, the aim is to ensure that investments in today's products will carry over to tomorrow's products in the same product family (Meyer and Utterback, 1993).

In the same way the strategy of attempting to define corporate visions of the future of technologies is again a way of accounting for the possible future benefits of investments in today's product families for future product families.

Core Competences

This perspective on management (Hamel, 1994) stresses that competitive success depends overall upon the effective management of organizational competences. Integrated organizational competences or 'know-how' are essential for effective technological innovation. This is particularly true in high-technology companies, because innovation rests on the input of many functional groups – some from the technology side and others from the operational and marketing part of the organization. Know-how incorporates bundles of both organizational and technological knowledge, tacit and coded, which grow over time with experience. Dyerson and Roper (1991) suggest that sudden breakthroughs in the accumulation of technological competences are rare. The ability of the firm to absorb and act upon knowledge depends in part on staff continuity. Practical steps to achieve this include on-the-job promotion and share options, or, more subtly, technology can be deployed strategically to 'lock in' staff.

Suppose that the organization sees its future competitiveness in terms of the deployment of its competences, rather than in terms of a collection of individual investments and projects. This shifts attention away from the returns to a particular investment within a particular project, and towards the contribution of that investment to the core competences of the organization. We have to recognize substantial measurement difficulties here, for, as Hamel (1994) points out, competences cannot simply be seen as assets to be measured and depreciated like other assets. Nevertheless, the concept of a core competence which will form the basis of a company's competitive edge over several product generations can in principle open up longer time horizons than those of the individual project. As such, this management philosophy is seen as a way of overcoming some of the under-investment recognized above.

Strategic Vision

Some see the company's vision of the future of a technology or a market as an essential part of its strategy (Knights and Morgan, 1990; Hamel and Prahalad, 1994; Metcalfe and Boden, 1993; Swann and Gill, 1993). These visions are often widely articulated within the organization, and sometimes widely publicized outside, especially in markets with rapid technology change. Our concern here is less with the *ex post* factual accuracy of these visions than with how the visions are articulated and publicized, and what are their effects on the subsequent development of the technology and market structure. Indeed, the literature on visions of technological futures does not see these technological paths as something exogenous to be forecasted; rather the existence of a strong corporate vision can be an essential tool in shaping the future to a company's vision.

The vision defines the range of technological and market outcomes for which the organization can be prepared. As Rosenberg (1969, 1976), Dosi (1982), Sahal (1985) and Georghiou et al. (1986) point out, the trajectory or vision can act as a focusing device, to help companies sort out from the wide range of alternative technology strategies a few leading paths along which they plan to progress. If the actual path of the technology strays too far from a company's vision, then that company may only be able to follow at a cost or time disadvantage. In such circumstances, and where most firms' visions have turned out to be incorrect, small organic firms may be at an advantage (Burns and Stalker, 1961; Tushman and Anderson, 1986; Swann and Gill, 1993). Conversely, when a large organization finds that the vision is accurate, that organization will be well placed to take advantage of economies of scale that arise from having an organizational structure designed to cater for that vision (Swann and Gill, 1993).

Visions can be updated, of course, but that is not unproblematic at the level of the organization, as firms become accustomed to organizational routines (Nelson and Winter, 1982), and visions become embodied in corporate or organizational structure (Metcalfe and Boden, 1993). To change the vision in a manner that will allow the economies of scale to be exploited requires a corresponding change in organizational routines and structure. Of course, this inertia is not necessarily inefficient. On the contrary, when the vision is correct, the mechanistic structure is a source of economies of scale. When a technology settles down, so that its path can be foreseen, it is firms of this type that will have an advantage. But when the technology is at an early stage, and trajectories are hard to predict, the organic structure will be able to adapt more readily to follow the emergent path. As Peters (1987) put it: some companies thrive on chaos.

It is useful here to classify visions of a technology according to two criteria: (1) are they tactical or strategic? (that is, short-term or medium- to long-term); (2) are such visions created for effects internal or external to the firm? The internal strategic use of visions of the future is as a long-term planning device. The principle is that if this vision permeates the organization, then change along that anticipated path is simply 'incremental' change, and the organization can cope with that.

Moreover, the internal strategic use of visions can help to resolve the under-investment problem identified above, because it gives the organization a framework within which to assess the potential relevance of investments in today's technology for tomorrow's technologies. A company with a clear vision of how the market for semiconductor memories will develop can assess what competences and scale economies are required to survive in the business, whether it is able to attain these and, if so, what investments today can be expected to realize relevant payoffs in future markets.

CONCLUSIONS

This chapter has had three aims. The first was to clarify when shortening business horizons are a consequence of financial short-termism, when a consequence of technological and market realism, and when simply a function of sheer uncertainty. The second was to clarify when these shortening business horizons will lead to under-investment. The third was to reinterpret two current management philosophies, defining core competences and building strategic visions, as ways of offsetting the problem of under-investment.

The chapter raises some issues that need further attention in future research. We have seen that strategies based on core competences and visions can overcome some of the firm's internal obstacles to longer-term investments. But how will such moves be understood by financial markets, and how will this influence the valuation of the company's shares? This interaction between company strategies and financial markets is crucial if the problem of under-investment is to be overcome. Moreover, while the present chapter does not go into this in detail, it is not a trivial matter for companies to achieve a clear consensus about what are their core competences and strategic visions. Equally, this difficulty extends to the task of assessing whether investments are indeed compatible with competences and visions. Nevertheless, we hope that the present chapter provides a motivation for exploring these important questions.

APPENDIX

A given investment is expected to yield future returns, but the timescale over which these returns accrue is uncertain. Moreover, while the initial returns are c per year, they are expected to decline over the lifetime of the project. For simplicity, assume that the probability that this investment is still yielding returns in period t is given by

$$e^{-pt}$$

and the best guess of the rate at which returns decline over the project lifetime is given by

$$ce^{-kt}$$

If it is conventional to discount future returns at the rate r, then the present value of the project is

$$\int_0^\infty ce^{-pt}e^{-kt}e^{-rt}dt$$

which is easily rearranged to

$$\int_0^\infty ce^{-(p+k+r)t}dt$$

NOTE

1. This chapter is an extended and revised version of an earlier paper written for the National Academies' Policy Advisory Group. I am grateful to Rod Coombs for helpful comments on an earlier version of this paper, and also to other participants at the Third ASEAT Conference, but none are responsible for remaining errors.

REFERENCES

Bosworth, D. and Wilson, R. (1993), 'Qualified Scientists and engineers and economic performance', in Swann, P. (ed.), *New Technologies and the Firm*, London: Routledge.

Burns, T. and Stalker, G. (1961), *The Management of Innovation*, London: Tavistock Publications.

Cosh, A., Hughes, A., Singh, A., Carty, J. and Plender, J. (1990), 'Takeovers and Short- termism in the UK', Institute for Public Policy Research, Industrial Policy Paper no. 3.

Dosi, G. (1982), 'Technological Paradigms and Technological Trajectories: A Suggested Interpretation of the Determinants and Directions of Technical Change', *Research Policy*, **11**(3), 147–62.

Dyerson, R. and Roper, M. (1991), 'When Expertise Becomes Know-How: The Management of IT Projects in Financial Services', *Business Strategy Review*, **2** (2), 55–73.

Freeman, C. (1982), *The Economics of Industrial Innovation*, 2nd edition, London: Pinter Publishers.

Georghiou, L. et al. (1986), *Post Innovative Performance*, London: Macmillan.

Geroski, P. and Machin, S. (1992), 'Do Innovators Outperform Non-Innovators?', *Business Strategy Review*, **3** (2), 79–90.

Geroski, P., Machin, S. and Van Reenan, J. (1993), 'The Profitability of Innovating Firms', *RAND Journal of Economics*, **24**, 198–211.

Goldberg, A. (1994), 'Fast Times, Fast Cycles', *Marketing Computers*, **14** (3), 20.

Goodacre, A., Ball, R., McGrath, J., Pratt, K. and Thomas, R. (1993), 'Accounting for R&D Costs: Does it Matter? Perceptions of Analysts and Company Management', in Swann, P. (ed.), *New Technologies and the Firm*, London: Routledge.

Haber, L. (1994), *Computer Reseller News*, 11 April, p. 120.

Hamel, G. (1994), 'The Concept of Core Competence', in Hamel, G. and Heene, A. (eds), *Competence-Based Competition*, Chichester, UK: John Wiley and Sons.

122   *Technological change and organization*

Hamel, G. and Prahalad, C.K. (1994), *Competing for the Future*, Boston, MA: Harvard Business School Press.

Hannan, M.T. and Freeman, J. (1977), 'The Population Ecology of Organisations', *American Journal of Sociology*, **83**, 929–64.

Hannan, M.T. and Freeman, J. (1984), 'Structural Inertia and Organisational Change', *American Sociological Review*, **49**, 149–64.

Jacobs, M.T. (1991), *Short-Term America*, Boston, MA: Harvard Business School Press.

Knights, D. and Morgan, G. (1990), 'The Concept of Strategy in Sociology: A Note of Dissent', *Sociology*, **24**, 475–83.

Lonie, A., Nixon, W. and Collison, D. (1993), 'Internal and External Financial Constraints on Investment in Innovative Technology', Chapter 12 of Swann, P. (ed.), *New Technologies and the Firm*, London: Routledge.

Marsh, P. (1990), *Short-termism on Trial*, London: Institutional Fund Managers' Association.

Metcalfe, J.S. and Boden, M. (1993), 'Paradigms, Strategies and the Evolutionary Basis of Technological Competition', in Swann, P. (ed.), *New Technologies and the Firm*, London: Routledge.

Meyer, M.H. and Utterback, J.M. (1993), 'The Product Family and the Dynamics of Core Capability', *Sloan Management Review*, **34** (3), 29–47.

Miles, D. (1993), 'Testing for Short-termism in the UK Stock Market', *Economic Journal*, **103**, 1379–96.

Nelson, R.R. and Winter, S.G. (1982), *An Evolutionary Theory of Economic Change*, Cambridge, MA.: Harvard University Press.

Newby, H. (1993), 'Innovation and the Social Sciences: The Way Ahead', *ESRC Innovation Agenda Pamphlet*, Swindon: ESRC.

Odagiri, H. (1981), *The Theory of Growth in a Corporate Economy: Management Preference, Research and Development and Economic Growth*, Cambridge: Cambridge University Press.

Odagiri, H. (1992), *Growth Through Competition, Competition Through Growth: Strategic Management and The Economy in Japan*, Oxford: Oxford University Press.

Peters, T. (1987), *Thriving on Chaos*, New York: Alfred A. Knopf.

Prahalad, C.K. and Hamel, G. (1990), 'The Core Competence of the Corporation', *Harvard Business Review*, **68** (3), 79–91.

Rifkin, G. (1994), 'The Myth of Short Life Cycles', *Harvard Business Review*, **72** (4), 11.

Rosenberg, N. (1969), 'The Direction of Technological Change: Inducement Mechanisms and Focusing Devices', *Economic Development and Cultural Change*, **18**, 1–24. (Reprinted in Rosenberg, N. (1976), *Perspectives on Technology*, Cambridge: Cambridge University Press.)

Rosenberg, N. (1976), 'On Technological Expectations', *Economic Journal*, **86**, 523–35. (Reproduced in Rosenberg, N. (1982), *Inside the Black Box*, Cambridge: Cambridge University Press.)

Sahal, D. (1985), 'Technology Guide-Posts and Innovation Avenues', *Research Policy*, **14** (2), 61–82.

Salop, S. and Scheffman, D. (1983), 'Raising Rivals' Costs', *American Economic Review*, **73**, 267–71.

Schmalensee, R. (1978), 'Entry Deterrence in the Ready to Eat Breakfast Cereal Industry', *Bell Journal of Economics*, **9**, 305–27.

Swann, P. and Gill, J. (1993), *Corporate Vision and Rapid Technological Change*, London: Routledge.

Tushman, M.L. and Anderson, P. (1986), 'Technological Discontinuities and Organizational Environments', *Administrative Science Quarterly*, **31** (3), 439–65.

Utterback, J. (1994), *Mastering the Dynamics of Innovation*, Boston, MA: Harvard Business School Press.

8. 'Upgrading' national systems of innovation: new technology-based firms

Margarida Fontes

THE ROLES OF NEW TECHNOLOGY-BASED FIRMS

Technological Dynamism Versus Fast Growth

The interest in the creation of new technology-based firms (NTBFs) originated in their association with a number of new technologies and the emergence of the new industries derived from them (Rothwell, 1984). This association conveyed the idea of NTBFs' potential contribution to technological change and more generally to economic growth, employment creation and industry regeneration (Bollinger et al., 1983; Cooper and Bruno, 1977; Rothwell and Zegveld, 1982).

An analysis of the arguments put forward permits us to suggest that the potential attributed to NTBFs derived from two factors: their *technological dynamism*, that is, the ability to identify and develop new technologies with high potential, and the entrepreneurial drive necessary to take them to the market; and their capacity for *fast growth,* on the basis of their success in the introduction of the new technologies. However, recently some doubts have been cast on NTBFs' ability to meet the expectations raised in respect of them (Oakey, 1991; Stankiewicz, 1994). In our view these doubts are largely based on the fact that, in spite of a few individual cases of outstanding success, NTBFs have not, as a group, matched the expectations of fast growth, although they have fulfilled their role as technology-dynamic firms, challenging existing ways of doing things.

The point is that maybe such expectations were 'inflated' (Stankiewicz, 1994) and most NTBFs did not necessarily have the willingness or the opportunity (or both) to grow. In fact, a large number of NTBFs expressed a preference for slow growth and showed reluctance to grow beyond a certain size (Autio, 1994; Jones-Evans, 1996), or chose alternative forms of expansion (Jarillo, 1989). The opportunity to grow depended on the conditions confronted by the firms. In some fields where technological opportunities are high, conditions may exist for new firms to grow on the basis of the appropriation of their technological knowledge (Pavitt, 1984). Therefore, some NTBFs did grow, but this was not a generalized phenomenon. The nature of the 'pioneering' process often means that early entrants experience great difficulties in getting established and in growing on the basis of the major innovation they have introduced (Olleros, 1986). This happens because these new firms lack the competences and resources in other (non-technological) areas necessary to exploit fully the results of their efforts (Teece, 1986). On the other hand, some large established firms have shown an ability to retain the lead for prolonged periods of time. They have survived potentially damaging 'discontinuities', have incorporated the radical changes introduced by young technology-based firms and have even recovered the leadership when they seemed to have missed a major opportunity (Pavitt, 1991). For the young firms, the result was acquisition, or situations of dependence or narrow specializations with a narrow margin for further growth (Granstrand and Sjolander, 1990; Freeman, 1991). The recent history of biotechnology provides a striking picture of this process (Walsh, 1993; Oakey, 1993).

Recently some authors have tried to dissociate NTBFs' activity from the fast-growth perspective. Stankiewicz (1994) argues that, at least in the case of academic spin-offs, the emphasis on growth and employment misses firms' most significant feature: the fact that they are an element in the process of knowledge and technology transfer from research organizations. The view that NTBFs' performance should be addressed in a broader context is also developed by Autio (1994), who points out that NTBFs' major role is played through their position in industrial innovation networks. A similar position is defended by authors addressing the network activity of small innovative firms (Rizzoni, 1994; Shaw, 1993). In directing the attention to NTBFs' role in the process of diffusion of new technology, these approaches shift the focus to aspects of NTBFs' behaviour that emphasize their potential as technologically dynamic firms. This perspective also provides a number of opportunities for NTBFs, often expressed as niches where fast growth is not necessarily the crucial issue (Autio, 1994; Mariti, 1993). According to Freeman (1991), the changes registered in the industrial organization – particularly those associated with the increased importance of networking – create a space for small innovative firms that are able to develop unique competences that are indispensable to their larger counterparts. Therefore, the fact that NTBFs remain small and specialized will not inevitably lead to their displacement.

Technological Dynamism as the Basic Feature of NTBFs

The above discussion permits us to argue that the role of NTBFs can be primarily expressed in terms of their technological dynamism and only secondarily in terms of their growth capacity. Fast growth is a 'bonus': it may or may not occur. But technological dynamism is an intrinsic factor associated with the very existence of the firm, and thus the relevance of NTBFs is based on it. We shall therefore examine in more detail the basic elements of this concept.

In our view technological dynamism should not be restricted to the ability to identify, develop and introduce a new technology/application. An analysis of the activities carried out by NTBFs suggests that their potential relevance as technologically dynamic firms is based on two factors: (a) the initial challenging role, implicit in the act of their creation; and (b) the more long-standing role of acting as a source of new technologies and as their diffuser, that is, their technology transfer role.

Each of these roles has been separately approached in the literature. The 'challenging' character of NTBFs is well summarized by Bollinger et al. (1983, p. 5): NTBFs not only often carry out major product innovations, making 'contributions which extend the boundaries and constraints of technical know-how', but they provoke existing firms, which view them as a threat and have to respond, into improving the existing technology or acquiring the new one. The technology transfer role is described by Autio (1994, p. 260) who points out that NTBFs 'develop technology internally and/or acquire it from external sources ... refine technology to achieve the best possible fit with customer needs ... deliver, or transfer, technology to customers through various interactions'.

These two roles are clearly complementary and together configure the major contribution of this type of firm. NTBFs are created to develop and/or introduce a new technology/application which improves or replaces the existing ones (often challenging the existing organizations). By that act a firm is established that is mainly a 'concentration of technology' (Autio, 1994), and whose basic role is to proceed as an agent of technology transfer, acquiring and delivering new technologies.

NTBFs as an Element of a Process

As young, small and technology-oriented organizations, NTBFs have a number of limitations (particularly with regard to resources and breadth of skills) that may hinder the performance of these roles. They may act as constraints on their ability to commercialize the technologies developed and/or to go beyond the early stages and proceed with their technology transfer role. Because of that, we shall argue that NTBFs' potential technological dynamism will only be fully expressed if other actors are involved in the process.

These actors include both established organizations and other NTBFs. They may be involved in the process of creation, participate in the introduction of the new technology/application, or act through time in a more or less symbiotic way with the young firm. There is ample evidence on the linkages NTBFs establish with their environment to compensate for their shortcomings: market-oriented agreements; finance-raising partnerships; and technical alliances (Ackroyd, 1995, Lawton-Smith et al., 1991, Roberts, 1990, Shan, 1990). Several authors have stressed the role of sophisticated customers and suppliers (Lipparini and Sobrero, 1994; Mustar, 1994; Saxenian, 1991) and the synergetic effects derived from location in knowledge-intensive environments (Feldman, 1994; Van de Ven, 1993).

Theorization about the 'dynamic complementarity' between large and small firms (Rothwell, 1983), about the emergence of the 'network organization' as a new organizational form (Miles and Snow, 1986) and the alternative of 'external growth' (Jarillo, 1989), about the social dimension in the emergence of new industries (Van de Ven and Garud, 1989) and in the building up of 'technological systems' (Carlsson and Stankiewicz, 1991), provide a more general framework which permits us to understand why NTBFs' role can only be clearly expressed in a relational context. NTBFs are only one element of the process of technical and industrial change. Their ability to perform a role in such a process depends on the presence of other elements and on the relationship they establish with them.

NTBFS IN LESS ADVANCED COUNTRIES

An Identification of NTBFs' Potential Roles

A review of the literature found few studies addressing NTBFs in less advanced countries, either Western countries (Abetti et al., 1987; Ayal and Raban, 1990; Martinez-Sanchez, 1992; O'Doherty, 1990; Ramos, 1989; Valls, 1993) or Asian ones (Brunner, 1991; Kim, 1988; Lee and Lee, 1994). It found even fewer references to the role of small technology-based firms in the development process. However, a careful analysis of the above studies leads to the conclusion that NTBFs appear to have some strengths, when a basic science and technology (S&T) infrastructure is present and some industrial development has occurred, permitting both access to technological knowledge and occurrence of market opportunities. It also suggests that, while being relatively similar in some respects to their counterparts in developed countries, these firms may be required to play different roles, given the context where they operate. One basic difference lies in the fact that large technology-intensive firms tend to be rare, and some of the roles usually played by them are not being performed.

NTBFs emerged from most of these studies as firms showing great dynamism in technological terms and an innovative behaviour considerably above that of the 'average' local firm. Two particularly important components of their behaviour were their close interaction with the local S&T infrastructure, and their ability to access and absorb externally generated technology, adapting it to local needs. These features appeared to make them well suited as one element in the process of gaining early competences in emerging technologies, in the 'catching-up' mode suggested by Perez and Soete (1988). However, the technological sophistication of the firms appeared to be largely a function of the sophistication of the markets – that is, more advanced firms will be more likely to emerge only when the market is receptive of them (Kim, 1988). This gives particular relevance to the role of government policies. Because the industrial structure is often weak and deficient in technological terms, and because technological and market opportunities are not sufficient (or at least are not perceived as such by potential entrepreneurs), some support or even incentive for NTBF creation and early operation will be needed (Kim, 1988; Ramos, 1989), involving mechanisms at the level of supply and demand.

Technological Dynamism and Less Advanced Countries

NTBFs' technological dynamism appears particularly important in the case of less advanced countries. There, too, the major role of NTBFs can be expressed along two lines: as technology challengers, breaking with the inertia of existing firms; and as diffusers of technology. However, the conditions prevalent in these countries mean that the ways such roles are performed and their impact on the countries' economic development are likely to be different.

Researchers addressing the development process have built a model (largely based on the case of newly industrializing countries – NICs), according to which a developing country would proceed along a number of steps (for instance Kim, 1980; Lee et al., 1988; Kim and Dahlman, 1992). These steps are: external acquisition of technology (through purchase or foreign direct investment); internalization (assimilation and diffusion); improvement and own development. The rationale behind this model is a view of development where the building up of technology capabilities is achieved through the ability to first implement (acquire and use), then assimilate, and only afterwards transform, the technology acquired.

We shall argue that NTBFs may, in certain fields, 'short-circuit' the above sequential process, by directly accessing new technology (both generated by the local S&T infrastructure and obtained from more advanced countries) and taking it to the market. In doing this they are acting more in accordance with the 'catching-up' mode described by Perez and Soete (1988, p. 459), where the 'capacity for participating in the generation and improvement of technologies as opposed to the simple "use" of them' is a crucial issue. They are also circumventing the bottleneck caused by the growing inadequacy between the 'kinds of the knowledge and skills required to operate given production systems, and the kinds of knowledge required to change them', described by Bell and Pavitt (1993, p. 165).

In fact, NTBFs can be a mechanism to exploit some of the new technological knowledge being developed by, or accessed through, public research centres. The low technological level exhibited by most local firms is likely to prevent them from profiting from such knowledge, whereas the few advanced companies may not be interested in exploiting it, due to the frequently 'niche' character of the opportunities provided. NTBF creation could thus be a way of achieving a greater industrial orientation of public research – that often accounts for most R&D undertaken at country level (OECD, 1992) – and overcoming the lack of integration of local researchers with the economy (Walsh, 1987). NTBFs may also act as channels to knowledge and technology generated in more advanced environments: accessing it, conveying it into the country, eventually combining it with existing skills, and applying it in the development of new products – which can be similar to others existing elsewhere, or truly innovative applications.

In market terms NTBFs can play a role in the introduction of new technology applications in small markets – which, given their size, would be neglected or poorly served by other (usually foreign) firms – thus meeting unmet demands, or responding more adequately to local application requirements (Kim, 1988; Perez, 1985).[1] They may even contribute to the upgrading of sectors traditionally important for the country's economy and eventually lead to the creation of a pool of distinctive competences, by achieving the integration between new technologies and traditional capabilities (Andersen and Lundvall, 1988; Jevons, 1992). Indeed, it is when the activities concerning the acquisition, development and diffusion of technology are carried out in this integrated mode that greater advantages are likely to be gained from the process, bringing about the formation of integrated clusters of development (Carlsson and Stankiewicz, 1991). Isolated and desegregated attempts, although important in raising local awareness about the technologies, are likely to be much less effective than more integrated ones (Van de Ven, 1993).

Obviously this process requires a basic S&T infrastructure, so that at least some new knowledge is generated indigenously and sufficient absorptive capacity exists to profit outside providers. It also requires a productive system with a given level of development, since new firms require a market for their products and some industrial experience behind them. The presence of a market for sophisticated products is particularly important, since only a certain level of national demand will provide the stimulus for local producers to pursue their innovative activities (Andersen and Lundvall, 1988; Rothwell, 1994). Its creation or strengthening is therefore one basic element for NTBFs' survival in less advanced economies (Kim and Dahlman, 1992; Deniozos, 1994).

In less advanced countries, as elsewhere, NTBFs are only one element in a process involving other actors and other types of intervention at different levels of the economy. Thus it is unlikely that this 'short-circuit' view can be applied to the less developed countries, where the above conditions are not present. But it applies to developing countries with a 'sufficient endowment of qualified human resources in the new technologies' and 'a reasonable level of productive capacity' (Perez and Soete, 1988, p. 477), as well as some sophisticated local buyers. On the other hand, this view may only be applicable to particular fields of technology, and within these, to the few segments that a small economy with scarce resources can master well enough to ensure an effective industrial application.

Empirical Research: the Case of Portugal

An in-depth study of the creation and early evolution of NTBFs in Portugal was used as the empirical setting to address the issues discussed above. The empirical study involved detailed interviews with 28 NTBFs and five young technology-based subsidiaries of existing companies, conducted between 1991 and 1994. These firms were selected from the 123 firms that responded to a mailed questionnaire, addressed to the universe of Portuguese NTBFs (identified by an extensive search). A definition of NTBF was devised for the purpose of this research: young independent firms involved in the development and/or diffusion of new technologies. Therefore the firms studied were: between one and 15 years old; launched by individual entrepreneurs; created to exploit a new technology, including firms developing frontier technologies and their early applications; and firms using them to create new or substantially improved products. Most firms operated in fields that can be broadly included under the 'information technologies' umbrella.

In analysing the ways NTBF founders acquired the technology, converted it into marketable products or services and brought them to the market, we attempted to evaluate whether they were performing the 'challenging role' and which particular forms it assumed in that context. In analysing the ways in which operating NTBFs went on upgrading and expanding their initial technology base, building up firm-specific competences and passing the results of their activities to the market, we attempted to evaluate whether they performed the 'technology transfer role' and the difficulties they might have encountered in achieving it.

One basic issue we investigated was whether, in performing these roles, NTBFs contributed to the upgrading of the technological capabilities of a country whose national system of innovation (Freeman, 1987) had a number of weaknesses. In other words, we were trying to evaluate whether NTBFs could in fact be an element in the 'catching-up' process of a less advanced country and what type of contribution theirs was.

The roles of NTBFs in the Portuguese environment
The empirical research confirmed that Portuguese NTBFs have undoubtedly performed the challenging role. Their founders identified technological opportunities not being exploited by existing organizations and created innovative organizations to do this. They acquired and developed new technologies not yet available in the country (or not used at industrial level) and took them to the market in the form of innovative products or services. The firms' active involvement in the development of the technologies (as opposed to the simple purchase) permitted the endogenization of competences, thus helping to increase the country's technological capabilities.

However, firms' ability to perform the technology transfer role varied. Being associated with continuity of innovative performance, this role required firms to be successful in the introduction of the new products, to survive as technology-intensive firms and to go on acquiring and developing new technologies and transferring them to the market. Firms showed different behaviours with respect to this issue, largely related to their market performance. Some firms were relatively successful in the market, being able to find early users for their products and to extend their activities to a growing number of clients. But several firms faced serious problems with regard to market acceptance of the technologies they were introducing: they had difficulties in convincing the potential users of the advantages of their products and/or were unable to go beyond a few advanced users. Some of these ended up being able to open a market after long 'desert-crossings', but others were forced to change more or less decisively the content of their activities, in order to adjust them to the reality. These 'adjustments', which indicate remarkable survival capabilities, included: (a) cases where firms were forced to move to another activity; and (b) cases where firms persisted in their chosen business, but were forced either to alter the character of their products, 'downgrading' them to conform to the effective needs of their potential clients, or to undertake less sophisticated activities in parallel. On the other hand, some initially successful firms were later confronted with the constraints derived from the limited market demand. This happened either when firms needed to replace the early lead-users, or when they envisaged further growth.

The research addressed these situations in some detail, since the problems at this level were found to have a negative impact on firms' ability to retain and expand the technological competences developed. In consequence, they reduced the impact of firms' efforts and, in the limit, led to a loss of expertise in country terms. It was concluded that the Portuguese market is undoubtedly difficult for NTBFs, given the limited demand for technology-based products, the conservative behaviour with regard to novelty, and the lack of trust in local suppliers.[2] Therefore, firms' problems were partly derived from market difficulties whose solution was beyond their means. But a number of problems resulted, to some extent, from firms' own behaviour. The conditions of the Portuguese environment called for even greater marketing skills than those required of NTBFs elsewhere, and for strategies targeted to the particular country circumstances. However, limited skills in non-technological fields and strategies based on role models derived from more advanced countries were found to be relatively widespread, particularly among the first NTBFs, who pioneered the introduction of technologies emerging elsewhere in a still very closed and unaware market. Nevertheless, it was also concluded that when marketing skills were present and when the founders adopted more 'prudent' strategies – because they had a better knowledge of the conditions of the market, or because they had learnt from the problems of their predecessors – difficulties still existed, especially in some fields. However, better approaches and several forms of external backing were found to afford firms better conditions to persist in their efforts or to achieve eventual adjustments (Fontes and Coombs, 1996).

The impact of NTBFs in the Portuguese National Systems of Innovation (NSI)

The above conclusions about the unequal ability revealed by Portuguese NTBFs to perform the roles hypothesized for this type of firm suggest that the impact of their technology acquisition and diffusion efforts would become clearer if it were expressed in terms of *levels* related to firms' evolution. Similarly, it also appears relevant to address separately the impacts relating to two domains where the firms revealed different capacities: (a) the process of acquisition of technological knowledge and development of competences in the new technologies at country level; and (b) the process of market diffusion of these technologies and of their applications. Three impact levels were identified.

Level 1: Introduce technology   This stage corresponds to the launch process, that is, to the activities performed by NTBF founders which led to the identification of an opportunity, the access to and further development of technologies that were new or not widely used in Portugal, and their conversion into products or services that were taken to the market. By developing capabilities in these technologies, NTBF founders have contributed to the creation of endogenous competences, which also led to an increase in the country's absorptive capacity for subsequent developments in the field. In bringing them to the market, they have, first, raised awareness about them and their applications among potential users, and, second, made them available to at least one set of more advanced users (Table 8.1).

Table 8.1   Level 1: Introduce technology

Activities	Impacts
	Technology:
Acquire new technology	Access technology not yet in the country
Develop marketable	Endogenous development permits the
applications	'internalization' of knowledge at country level
	Market:
Create firm to	Raise the awareness about the uses of the
commercialize applications	technology
Introduce applications in	Make its applications available to at least one
the market (i.e. sell them to	set of more advanced clients – by introducing
at least one or a small set	completely new products, or by increasing the
of initial clients)	accessibility of products similar to others
	existing elsewhere

Note: This is a transitory stage, although it can be pursued for some time (depending on firms' resources and requirements). At some point, firms will either evolve to another stage or go out of business.

Level 2: Improve accessibility   This stage corresponds to a situation where NTBFs have been able to establish a good user–supplier relationship with one or a small group of clients – usually more aware users. The guarantee of a certain continuity of demand provides an incentive for firms to upgrade and expand the initial technology base and to pass the results to their clients. However, given their dependence on a few clients, firms are in a vulnerable position, which may threaten the continuity of their technology acquisition and diffusion efforts (Table 8.2)

Table 8.2   Level 2: Improve accessibility

Activities	Impacts
Firms gain the guarantee of a certain continuity of demand from a small set of advanced clients for: • the first product/service • other products/services Continue acquiring/developing new technology to upgrade existing products or to develop new ones	**Technology:** Develop motivation to upgrade and expand initial technology base Build firm-specific competences to consolidate technological capabilities in the field, at country level Likely to establish links with other organizations to complement internal acquisition, contributing to a denser network in the field **Market:** Contribute to diffuse advanced technology among a set of more aware users by: • providing access to technology they might not know about otherwise; • devising applications that satisfy more closely their needs; and • guaranteeing local supply of a technology they would otherwise import

Note: Firms are vulnerable, given the dependence on one or a few clients, which may fail at any moment. This may threaten the continuity of technology acquisition and the retention of developed competences. It may also make firms less reliable as suppliers, because there is no guarantee of continuity of supply.

Level 3: Contribute to diffusion   In this stage NTBFs have been able to extend their activities to a wider range of clients, either expanding the client base with the same product or its extensions, or developing new products oriented to other niches (in this case, often still relying on a set of advanced clients). Given the greater stability achieved by these firms, they have better conditions to develop their in-house technological competences, with implications for the continuity of technology acquisition and for the level of resources devoted to it. They are also more effective as suppliers (Table 8.3).

Table 8.3   Level 3: Contribute to diffusion

Activities	Impacts
	Technology:
Expand range of clients:	
(1) on the basis of the same product (or its extensions), either by reaching other clients, or by moving to other (often foreign) markets;	Same as Level 2, but with greater guarantee of continuity and possibly with more resources (human and financial)
(2) through diversification, developing new products in other niches (often also targeting advanced clients) based on their technological competences	**Market:** Continue performing the roles described in Level 2 for the 'core' portfolio of more advanced clients, but simultaneously:
Where firms fail to expand their range of clients, resort to maintaining a 'core' portfolio of more advanced clients or continue acquiring/developing new technology to upgrade existing products or develop new ones	(1) bring the applications to a wider range of clients, some of whom might not be aware of it, if the firm imported technology instead of using a solution more geared to their specific needs
	(2) have as main target relatively advanced clients, but have a wider impact because of the broader range of clients reached, in the different areas being addressed

Note: Level 3 firms are less vulnerable than Level 2 firms. From the technological capabilities standpoint, this means that they are better prepared to retain the competences and to upgrade and expand them. They are also more reliable as suppliers, guaranteeing a continuity of supply, and passing on their technological evolution to the clients.

Firms in Level 2 and Level 3 similarly contribute to improving the technological capabilities at country level, although the lower vulnerability of Level 3 may make their efforts more consistent. However, because the range of users they reached is different, the impacts of their technological efforts in the market will vary. Firms in Level 2 will be particularly important in facilitating access to new developments of a set of more aware users, and in devising applications more geared to their needs. Depending on the forms assumed by their expansion, firms in Level 3 will either make the same type of contribution towards a wider range of advanced clients, or will have a greater diffusion role by taking the technology to clients who might not have been aware of its potential if the firm had not made it available to them, or might have resorted to standard imported technology instead of using a solution more geared to their requirements.

The expansion beyond the early stage associated with Level 1 was not always straightforward, with several firms being unable to impose their products. This situation forced these firms to close down, or to adopt one of the responses described above: to 'downgrade', or to move to a new field. In the case of firms closing down, a loss of expertise is inevitable, unless some of the competences are re-absorbed (for example, by acquisition; or if founders or employees move to other companies or create new ones). NTBFs forced to 'downgrade' are a particular case, the degree of loss in country terms depending on whether they keep some activity in the initial field. If they do, they may be able to retain the technical competences acquired, although they may not be motivated to upgrade and expand them consistently, thus reducing their contribution in purely technological terms. But in terms of use of the technologies, firms that move closer to the technological needs of their clients, bringing them the new advances in a 'simpler' form, are performing an important role in the process of diffusion. If they are successful in this approach and expand the client base among this subset of less sophisticated users, they may approximate the Level 3 market impacts. If they are also able to raise the awareness of these clients, leading them to increase their technological requirements (or are able to maintain some more sophisticated clients in parallel), they may equally continue to contribute to expanding the technological competences in the field.

Among the firms interviewed, several had moved to Level 2 – after more or less troubled start-up periods – but relatively few had attained Level 3.[3] Most of the latter achieved this through diversification of products and hence of the niches addressed, and only a few by substantially expanding the number of clients for a given product. A number of firms were nevertheless attempting to achieve this type of expansion, namely by addressing foreign markets.

Therefore, one of the basic conclusions of this research is that most NTBFs interviewed were particularly effective in acquiring, absorbing and developing new technology and in bringing its applications to the market, making them available to a set of advanced users. But they were generally less effective in diffusing these applications beyond a relatively limited number of more aware clients.

NTBFs as Acquirers, Synthesizers and Developers of New Technology

Considering the above conclusion about the domains where NTBFs have a more consistent impact, it seems pertinent to underline the most salient aspects of firms' contribution with regard to technology acquisition, absorption and development.

Whereas all firms can be said to have been involved in the acquisition and development of new technology in their initial stages, and several continued doing it with more or less intensity over time, the forms such activities assumed and their impacts at country level were different. The network of linkages that firms had established with their environment was one differentiating aspect, since it had implications both for the ways in which firms accessed technological knowledge and for their ability to share it with other organizations.

Table 8.4   Typology of firms according to their technological relationships

---

SYMBIOTIC
Firms with a symbiotic relationship with a source of science and technology, since start-up, which they use extensively to leverage their capabilities in core areas (frequently spin-offs from research)

LINK +
Firms with a privileged link with a source of science and/or technology, since start-up or early years, which supplements their in-house capabilities, in fields where these are recognized as weaker

INDEPENDENT
Firms that rely largely on their in-house capabilities, and use a variety of formal and informal links with local sources on an 'opportunistic' basis, to acquire skills and/or knowledge which complement their own

AUTONOMOUS
Firms whose relationships with local sources are weak or virtually absent – either because competences do not exist, or because they are unable to access them – and which have built an extensive in-house autonomy. The more technology-intensive firm considers it indispensable to complement in-house activities with external inputs and searches for expertise elsewhere, either by building links locally which facilitate access to foreign sources or by integrating international networks, generating a major subgroup labelled 'Autonomous–integrating'

Previous research about the process of technology acquisition by Portuguese NTBFs (Fontes and Coombs, 1995) led to the definition of a typology of firms, on the basis of their relationships with the external environment,[4] which is presented in Table 8.4. This typology is relevant to the analysis, since firms belonging to each type exhibited different behaviours with respect to technology acquisition and hence their contribution was also different.

The functions performed by Portuguese NTBFs as vehicles of technology acquisition (which will subsequently also be used to encompass the absorption and development elements) can be described in two main ways:

(a) transferring knowledge and technology from local academic research to the market; and
(b) acquiring and absorbing technological knowledge developed outside the country and turning it into national competences.

Transfer of technology between local research and industry
This transfer was carried out at various levels and with a number of benefits for both the firm and the research organization. Table 8.5 summarizes the more relevant impacts identified, and the role played by every type of firm. The relationships established by these firms, whether of an 'organic' type such as the 'Symbiotic' or, more rarely, the 'Independent', represented a 'short-circuit' of the laborious and frequently ineffectual process of transfer between the two 'worlds', was thus an important achievement of NTBFs. They contributed to an increase in the technical networks in some fields, and more generally to leverage the individual efforts of every participant, with a positive impact on the overall capabilities at country level.

The bridge that was created between the two environments permitted more than the movement of information or technological knowledge. It also allowed a certain adjustment: industrial companies became better able to define their needs and therefore to gain access to the inputs more relevant to them; research organizations gained a window on market requirements, helpful in defining research directions more appropriate to the needs of local industry. In the limit firms' particular needs led research organizations to address fields neglected up to then, filling a 'gap' at country level. More generally, the development of a common language precipitated further relationships with similar organizations. Finally, links with local research organizations functioned as channels to foreign sources. Even some 'Autonomous' firms, which held that links with research organizations were not very useful, would end up recognizing their relevance in accessing inputs originating from outside the target organizations, but accessible through them.

Table 8.5   Impacts at the level of the relationship between academic research and industry

	Symbiotic	Link +	Independent	Autonomous
Direct transfer of knowledge and technology originating from research in the process of creation	H	S	–	–
Preferential relationships: keep a channel open between organizations, permitting a movement of information, knowledge and people (both ways)	H	H	L	–
Occasional contacts: greater use of research inputs by industry; increased awareness of research organizations about industry and market requirements	L	M	H	L
Creation of a bridge between two different environments, permitting developing of a common language, which facilitates further contacts	H	H	H	L
Presence of firms operating in a field stimulates research organizations to reorient their research to its development	–	–	M	M
Local research organizations act as channels to foreign sources, where other inputs can be obtained	H	H	M	M

H – high impact or very frequent; M – medium impact or less frequent; L – low impact or infrequent.

Accessing and absorbing foreign technology

A second fundamental role performed by NTBFs entailed acquiring and absorbing technological knowledge developed outside the country and turning it into national competences. This process involved: (i) accessing technological knowledge not available in the Portuguese context (or whose development was not carried out with an industrial orientation); and (ii) achieving a synthesis between knowledge obtained elsewhere and knowledge and skills developed locally, with the firms (or their founders) functioning as the 'meeting point' and the 'integrator' for inputs coming from several origins: local research; local industry; and abroad. In gaining competences in these 'absent' technologies, and in applying them in the development of products or services (often oriented to the needs of the local market), as opposed to just purchasing and using them, NTBFs acted as agents of their endogenization at country level, rather than of their simple introduction. This process can thus be described as a higher-level transfer of technology from more advanced environments, which contributed to improve national technological capabilities.

This role was performed both at start-up and over time. At start-up their principal performers tended to be 'Autonomous' and 'Independent' firms, often formed on the basis of technologies of limited or no development at national level. Although 'Symbiotic' firms were associated with transfer to the market of technology developed locally, there were also some cases of combination with foreign technology among them (Table 8.6).

But the search for foreign sources of technological knowledge was a requirement for all operating NTBFs. The firms were either required to continue resorting to them, or were at some point forced to look for them, when new knowledge not available locally became necessary. The extent of this acquisition process depended on firms' ability to build (or keep open) the channels to the places where expertise existed. The forms it assumed differed according to the methods favoured by each type of firm to access these inputs (Table 8.7).[5]

For a substantial number of start-ups as well as for firms already in operation, the absorption and further development of the technological knowledge acquired entailed the combination of the new skills and knowledge with those gained through founders' work in local organizations (in the case of start-ups), or with the competences obtained through in-house acquisition practices (in the case of existing NTBFs). Links, close or opportunistic, with other local organizations were also used. Finally, awareness of the requirements of local customers was a relevant element in this process. Although some founders already possessed it, it was particularly evident in the case of operating NTBFs, whose activity had permitted them to develop a better perception of market needs. The result of this process was often a 'new

Table 8.6   Forms of access to foreign technology at start-up

	Symbiotic	Link +	Independent	Autonomous
Founders acquire and apply technology generated outside the country (alone or in combination with existing skills and knowledge)	L	L	M	H
Founders apply knowledge and skills obtained outside the country, e.g. PhDs abroad; work in foreign firms; exposure through local firms or MNE subsidiaries	M	L	H	H
Founders base new firm on information and research spill-overs gained through diverse means, complemented with 'self-learning' (always combined with existing skills)	–	–	M	H

H – high impact or very frequent; M – medium impact or less frequent; L – low impact or infrequent.

combination', encompassing elements from a variety of origins (local and foreign), for which the new start-up or the existing NTBF acted as the integration vehicle.

The importance of this process of acquisition and internalization of technology generated outside the country does not rule out, but rather runs parallel to, the efforts to create locally a 'critical mass' in a number of fields, which functions as a seed-bed for the creation of new firms and leverages the activities of the existing ones. These can indeed be seen as complementary forms of technology acquisition and diffusion. The development of strong local competences can have an important impact. This is shown by the case of communications systems and software, where a number of research organizations with a consistent industry-oriented activity have encouraged and supported several spin-offs. Benefits have also been derived by a group of 'Symbiotic' firms, with spin-offs from the same research organization, from their networking activities with the centre and amongst themselves. (Benefits

Table 8.7   Forms of access to foreign technology by NTBFs in operation

	Symbiotic	Link +	Independent	Autonomous
(Close) relationships with foreign suppliers	M	M	H	H
Partnerships or supplier relationships with foreign companies or with MNE subsidiaries acting locally	L	L	L	L
Integration in international networks in the field	L	–	–	L
Participation in international collaborative R&D projects	H	L	M	M*
Use of local research organizations as intermediaries to foreign sources	H	M	M	M*
Extensive use of a variety of scanning mechanisms to access research spill-overs	M	M	H	H

H – high impact or very frequent; M – medium impact or less frequent; L – low impact or infrequent.
* Research-intensive autonomous: when scanning mechanisms existed they were particularly relevant at these two levels.

extended in some cases to a few 'outsiders' acting in adjacent fields.) But the ability to access and apply technologies, which is not being addressed in Portugal, is equally important, since it permits identification of the constraints on their diffusion caused by the inevitable gaps in the Portuguese system. Therefore, a situation in which NTBFs acquiring new technologies elsewhere achieve some sort of integration between the new technological knowledge and the competences developed locally in a particular field, thus contributing to expansion and upgrading of the country's competences in it, appears to be the one that would have the most impact upon the country's development.

NTBF Weaknesses and the Limited Scope for Complementarity: some Policy Recommendations

As was argued above, NTBFs have a number of intrinsic limitations and, therefore, their potential role can only be completely fulfilled if other actors are involved. Portuguese NTBFs are not different in this respect, sharing some of the weaknesses of their counterparts in more advanced economies. However, the characteristics of the Portuguese NSI not only bring additional difficulties, but also imply that NTBFs' weaknesses cannot be compensated by the actions of other actors, which are present in other contexts, but are absent or show lower initiative in Portugal. We now focus on the problems derived from NTBFs' weaknesses and from their complex interaction with the Portuguese NSI, which constrain the full realization of these firms' potential, and advance some suggestions concerning ways to address these problems.

One limitation derives from the fact that Portuguese NTBFs are relatively few. Therefore, with the exception of some 'pockets' where firms were created on the basis of development of local competences in a given field, they tend to be relatively isolated, which makes their efforts less effective. This happens because the Portuguese environment is not particularly favourable for this type of firm: technological opportunities are not extensively generated, and the low demand for technology-based products does not encourage their exploitation very much. If NTBFs' importance is accepted, it may be necessary to act at a number of levels to facilitate their formation. To be effective such intervention should go beyond the simple mechanisms to support firm creation, with actions being oriented to the root of the problem: the supply of and especially the demand for technology.

Second, Portuguese NTBFs have weaknesses intrinsic to their youth, their scarcity of resources, and their sometimes low competence in non-technological areas. These limitations, which also hinder NTBFs in other contexts, may make them poorly equipped to confront the difficulties present in some of the markets they address in Portugal. These shortcomings are especially restrictive when NTBFs operate in fields where there are few or no other organizations that can compensate for their deficiencies or allow for complementarities.

A striking example of NTBFs' difficulties (or even inadequacy) to address some markets/clients was the case of firms that attempted to introduce new technologies oriented to the upgrading of less advanced industrial sectors. NTBFs were faced with firms which still preferred low wages to technological upgrading and which were not prepared to deal directly with a technology-intensive supplier, particularly one that was national, had no reputation, and was frequently too close to academic research. Thus the voluntarist efforts of NTBFs towards this group were bound to fail, despite the fact that NTBFs might be better prepared than foreign suppliers to adjust the technology to their needs, as was shown by the experience of firms in more modern sectors. These cases show that the potential carried by NTBFs to achieve integration between traditional country capabilities and new technologies can only be turned into a real advantage if other elements are present: intermediaries and mechanisms directed to improve the technological awareness of potential clients; market pressures forcing them to upgrade technologically; and government policies to foster the use of local suppliers, rather than imported technology, to achieve such upgrading. On the other hand, the prevalence of variants on the above behaviour among the Portuguese firms (particularly in the manufacturing industry) and the relatively low number of advanced clients prepared to act as 'lead-users' or at least to recognize quickly the advantages of the products commercialized by NTBFs – which in other contexts are a powerful impulse to innovation – are real constraints on the development of local NTBFs, inhibiting the full exploitation of their potential.

Market resistance to the new technologies – a problem whose solution often requires a conjugation of efforts much beyond the possibilities of a small firm's resource constraints, especially when combined with NTBFs' intrinsic weaknesses, absence of reputation, and limited market knowledge and skills – means that, if NTBFs' challenging behaviour and their technological competences are to be profited from, they should be helped to overcome their weaknesses, and generally supported in their efforts. This assistance can come from existing organizations or from government initiatives. The involvement of the first has the advantage of favouring the building up of 'complementarities', as is shown by the case of other countries and was confirmed in the Portuguese case by some experiences of partnerships, close user–supplier relationships and risk-capital initiatives. But government intervention may also be necessary, especially in areas where the complementary organizations are absent from the Portuguese context.

The results of this research suggest that assistance could be more fruitful when it: (a) supports firms in overcoming their critical weaknesses at the level of the market, and sometimes also at the level of production; (b) provides resources to back their initial efforts or the expansion of their activities (for example, risk capital); (c) assists their internationalization (which may be a condition of obtaining the resources to pay for their continued development); (d) contributes to the promotion of the technologies being developed and commercialized; and (e) facilitates access to sources of technology and support mechanisms that allow firms to upgrade and expand their technological competences (for example, support to R&D and product development). Additionally, in more complex markets, the government can make an important intervention with regard to expanding the level of demand. This can be achieved directly through public procurement, or indirectly through actions that stimulate the demand for some technologies and their applications (for example, supporting adoption by laggard firms) and convey the idea that they can be supplied by local firms. Finally, in the limit, the acquisition by other firms may be a solution to be considered (although with care) when it appears to be the best path to retain the acquired competences and/or to ensure that they are more efficiently transferred to the market.

CONCLUSIONS

The analysis of a group of Portuguese NTBFs has shown that in less advanced countries these firms can make a relevant contribution to the strengthening of national technological capabilities. They can have an important role as vehicles for the acquisition, absorption and development of technological knowledge at country level, at least in some fields. They accomplish it by accessing the knowledge generated in the local S&T infrastructure and turning it into market-able applications, and by absorbing technological knowledge developed outside the country, eventually making a synthesis with local knowledge and skills. In developing competences in the new technologies and their application, as opposed to its simple purchase and use, NTBFs can be said to be performing a higher level of technology transfer. If they also achieve integration between the new technology and traditional capabilities, their activity is contributing to the development of country-specific competences.

But NTBFs' effectiveness in passing the results of their efforts on to the market was found to be frequently hindered by the local market conditions, and aggravated by firms' own limitations. Whereas NTBFs are usually able to bring the new technology applications to a set of already aware users, they often have greater difficulties in conveying their products or services beyond these few clients. This means that the market impact of their efforts tends to be relatively limited, in spite of a few cases where firms revealed the ability to reach a wider range of customers, including less advanced ones. Moreover, the market resistance to novelty and the limited number of sophisticated users act as a constraint on NTBFs' evolution, and, in the limit, may even be a threat to their survival. The NTBFs' intrinsic weaknesses of resource constraints, absence of reputation, and limited market skills may aggravate the problem, leaving the firms poorly equipped to face the predictable difficulties. Moreover, while in other contexts NTBFs' weaknesses can be compensated by the interventions of others in the process of technological development, in Portugal these other actors are absent or show lower initiative, frequently leaving the firms very isolated.

Demand problems emerged as the most serious constraint on Portuguese NTBFs, inhibiting the full exploitation of their potential. The limited market success, or even the failure to pursue their initial activities, had further implications for firms' ability to retain the technological competences developed and to go on upgrading them. This reduces even more the impact of their efforts and, in the limit, represents a loss of expertise in country terms.

Therefore, if NTBFs' competences and innovative drive are to be fully exploited, helping to endow Portugal with the conditions to face the technological and industrial challenges of the turn of the century, they need to be assisted in their efforts. Such assistance may come from existing organizations, thus permitting the development of beneficial two-way relationships. But the intervention of the government will also be necessary, especially at the level of demand, where measures to increase the awareness about the available technologies and to encourage existing organizations to upgrade their technological knowledge, accepting local firms as suppliers, appear to be fundamental.

NOTES

1. This does not mean exclusive concentration on local markets, which beyond the short term can be a dangerous strategy for firms in countries with consistently small markets. The best approach is to exploit sophisticated niche markets that can also provide opportunities for international expansion (Lemola and Lovio, 1988; O'Doherty, 1990).
2. The constraints of the national market can be avoided through entry into foreign markets, and a number of NTBFs (whose type of activity permitted it) attempted this. However, at this level NTBFs confronted both the problems of a small firm with scarce resources *and* the image of Portugal in the international arena, which complicated their acceptance as technology-intensive producers.
3. A sequential move to Level 2 and then to Level 3 was more likely, but some firms moved directly to Level 3 or else stayed at Level 2 for longer periods This latter situation usually ocurred when firms operated in fields where there were only a few clients prepared to buy their products, but this could also be caused by firms' lack of skills to go beyond the more aware clients.
4. The basic factors behind this classification were: (i) the type of technological linkages firms had established at start-up and their evolution, and (ii) the role firms had attributed to relationships with external sources of technology.
5. A more complete description of the forms used to identify and access the foreign technology and of the conditions in which it was combined with existing skills and knowledge – both at start-up and over time – can be found in Fontes and Coombs (1995).

REFERENCES

Abetti, P., O'Connor, J., Ehid, L., Rocco, J. and Sanders, B. (1987), 'A Tale of Two Parks. Key Factors Influencing the Location Decision Process of New Entrepreneurial Companies', in Churchill, N. et al. (eds), *Frontiers of Entrepreneurial Research*, Wellesley, MA: Babson College, pp. 26–41.

Ackroyd, S. (1995), 'On the Structure and Dynamics of Some Small, UK-Based Information Technology Firms', *Journal of Management Studies*, **32** (2), 141–61.

Andersen, E.S. and Lundvall, B. (1988), 'Small National Systems of Innovation Facing Technological Revolutions: An Analytical Framework', in Freeman, C. and Lundvall, B. (eds), *Small Countries Facing the Technological Revolution*, London: Pinter Publishers, 9–36.

Autio, E. (1994), 'New Technology Based Firms as Agents of R&D and Innovation: An Empirical Study', *Technovation*, **14** (4), 259–73.

Ayal, I. and Raban, J. (1990), 'Developing Hi-Tech Industrial Products for World Markets', *IEEE Transactions on Engineering Management*, **37** (3), 177–83.

Bell, M. and Pavitt, K. (1993), 'Technological Accumulation and Industrial Growth: Contrasts Between Developed and Developing Countries', *Industrial and Corporate Change*, **2** (2), 157–210.

Bollinger, L., Hope, K. and Utterback, J. (1983), 'A Review of Literature and Hypotheses on New Technology Based Firms', *Research Policy*, **12**, 1–14.

Brunner, H. (1991), 'Small Scale Industry and Technology in India: The Case of the Computer Industry', *Small Business Economics*, **3** (2), 121–9.

Carlsson, B. and Stankiewicz, R. (1991), 'On the Nature, Function, and Composition of Technological Systems', *Journal of Evolutionary Economics*, **1**, 93–118.

Cooper, A.C. and Bruno, A.V. (1977), 'Success Among High Technology Firms', *Business Horizons*, **20** (2), 16–22.

Deniozos, D. (1994), 'Steps for the Introduction of Technology Management in Developing Economies: The Role of Public Governments', *Technovation*, **14** (3), 197–203.

Feldman, M.P. (1994), 'Knowledge Complementarity and Innovation', *Small Business Economics*, **6** (5), 363–72.

Fontes, M. and Coombs, R. (1995), 'New Technology-Based Firms and Technology Acquisition in Portugal: Firm as Adaptive Responses to a Less Favourable Environment', *Technovation*, **15** (8), 497–510.

Fontes, M. and Coombs, R. (1996), 'New Technology-Based Firm Formation in a Less Advanced Country: A Learning Process', *International Journal of Entrepreneurship Behaviour and Research*, **2** (2), 82–101.

Forrest, J.E. and Martin, J. (1992), 'Strategic Alliances Between Large and Small Research Intensive Organizations: Experiences in the Biotechnology Industry', *R&D Management*, **22** (1), 41–53.

Freeman, C. (1987), *Technology Policy and Economic Performance. Lessons from Japan*, London: Pinter Publishers.

Freeman, C. (1991), 'Networks of Innovators: A Synthesis of Research Issues', *Research Policy*, **20**, 499–514.

Granstrand, O. and Sjolander, S. (1990), 'The Acquisition of Technology and Small Firms by Large Firms', *Journal of Economic Behaviour and Organization*, **13** (3), 367–86.

Jarillo, J.C. (1989), 'Entrepreneurship and Growth: The Strategic Use of External Resources', *Journal of Business Venturing*, **4**, 133–47.

Jevons, F.R. (1992), 'Who Wins From Innovation', *Technology Analysis and Strategic Management*, **4** (4), 399–412.

Jones-Evans, D. (1996), 'Technological Entrepreneurship, Strategy and Experience', *International Small Business Journal*, **14** (3), 15–39.

Kim, L. (1980), 'Stages of Development of Industrial Technology in a Developing Country: A Model', *Research Policy*, **9**, 254–77.

Kim, L. (1988), 'Entrepreneurship and Innovation in a Rapidly Developing Country', *Journal of Development Planning*, **18**, 183–94.

Kim, L. and Dahlman, C.J. (1992), 'Technology Policy for Industrialisation: An Integrative Framework and Korea's Experience', *Research Policy*, **21**, 437–52.

Lawton-Smith, H., Dickson, K. and Smith, S. (1991), '"There Are Two Sides to Every Story": Innovation and Collaboration Within Networks of large and Small Firms', *Research Policy*, **20**, 457–68.

Lee, J., Bae, Z.T. and Choi, D.K. (1988), 'Technology Development Processes: A Model for a Developing Country with a Global Perspective', *R&D Management*, **18** (3), 235–50.

Lee, J. and Lee, J. (1994), 'Competitive Structure and Strategic Types in the Korean Software Industry', *Technovation*, **14**, 295–309.

Lemola, T. and Lovio, R. (1988), 'Possibilities for a Small Country in High-Techno-logy Production: The Electronics Industry in Finland', in Freeman, C. and Lundvall, B. (eds), *Small Countries Facing the Technological Revolution*, London: Pinter Publishers, 139–55.

Lipparini, A. and Sobrero, M. (1994), 'The Glue and the Pieces: Entrepreneurship and Innovation in Small Firm Networks', *Journal of Business Venturing*, **9**, 125–40.

Mariti, P. (1993), 'Small and Medium-Sized Firms in Markets with Substantial Scale and Scope Economies', in Humbert, M. (ed.), *The Impact of Globalisation on Europe's Firms and Industries*, London: Pinter Publishers, pp. 191–8.

Martinez-Sanchez, A. (1992), 'Regional Innovation and Small High Technology Firms in Peripheral Regions', *Small Business Economics*, **4** (2), 153–68.

Miles, R.H. and Snow, C. (1986), 'Organizations: New Concepts for New Forms', *California Management Review*, **28** (3), 62–73.

Mustar, P. (1994), 'Organisations, Technologies et Marchés en Création: La Genèse des PME High-Tech', *Revue d'Économie Industrielle*, **67**, 156–74.

Oakey, R.P. (1991), 'High Technology Small Firms: Their Potential for Rapid Indus-trial Growth', *International Small Business Journal*, **9** (4), 31–42.

Oakey, R.P. (1993), 'Predatory Networking: The Role of Small Firms in the Develop-ment of the British Biotechnology Industries', *International Small Business Jour-nal*, **11** (4), 9–22.

O'Doherty, D. (1990), 'Strategic Alliances – an SME and Small Economy Perspec-tive', *Science & Public Policy*, **17** (5), 303–10.

OECD (1992), *Technology and the Economy: The Key Relationships*, Paris: OECD.

Olleros, F.J. (1986), 'Emerging Industries and the Burnout of Pioneers', *Journal of Product Innovation Management*, **3** (1), 5–18.

Pavitt, K. (1984), 'Sectoral Patterns of Technical Change. Towards a Taxonomy and a Theory', *Research Policy*, **13**, 343–73.

Pavitt, K. (1991), 'Key Characteristics of the Large Innovating Firm', *British Journal of Management*, **2**, 41–50.

Perez, C. (1985), 'Microelectronics, Long Waves and World Structural Change: New Perspectives for Developing Countries', *World Development*, **13** (3), 441–63.

Perez, C. and Soete, L. (1988), 'Catching Up in Technology: Entry Barriers and Windows of Opportunity', in Dosi, G. et al. (eds), *Technical Change and Economic Theory*, London: Pinter Publishers, pp. 458–79.

Ramos, R. (1989), 'High Tech Entrepreneurship in Madrid', in Birley, S. (ed.), *European Entrepreneurship: Emerging Growth Companies*, Proceedings of the First Annual EFER Forum, Cranfield School of Management: EFER, pp. 159–85.

Rizzoni, A. (1994), 'Technology and Organization in Small Firms: An Interpretative Framework', *Revue d'Économie Industrielle*, **67**, 135–55.

Roberts, E.B. (1990), 'Initial Capital for the New Technological Enterprise', *IEEE Transactions in Engineering Management*, **37** (2), 81–94.

Rothwell, R. (1983), 'Innovation and Firm Size: A Case of Dynamic Complementarity; Or, Is Small Really So Beautiful?', *Journal of General Management*, **8** (3), 5–25.

Rothwell, R. (1984), 'The Role of Small Firms in the Emergence of New Technologies', *Omega*, **12** (1), 19–29.

Rothwell, R. (1994), 'Issues in User–producer Relations in the Innovation Process: The Role of Government', *International Journal of Technology Management*, **9** (5/6), 629–49.

Rothwell, R. and Zegveld, W. (1982), *Innovation and the Small and Medium Sized Firm – Their Role in Employment and in Economic Change*, London: Frances Pinter.

Saxenian, A. (1991), 'The Origins and Dynamics of Production Networks in Silicon Valley', *Research Policy*, **20**, 423–37.

Shan, W. (1990), 'An Empirical Analysis of Organizational Strategies by Entrepreneurial High-Technology Firms', *Strategic Management Journal*, **11** (2), 129–39.

Shaw, B. (1993), 'Formal and Informal Networks in the UK Medical and Equipment Industry', *Technovation*, **13** (6), 349–65.

Stankiewicz, R. (1994), 'Spin-off Companies from Universities', *Science & Public Policy*, **21** (2), 99–107.

Teece, D.J. (1986), 'Profiting from Technological Innovation: Implications for Integration, Collaboration, Licensing and Public Policy', *Research Policy*, **15**, 285–305.

Valls, J. (1993), 'Small Firms Facing Globalisation in R&D Activities. Lessons From Case Studies of Spanish Small Firms', in Humbert, M. (ed.), *The Impact of Globalisation on Europe's Firms and Industries*, London: Pinter Publishers, 200–10.

Van de Ven, A.H. (1993), 'The Development of an Infrastructure for Entrepreneurship', *Journal of Business Venturing*, **8**, 211–30.

Van de Ven, A.H. and Garud, R. (1989), 'A Framework for Understanding the Emergence of New Industries', in Rosenbloom, R.S. and Burgelman, R.A. (eds), *Research on Technological Innovation, Management and Policy*, Greenwich, CT: JAI Press, pp. 195–225.

Walsh, V. (1987), 'Technology, Competitiveness and the Special Problems of Small Countries', *STI Review*, **2** (2), 81–133.

Walsh, V. (1993), 'Demand, Public Markets and Innovation in Biotechnology', *Science and Public Policy*, **20** (3), 138–56.

9. Foresight for research and technology policies: from innovation studies to scenario confrontation

Bastiaan de Laat and Philippe Larédo

INTRODUCTION

Foresight is booming in Western Europe. More than seeing this as a fashionable venture, we think that it reveals a renewed interest in the articulation between research policies and socioeconomic stakes.[1] Whereas several countries have set up wide-ranging foresight exercises, generally involving huge numbers of experts, researchers, companies and policy makers, systematic thinking about methods and concepts for such exercises is lagging behind. It is even said to be in crisis by practitioners themselves, such as Coates.[2] We argue that this is linked to the limited attention given to innovation studies. Taking up their results might help to overcome this so-called crisis.

We propose to use the concept of techno-economic network (TEN)[3] to analyse the scenarios actors elaborate. 'Scenario', however, has different meanings. Two of them will be used in this chapter. These are, on the one hand, the formal scenarios as used in foresight exercises; on the other hand, we are concerned with the trajectories actors envisage and construct. These scenarios represent the future world actors try to build and are inscribed in their attempts to stabilize new or modified TENs. The development of foresight exercises pushes actors to formalize such attempts and to confront them with each other in the 'hybrid fora' such policy actions promote. The purpose of this chapter is to show that four main configurations in which scenarios oppose each other can be distinguished. They can be characterized by four metaphors borrowed from economics: monopoly, oligopoly, monopsony and pure competition. We shall finally argue that, while the first three configurations can clearly be made explicit for debate, the fourth configuration, where incompatible anticipated future worlds proliferate, is difficult to deal with through foresight approaches, although they are often the main reason that politicians launch such costly processes.

The chapter is structured as follows. The first section will outline why, despite all the activity presently observed, foresight is said to be in crisis. In the second section recent results from innovation studies will be discussed so as to outline how attempts to stabilize new TENs can be identified. The third section will discuss the two meanings of the word 'scenario' that are used in this chapter. And the fourth section will propose a taxonomy of scenario confrontations that were encountered during the fieldwork. The chapter concludes with a set of implications for foresight and policy and with proposals for future research.

The four configurations will be illustrated with examples from fieldwork. Like the work presented by Larédo and Mustar (1996), they will be drawn from several studies conducted by the Centre de Sociologie de l'Innovation (CSI) from 1992 to 1995, in particular by Barbier on municipal waste management, de Laat on technology foresight with French and Dutch environmental agencies, and Rémy on emerging environmental issues.[4]

FORESIGHT – IS THERE A CRISIS?

Foresight is undoubtedly undergoing a strong revival. In Western Europe no one can ignore the manifold activities in this area: the huge German Delphi, the United Kingdom's Technology Foresight Programme, the Dutch Foresight Steering Committee, the French Ateliers Prospectifs.[5] These activities do not merely represent some fashionable venture. Like the upswing in research evaluation a few years ago,[6] the increasing growth of foresight exercises reveals a renewed interest in research policy. It marks a shift from more traditional science policies to the direct and explicit articulation between research activities, economic issues and social needs. In short, the focus is on innovations.

Two parallels can be drawn with research evaluation. First, foresight exercises are local in several respects. They are set up to apply to a circumscribed domain. This can be a nation's research system or a firm's environment. But it can also be a scientific discipline, for instance chemistry, or a problem area like public health (for example, Van den Heuvel, 1994 or ANRS, 1995, respectively). They are also local since they are conducted by people, mobilize other people (experts, scientists, lay persons and so on), and take place within specific settings: 'futures studies are always centrally concerned with uniqueness of time and place, not just timeless conditional regularities' (Adelson, 1989, p. 32). And if not completely incorporated in policy makers, as Hauptman and Pope (1992) argue, they are deeply embedded in policy processes.

A second and related parallel with research evaluation lies in its changing perspective. Traditional research evaluation was characterized by its focus on one preoccupation, that is, on assessing whether and to what extent initial technical objectives had been attained. As shown by the recent state of the art in evaluation practices and methods, evaluation is shifting to the analysis of how results relate to the present world (Callon et al., 1995). When it is known that both evolve simultaneously, it does not make much sense to evaluate today's results against yesterday's problems.[7] Symmetrically, present foresight activities should no longer be seen as predictive exercises but as a way to see present problems through anticipatory glasses.[8] They have lost their 'crystal ball'-type character and become a managerial tool within public policies.

Nevertheless a paradox remains: despite all the ongoing activity, foresight concepts and methods are said to be in an impasse (Linstone, 1989, 1994). They are stuck in old regimes,[9] and even worse – according to Coates et al. (1994) – the situation has severely deteriorated over the past decades:

> Overall, we see [foresight[10]] as underdeveloped. It was better developed in the 1960s and has decayed in methodological quality and substantive content. The more recent [foresights] are more often informal side commentaries, or poorly defined and executed, without much attention to assumptions, time horizons or the author's intentions (pp. 23–4).

This is exemplified when analysing, for instance, the latest volumes of *Technological Forecasting and Social Change*, one of the leading journals in the field. In most articles a complete separation is maintained: foresight studies focus either on 'technological potential' only, or on actors (social groups, industrial sectors, and so on) and their needs. Within innovative processes however, the two are continuously linked. Foresight methods and concepts seem to ignore the conditions under which innovations unfold.

This dual dimension is also clear in practice. On the one hand, foresight exercises produce an enormous number of statements on research priorities, promising fields or new technologies. On the other hand, through expert committees, workshops, seminars and other meetings, they also produce a great deal of social networking.[11] Foresight processes are definitely a social as well as a technical enterprise. Yet formally the two remain strictly separated, as is well illustrated by one of the comments on the recent British Technology Foresight Programme made by a former chief adviser on science and technology at the British Department of Trade and Industry, and present director of the British IBM laboratory:

> considering the practical uses to which the results of foresight may be put, we must not overlook the potential inhibitors to the successful exploitation in the UK of opportunities identified by the programme (Robinson, 1994).

The 'inhibitors' relate to specialized skills, networks of suppliers and distributors, regulatory barriers, or international collaboration, to cite just a few. According to the author, these are crucial elements, ignored by the foresight exercise. These 'inhibitors', however, are among the many topics that innovation studies have focused on over the last decades, whether in sociology of science, economics of technical change, history or anthropology.[12] The next section identifies three lessons that have strong implications for technology foresight.

RECENT RESULTS FROM INNOVATION STUDIES

This section discusses three recent results from innovation studies and their implications for foresight. First, innovation is not a linear process from science to market but consists of the gradual establishment of links between actors. Second, innovation processes lie in the formation of heterogeneous assemblies, that is, they are simultaneously social as well as technical. Last, innovations can become irreversible rather early and are path-dependent. The concept of techno-economic network (TEN), elaborated by CSI, accounts for these three observations. Innovation processes can thus be interpreted in terms of the attempts actors make at stabilizing new TENs. An instrument has been developed elsewhere to identify such attempts.[13] It formalizes the 'anticipations' actors make.

First, there is the problem of linearity. Innovation has long been described as a stepwise process from science to the market (Freeman, 1982). Likewise a relay race, in which actors deliver their products sequentially – first knowledge, then a concept or patent, then a prototype, and so on. Then each withdraws, after delivering a finished contribution. This process was supposed to be governed either by a science-push or by a demand-pull logic.[14] Empirical studies, however, show that innovations do not follow such a sequence. The objects elaborated by actors rather describe a whirlwind pattern – see for instance the synthesis by Vinck (1991). Products, whether they are consumer products or scientific articles, are developed and tested, maybe normalized, encounter problems (resistance, opposition), are reshuffled, redefined, tested again, and so on. They can go from science to market, but they can also find their origin in a certain demand. In other words, scientists sometimes play a dominant role, but Von Hippel showed that users can be equally important in this process.[15] No general factor or single social group can be held solely responsible for the development of an innovation. While economists in the meantime have proposed new models to deal with the non-linear character of innovation,[16] the traditional linear concept still very often forms the basis for foresight thinking.[17] Instead, innovation studies suggest that innovation is not a process whereby actors (laboratories, firms, users and so on) intervene sequentially, but a process during which durable links are created between them. This collective character of innovation processes is an integral part of any foresight exercise, though rarely in explicit form.

This leads to the second lesson to be learned from innovation studies. It concerns the relation between the technical and the social. The technical, and more generally, the construction of technical systems, has until recently been the privileged domain of the technologist, the scientist or the engineer. The social, the interactions between human beings, was the locus of enquiry exclusively reserved for the sociologist or maybe the behavioural psychologist. Micro studies of innovation have, however, shown that the two are intimately linked. Whether it is bicycles or bakelite at the beginning of this century, a gasifier in a developing country or high-tech subway or aircraft projects,[18] in all cases the social and the technical are formed together. Techniques are shaped by collective social action, simultaneously shaping the politics, the users, and the infrastructure – the networks – associated with them.[19] And once established, techniques act themselves.[20] Hence a technical object does not only reflect social relationships[21] but 'transcribes and displaces the contradictory interests of people and things' (Latour, 1992, p. 226; see also Akrich, 1992a). In sum, innovation – the process as well as its outcomes – is a sociotechnical assembly in which multiple heterogeneous actors play a role. The consequence for foresight can be described as follows. Coming up with sets of research priorities, foresight cannot ignore that these are connected to certain configurations of actors. In other words, every technical choice implies or presupposes a social configuration, and vice versa.[22] Technology foresight is sociotechnical foresight in all its aspects.

The third implication for foresight studies stems from the work of economists of technical change and their observation that innovations are path-dependent. Dosi's or Nelson and Winter's 'technological' and 'natural' trajectories or Sahal's innovation avenues account for the existence of paradigms within technical innovation that are relatively fixed over long periods of time.[23] Such paradigms are built up little by little, resulting in a framework shared by everyone. As David has demonstrated for the QWERTY keyboard, such trajectories are not necessarily 'rational' or 'optimal' with regard to the technology under consideration. They depend heavily on initial choices which become irreversible.[24] Other authors argue that stabilization occurs rather early, fostering the development of a certain path and hindering others. Small but critical events appear important in any technical development, whether it is within research programmes,[25] in the case of products competing for a market share[26] or for complete technological systems.[27] Hence the third consequence for foresight studies is to identify those areas where early closure of sociotechnical choices is at stake. Popular methods within the forecasting community such as regression analyses, logistic – so called 'S' – curves, envelope curves, or other types of extrapolation[28] can only be used to describe trajectories after irreversibilities have been created.

The concept of techno-economic networks allows these three features to be integrated. The notion of network refers not only to the actors that make it up but simultaneously to the intermediaries that circulate between them. It is techno-economic not only because it associates heterogeneous actors – belonging to the scientific or technical sphere, industrial production, commercial distribution, consumption, administration or other – but because coordination mechanisms are those traditionally described by economics (markets, hierarchies and trust),[29] as well as those linked to science and technology (texts, embodied knowledge and objects).[30]

The relation between techno-economic networks and foresight can now be described as follows. Potential future trajectories, whether they turn out to be successful or not, are being inscribed by actors in their attempts to stabilize new techno-economic networks or modify existing ones. A laboratory focusing on gene mapping, a public research programme financing soil cleaning techniques, the writer of computerized simulation models to predict oil wells: all anticipate a specific network in which their results are to be taken up. Here, a potential future world is shaped where a market for genetic techniques exist. There, a general agreement exists to define and locate contaminated soils which have to be cleaned up, and so on. These worlds, or at least some parts of them, are inscribed in the routines used, the articles put into circulation, the instruments developed, the labs that work together or the industrial partners involved. In short, any research project promotes a specific techno-economic network. It contains an anticipation of tomorrow's world, which all those who support the project share (explicitly or implicitly).[31] In such an approach, one of the tasks of a foresight exercise consists in the identification and analysis of the anticipated trajectories that are linked with the attempts made by actors to stabilize techno-economic networks.

Can such stabilization attempts be formalized? This was the object of recent work with the French environmental agency ADEME.[32] It is based on the translations actors make to link a precise stake to a precise research programme (cf. Callon, 1986). Partially inspired by the characterization of European medical networks (Larédo et al., 1992), three analytical dimensions in the interventions conducted by this agency were distinguished. A first translation step is the transformation of a political stake, for example, the greenhouse effect, into objects that are expected to be able to respond to that, that is, to solve an identified problem. In our case these 'objects' were mainly technical research priorities, but they can be other ones, such as new regulations, and the like. The second step concerns the intervention within techno-economic networks, for example, funding of a laboratory or a firm, creation of an interest group, or support for new standards which internalize the corresponding stake. Such intervention serves to transform the research priorities into concrete technical objects and technologies. Last, the formalization focuses on the hypotheses about the future networks that are made through them: what should be in place for the object to work? Or to put it more simply: what will the world look like in which the desired technical object should be embedded?[33]

The work with ADEME has led to a procedure that serves to identify, track and describe the stabilization attempts within one organization. But it also rendered explicit the multiplicity of *de facto* scenarios elaborated within the agency and, when applied to its Dutch counterparts, between agencies.[34] The following section will argue that such formalized anticipations would correspond to formal scenarios found in most foresight exercises, if they took on board the conditions under which innovations unfold.

FORMAL SCENARIOS AND DE FACTO SCENARIOS: TWO SIDES OF THE SAME COIN?

Apart from its most common use in movie making, in different branches of innovation-related literature the word 'scenario' designates different things. At least two meanings deserve special attention when technology foresight is at stake. The first relates to scenarios used in the foresight or forecasting literature. The second relates to the idea of 'actor-worlds', 'scripts' or 'set-ups' encountered in sociology of technology literature.[35] Both types are discussed below.

Scenarios as formal forecasting tools were initially developed by the military in the 1950s.[36] They were taken up in the public domain in the 1960s and are currently employed by a large number of institutions – public authorities, firms, research institutes and others.[37] Although their uses and the different methods underlying them are rather heterogeneous, all scenarios share one element. A scenario provides an image of a certain future or envisaged end-state of the system under scrutiny; according to Amara it is 'nothing more than a description of an internally consistent, plausible, future' (Amara, 1989). Additionally, in some cases, the sequence of events that should lead from a given initial state to this end-state is also described. Scenarios as foresight tool always rely on previously established predictions, analyses, expert opinions, and so on. They are an aggregate and synthesis of a set of expectations about future developments.

But scenarios are not only found in this highly formalized form. The definition of a combined end-state/path is an inherent feature of research activity and its results. In technical research, implicit or explicit anticipation of new future worlds is the rule. This idea of a scenario can be seen as an extension of Callon's 'socio-technical scenarios' (Callon, 1987), with a stronger emphasis on the trajectories defined by actors, that is, the conditions under which, according to them, these worlds will be realized. Moreover, it is complementary to Akrich's script, which is the theory of actors' behaviour inscribed in technical objects (Akrich, 1992b). The example of the electric Peugeot 106, a vehicle introduced in 1995, might serve to illustrate this complementarity. The batteries of this vehicle are placed in three different places in the car. They are fixed and hence cannot be easily removed. This car then *de facto* presupposes an environment built in such a way that recharging is possible. It excludes rapid exchange of batteries at our current petrol stations. This can be called the script of the electric Peugeot 106. The scenario then would be Peugeot's story of how the world in which the vehicle functions should be created. It contains the specifications of the object (the electric vehicle), the actors it defines (users, recharging stations, electricity, transport, and so on), and the sequence of 'obligatory passage points'[38] defined by Peugeot which would lead to the realization of this world (the technical barriers to overcome, the development of new laws, changes in user behaviour, and the like). Hence the end-state is the script defined by the object – the specific car – and a world that obeys the script, whereas the scenario concerns the way in which both should be realized. What is the relationship between the two types of scenario? The increased use of scenarios – in the first sense – as a tool for research policy within foresight exercises forces actors increasingly to formalize the implicit scenarios they elaborate through the TENs they promote. One could say that actors try real *coups de force* to have their scenarios accepted, taken over and integrated into the 'political' ones. In other words, they have to translate their projects, their TENs and the worlds they promote so that they fit into the formal scenarios others promote. This is all the more possible since, as outlined above, formal scenarios focus on end-states, and mostly leave open pathways which should lead to them. This means that a script-producer – an actor promoting one or several TENs – will try to have his or her specific pathway adopted. It can either win – in which case the proposed scenario is accepted as such – or lose – in which case it is rejected. In the latter case the script will have to be modified to be of interest again.[39] Viewed in this way, a foresight exercise is a forum where actors put forward their anticipations and postulate not only 'technological options' but, often implicitly, also the scripts and scenarios that correspond to these options. Moreover, it is a hybrid forum[40] since in most of the cases it appears that no absolute criteria (shared by all actors) have yet been constructed that would allow for comparison between scripts and selection of the TENs. This is part of the foresight process itself.

Such a view of foresight emphasizes the process rather than the result, and the arena in which it takes place. In such arenas promoters push forward their scenarios, confront them with other scenarios, and try to align, absorb or discard all those with future worlds incompatible with theirs. It is in this promoting action that actors simultaneously define the relevant fora and the complementary/competing futures. The question is thus not one of building criteria for comparing scenarios but of following the promoters of different futures both to identify these relevant fora and the articulation between anticipations made through TENs on the one hand, and wide-ranging policy scenarios on the other. Following the sociology of science,[41] the focus will inevitably be on controversies and disputes in order to identify conflicting TENs and anticipated worlds, in other words, conflicting views of the future. For the foresight practitioner, then, one problem immediately arises concerning the process. Are all hybrid fora specific or can we observe typical configurations which can help in the 'handling' of the process? The work undertaken at CSI in the last three years suggests a limited set of configurations. This will be the focus of the last section.

COMPLEMENTARY AND CONFLICTING SCENARIOS – FOUR MAIN CONFIGURATIONS

Working on energy and environmental issues, we have observed four main configurations through which scenarios relate to one another in the specific arena of research policy making. First, we found a dominant scenario around which all others are built or which all integrate in their own scenario making. In the second configuration, two 'complete' networks aimed at providing a full solution to the same problem face each other without any accepted means for comparison. In contrast, the third configuration is based on a shared end-state but on partly differing paths. Finally, in the fourth situation translations proliferate. These four configurations can be characterized by economic metaphors: monopoly, oligopoly, monopsony and 'pure' competition. This section presents them in turn, using examples from the 'prospective' studies undertaken at CSI.

Monopoly

Some 80 per cent of French electrical power is generated by nuclear energy. Electricité de France manages and builds the nuclear power stations. As of 1 January 1992, 52 units were installed, with a total capacity of 56 808 net MWe (CEA, 1992). The CEA[42] conducts nuclear and related research, Framatome builds the reactors, while Cogema is responsible for the regeneration of nuclear waste. Apart from these huge[43] operators, a whole set of other actors is more or less directly linked to French nuclear energy: firms, laboratories, public authorities, and foreign countries as importers of French electricity. They constitute a real 'network of power'[44] that has been slowly built up since the end of the 1960s.

Despite the power of the nuclear 'complex', alternative solutions to electricity generation are and have been proposed, for instance through research programmes initiated by ADEME or its predecessor AFME.[45] The agency promotes research on the mast, blades and rotor for wind turbines. It also focuses on the diffusion of small windmills or on environmental standards of hydroelectric power stations. Firms and laboratories in the field of active and passive solar energy are sponsored. Thus, ADEME inscribes electricity production in an entire set of other networks besides the nuclear one we described earlier. It appears, however, that these alternative energy routes are expected to be complementary to the central one. For instance, solar power and wind power combined with diesel engines should be used in remote places or overseas, which is where the test-beds are installed, not in the centre of Paris. These alternative networks can only grow where calculations have shown that it will be too expensive to lay cables for transporting nuclear electricity. Niche markets, deliberately left open by nuclear energy, are created for these other types of energy.

This holds even more for electricity production from biomass. As will be further elaborated under the next heading, wood can be gasified. Depending on the techniques employed, it can be transformed either into syngas or into fuel gas. The first can be used by the chemicals industry as a raw material – hence its name: synthesis gas. Fuel gas can be used for electricity production. The alternative, renewable sources discussed in the preceding paragraph take the form of small units and it is expected that this will continue.[46] However, a future world associated with electricity production from wood depends on economies of scale: vast areas of production forests which supply wood to huge gasification plants. Centralized power generation is a common feature in the wood-for-electricity scenario, the traditional coalmine or gas well being replaced by a highly productive forest. Since it concerns central power generation, such an option definitely anticipates the substitution of nuclear power generation, or at least part of it. Biomass for large-scale electricity production does not appear in French energy scenarios.

The essence is that in any (present) energy scenario elaborated in France, nuclear power is central. Alternative solutions to central power generation appear doomed – which was surely not the case when the first oil crisis occurred.[47] At present, however, as future worlds promoted through research networks, proposed new electricity options do not anticipate substitution of nuclear energy, but rather expect to manoeuvre in the few spaces left open by it. This is not to say that all-renewable scenarios have never been envisaged in France. But they have – at least temporarily – lost the battle for a central place and have to be satisfied with a 'complementary-to-nuclear' position.

The typical morphology of French energy networks constitutes a good, and surely very specific, example to illustrate our first configuration. It represents a situation where every actor who promotes new options – in this case for electricity generation – has to articulate his scenario and the corresponding network around a central and uncontested techno-economic network.

In economic terms, a monopoly exists when one firm dominates the market, and when there is thus an exclusive possession of the trade in some commodity.[48] This image corresponds very well to this first interscenario configuration. One techno-economic network dominates other potential ones. Every scenario elaborated by actors has to account for, and build alongside with, this central network, which turns out to be uncontested. Alternative options and potential new networks proposed by actors are built around the central one and leave it intact. They do not aim at replacing it, or even parts of it. They are complementary, meaning that they anticipate operating at its margins. These margins are determined, not by these opposing networks, but by the central network itself. It is the dominating TEN that has the capability of deciding its own boundaries and hence fixes those of others.[49] Moreover, networks that anticipate even a partial substitution, like other solutions to large-scale power generation, do not appear in the scenarios. They might have existed as germs of an idea, but could not get recognition in the hybrid forum dominated by the central network.

Oligopoly

In the former section biomass was introduced as a potential techno-economic network aimed at electricity generation. We concluded that biomass (wood) for electricity production was not part of French energy scenarios. However, different biomass networks are and have been under construction. And scenarios exist in which they play an important role. They will serve to illustrate the second configuration, when we add to French scenarios those promoted through Dutch networks.[50]

To simplify, both in the Netherlands and in France actors have tried to translate the same problem, the greenhouse effect, involving carbon dioxide emission and the 'set-aside policy' of the European Union concerning agriculture.[51] In both countries, these problems have been translated into the development of non-food agricultural activity since, in the same action, carbon dioxide can be fixed, and fallow land used. These translations – which are relatively well shared by actors in both countries – build a common framework (or policy scenario) under which TENs can be further elaborated. However, they do not say anything about how these scenarios might be realized. And indeed, different ideas oppose themselves to each other, so that a hybrid forum is born. In this specific case, the number of options proposed is not that large, and appears to be mainly centred around the following question: what should be put on the land? Then grosso modo two constructions are envisaged: perennial plants, that is, trees, or annual plants, traditional cultures like wheat, beets, sweet sorghum or rapeseed.

Both cases constitute typical examples of technological controversy,[52] which in addition expand from a national level to a controversy between countries in international fora like the IEA.[53] For the analyst, all instruments are there to follow closure. Closure in France is indicated by the '*rapport Lévy*', which concludes with a national choice for biofuels, whereas two years before nothing had yet been played out.[54] Until that time, the wood option was still open as a potential response to the set-aside policy. Fifteen years of genetic research into different tree species had been conducted. Harvesting machines had been developed or adapted to the irregular surfaces of the French forests. Also a pilot plant to transform wood into syngas had been built at Clamecy.[55] Simultaneously, research activity into the biofuels route, though at a rather low level, had been maintained.[56] So, both routes had been deliberately kept open for several years without making one or the other irreversible. The end of the controversy between the biofuel and the wood trajectories was marked by the official closure of the pilot plant at Clamecy in the summer of 1994.

Whereas the French case is closed, the Dutch controversy was still active in 1996.[57] The options were initially laid down in a report commissioned by NOVEM.[58] It described the scenarios for different types of biomass production for the Netherlands on the basis of an 'enlarged' cost–benefit analysis. 'Enlarged' since it integrated not only internal costs, but also tried to account for so-called externalities such as the costs of cleaning up the emissions of different pollutants, transport costs and so forth. *De facto*, it not only proposed options, but, by bringing all 'factors' down to cost, it implicitly defined the conditions under which other actors had to choose between the options the report proposed. However, after all the difficult cost calculations, this one appeared to be a miscalculation. Whereas 'scientifically' the analysis seemed perfectly in order, the conditions were not accepted by the Ministry of Agriculture, the National Farmers' Association or the sugar companies. One of the main reasons put forward did not concern the quality of the report, but the criteria that were proposed for selection. The report ignored the fact that, for farmers, agricultural practices – the pattern of revenue generation and so forth – differ drastically between an annual and a perennial crop. Whether it was a 'farmers' lobby' – as the proponents of the wood option said – or not, the fact was that in 1994 DLO, the Dutch agricultural research institute, an obligatory passage point for anyone envisaging doing agricultural research, placed an embargo on both routes – and no funding was allocated.[59] But actors' scenarios can change, and so did DLO's: the institute's research plan for 1995 onwards announced a new research programme studying the feasibility of electricity generation from biomass, in particular from wood. Without explicitly referring to it, this plan takes up some of the considerations of NOVEM's biomass report. However, it adds explicitly: 'by viability we do not understand only if the costs are covered in an economic sense, but also if other effects of biomass-energy are societally desired or acceptable'.[60] Moreover, the programme consists of the integration of the different emerging (and very incomplete) networks that were investigated by us some 18 months earlier. A scenario becomes established with the networks that support it – electricity from wood might turn out to be a successful *coup de force*.[61]

This case exemplifies the main characteristics of the second configuration: few constructions are opposed but the networks they define are radically different. If one network is constructed above the other, and gains 'momentum', in Hughes's terms, coexistence, let alone synergy, is said to be impossible. Within the same forum, the networks are mutually exclusive. Two radically different TENs are anticipated and partially inscribed, without the conditions yet being laid down (and hence no decision taken) for choosing one or the other. We propose to call this situation an oligopoly situation.[62] In economic terms, in an oligopoly a small number of producers face a huge number of consumers. In our example, it is a small number of TENs having to interest and align a large number of heterogeneous actors. The oligopoly situation is not a stable one: we observe that in the case where few constructions are opposed to each other, actors try nearly everything to create the conditions for their network to win. In other words, the networks in an oligopolistic situation are stable as long as the conditions that allow a choice between them are not. This implies that networks are not yet complete and that a market still has to be established.[63] The criteria which render both networks commensurable are the same as those which will enable the interessment (see n.70) of all the actors – future users of the technique, future users of the product, environmental representatives, as well as politicians, and so on – who at the moment are still to be convinced. The criteria might hence be economic (proving that the technologies will be low-cost), social (suggesting that one cannot expect farmers to change from annual to perennial crops), technical (demonstrating that biofuels are the best environmental option), or other. Agreement between actors on the criteria – and thus potential agreement about the conditions under which this or that network might be created – implies that losing TENs give way to the winning one.

What is further shown by this case is that the same controversy can take place in different fora with different outcomes. It is interesting to note here that French and Dutch agencies only became aware of the radical differences of their respective networks through our comparative exercise and thus recognized the 'sociotechnical' content of any research programme definition.

From the point of view of dynamics, the oligopoly configuration appears as a transitory one whereby, once common criteria are recognized within a forum, such oligopoly anticipations turn into 'local' monopolies. Following the controversies studied by the sociology of science and technology, our hypothesis is that this is a compulsory trajectory and that, within a given forum, there can be no conditions under which opposite scenarios can develop fully, including the construction of a market. How long can such 'local' monopolies survive? In other words, in the long run, how viable are radically different local monopolies? Energy, in which global firms operate, tends to prove that no definite trajectory exists and that different local constructions – like the nuclear one in France – can be stabilized for long periods of time within so-called global markets, re-opening the door for specific 'prospectives', 'actions' and 'constructions'.

Monopsony

In the second case study, we looked at a shared policy scenario associating carbon dioxide emissions and EU agricultural set-aside policy. But TENs developed under this broad framework became radically opposed. Other situations were faced whereby a shared technical goal defined a sociotechnical end-state which left less room for interpretation: such is the case of the French household waste policy. By 2002, all landfills are to disappear, except for new ones which will be dedicated entirely to stabilized (ultimate) waste – a residue after recycling. This accords with a broader definition of recycling, including not only materials and compost, but also energy. The prohibition-of-landfill scenario had two major effects. First it organized the debate between actors about what was to be understood by 'stabilized' waste. It also provided actors with a shared future in which different recycling techniques coexist,[64] and where the confrontation between routes and networks lies less in the search for a monopoly position than in the search for an 'adequate' relative positioning compared to others.

This is typically the case of household waste collection, which has rapidly emerged as the key point in the transformation of waste management. The critical issue on which networks are deployed lies in the organization of the separation of waste. A survey of 11 'innovative' approaches in France has shown that everywhere it required a changing attitude to waste production and a transformation of users of the public service into effective sorters (Barbier and Larédo, 1994). As in any innovation, it required trial-and-error processes through which learning took place, and through which all participants progressively became aligned. This then crystallized into equipment specially adapted to household waste, and the establishment of a new type of service. All arrived at a similar end-state where waste was transformed into 'new' materials entering nationally or internationally established markets (paper, aluminium, iron, glass, and so on). Locally, however, systems were very different. In some places inhabitants were asked to keep 'clean and dry' wastes in one blue bin which was specifically collected and sorted in a manual separating centre; in other places, separation of 'clean and dry' was done at home and each material (glass, plastics, metals, and so on) collected in turn for immediate delivery to the national markets; elsewhere, the task of separation was split between inhabitants and garbage men using a compartmentalized truck. In another large city, waste is separated into four categories – 'corps creux', 'corps plats', 'fermentescibles'[65] and others – which require two double bins, newly developed trucks and a mechanical separating centre (representing a radical innovation *per se*). In sum, a multitude of different local networks link the producer of waste to more global structures such as an incinerator, or different 'materials chains' or 'filières'. The global result – the end-state – is, however, the same for all actors, which was not the case in the previous configuration.

This is not to say that under such an inclusive umbrella no alternative (sub)networks are proposed. When examining the elements of such networks more closely, comparable situations – competition for fulfilling the same goal – are encountered. In the case of incineration, for instance, actors' questions shift to the optimal production of heat, electricity and inert residues from mixed wastes. Different approaches – at source or end of pipe – and different techniques are in competition, through rather traditional innovation processes and TENs.[66] This reminds us of another, less well-known, but nevertheless typical situation in economics, that is, one in which different suppliers depend on a single client. Such an economic situation is called a monopsony.[67] In the case discussed here, the 'client' is defined as in marketing and this definition is typically based on functional operation: for instance, in one case 'incineration' represents the client role, in another this role is taken by 'waste separation'. The 'suppliers' are then the different 'ensembles' of techniques supporting and serving these purposes, that is, the incineration or the collection and separation of waste. In other words, the 'single client' is the single envisaged end-state of the *de facto* scenario resulting from the operations relating to household waste. The multiple suppliers are the different (sub-)trajectories which actors propose to lead to this end-state. Read in this way, we can identify classical industrial situations, in which suppliers progressively work their way through from demonstration to dissemination, and from first realizations to 'achieving significant market share'. At a certain level, the difference is crucial: in one place a certain network dominates (for instance waste collection based on mechanical separating centres in large cities) while in another a different one has gained momentum (let us say a division of labour in waste separation between household and garbage in rural areas). But at another level – the national policy or the distinct product chains – the coexistence of different techniques and networks does not matter. In this monopsony scenario the same future is promoted through different routes by different actors.

This situation is the only one which sees both formal and script-based scenarios working together. Within one forum, the same end-state is postulated by all networks, a situation which can be read as the result of previous alignment. A monopsony configuration thus corresponds to a partly irreversible situation: a unique future world with different technological–organizational routes. It should be clear, however, that like the oligopoly configuration, this is a transitory situation. The sole fact of choosing one route (or choosing it more often) will enable a learning process to be entered on, foster irreversibility and, through the refining of performance criteria, progressively co-adapt the path and the end-state.

Pure Competition (or the Proliferation of Future Worlds)

The three preceding configurations have in common the existence of a limited set of well-developed networks. These networks are effective in translating a debated issue into a proposed trajectory: to solve the energy dependency demonstrated by the first oil crisis, only nuclear power appeared feasible to French policy makers. In the second case, reduction of carbon dioxide emissions is connected to the agricultural set-aside policy to propose generation of either electricity or car fuels from biomass, which are radically different paths. In the third case different routes for waste collection and elimination should lead to the same future. It may be that in many 'sectoral' policies these three are the only configurations encountered; within research policies, however, situations exist where both the issues and the ways to deal with them are unspecified.

Who was aware, for instance, of the ozone hole before scientists went to the Antarctic and built observation stations? And, before that, how could such a research programme be decided upon? The uncertainty not only lies in the path to follow (which direction to take to cure insulin-dependent diabetes, for instance) but on the end-state postulated: will oceans rise and cover more land if we experience global warming? Should we believe that biodiversity is threatened? And so forth.

A recent survey of research priorities in the environment presents us with hundreds of claims from scientists about future environmental problems which require specific new research programmes.[68] We are here simultaneously faced with differences in the phenomena that we are told will emerge in the next 10, 20 or 50 years, and different corresponding universes and frames of reference. To put it bluntly: each actor defines a different scenario, with different research priorities, that is, a different trajectory to solve it. Each position is somewhat different (relatively unshared with others) which means that nothing has yet been established. Most of the time such positions are not even inscribed into recognized research results. It is a proliferation of future worlds.

It should be no surprise to have to face such different claims and future worlds. This is typical of research activities, as Latour demonstrated.[69] The same thing happens with any call for proposals. But answers have rarely been selected which take account of the differing future worlds promoted. Criteria are often quite different: at the Social Science and Humanities research Council (SSHRC) in Canada track records of excellence dominate; in EU research programmes answers must bring together teams from more than one country, coming from both public and private research, large and small countries, and so on; for the Dutch Technical Foundation STW, relevance to industrial problems has to be explained in the calls for proposals.

Foresight exercises on research priorities reverse this approach. Here, the claims for inclusion into a policy framework are put forward. By changing arenas, foresight exercises could radically transform the conditions under which researchers articulate and promote their projects. Still, the question is open about how to handle such claims. Will it rely upon the long-standing *intéressement*[70] process illustrated by Latour in respect of Joliot and nuclear energy?[71] In this case, recognition by peers in the 1930s contributed to encouraging what we would now call an École de Doctorat (a doctorate school), promoting the new energy option in the media, convincing industrialists to provide Joliot with a factory and uranium (against a share in the future returns), and obtaining from the war ministry (already!) the necessary equipment, money and manpower. Or should new procedures be developed to formalize the debate about which claims should be taken on board by policy and thus to organize public action?[72]

SCENARIO ADOPTION AND POLICIES

The cases have been useful in highlighting typical confrontations between scenarios. At the same time they answer one strong methodological question. By pointing to these situations, we do not compare scenarios, let alone perform a ranking exercise. We follow processes through which TENs connect themselves to other TENs. Nuclear power does not dominate because it has eliminated all other options. It is there since those in France who make anticipations today, do so by taking into account the dominating position of nuclear. As mentioned, this was not the case 20 years ago. The same arises when both ADEME and NOVEM describe similar issues when they connect global warming with EU set-aside policy. These are established political or scientific facts. It is the explicit mission of the environmental agencies to assist in finding and co-constructing solutions – in other words, to help make some trajectories irreversible. By doing so, they make it possible for a hybrid forum to develop in both countries, whatever the outcome might be.

We do not deny that interference is generated when scenario makers start to involve innovation sociologists in their strategic reflections. In the present case, our involvement satisfied a need for systematization and the integration of 'future worlds' into the repertoire of criteria for choice. The formalization of anticipations, and previously at ADEME the formalization of emerging TENs and their adoption as management tool by this agency,[73] does not provide some actors (for example, policy makers) with 'best' solutions. It clarifies potential choices and thus serves as a base for reflecting on potential intervention – where in the end the final choice remains essentially political. The following paragraphs describe directions for intervention.

As in any innovation process, a scenario gains momentum by gaining allies. This is inscribed in the way other scenario makers adopt it.[74] When focusing on science and technology policy, the typology has the following relevance. Every set of technical research choices expresses a view about the future world. Although each specific configuration will be made up of other actors, which makes policy interventions differ qualitatively from case to case, it can be argued that if the number of scenarios within a configuration is limited, so will be the typical choices for policy intervention. Once certain scenarios start to oppose themselves to each other in a certain way, the resulting configuration defines potential policy measures. In the monopsony configuration, for instance, the goal, say, incineration, is fixed, but how one should arrive at it is open. It thus simultaneously defines a possible public intervention – a demonstration programme for new technologies that are able to reach the desired goal, for example, satisfy certain emission requirements with regard to nitrogen oxides, sulphur dioxides or dioxins. Thanks to 'internetwork' alignments already created, different techniques can be compared.[75] In reverse, when faced with an oligopoly configuration, policy makers may choose to join one or the other network – NOVEM joining 'wood for electricity'. But they may also find that the time is not yet ripe to intervene actively, and may wait for others (the market, constituencies, lead-users, and so on) to tip the balance one way or another – ADEME's present position as regards local choices about household waste collection. Finally, they may find it crucial for both directions to be left open and choose to support the weaker network so as to enhance balanced learning – annual versus perennial crops as in the French case until two years ago.

In the first three cases we discussed – monopoly, oligopoly and monopsony – the situation has been stabilized to a great extent and, thereby, the type of policy priorities that can be articulated. But how to deal with a proliferation of 'future worlds', with unstable or undeveloped networks? Which claims to foster and support? For which reasons and with which selection criteria? If one wishes systematically to think out research and technology policy along 'problem-geared' lines, new procedures will have to be developed which favour the expression of such claims and the development of hybrid fora where they get a chance to be convincing, and start gaining allies. Hence we are both very far from our initial question – no longer dealing with foresight in the usual sense – as well as very near the need for articulation between research and societal priorities – by tackling the problem which, in our view, at least partly explains the boom in foresight activities.

We summarised the four situations in which actors' *de facto* scenarios are confronted with each other in Table 9.1. Taking on board lessons from innovation studies has served to establish a simple typology in which the number

Table 9.1   Summary of the four situations of scenario confrontation

Type	Description	Actions encountered
Monopoly	Every actor promoting new options is confronted with a stabilised, dominant and central techno-economic network	Niche strategies, price competition
Oligopoly	A limited set of radically different scenarios is proposed by different actors in response to the same problematic issue; trajectories and end-states differ; no criteria have yet been constructed which would allow choice	Internalizing externalities, construction of criteria for choice between different networks
Monopsony	All networks proposed by actors postulate the same end-states, but trajectories differ	Demonstration programmes according to existing criteria
Proliferation (free competition)	A situation in which all actors propose different scenarios as well as different criteria to choose between them	Inventory of the futures proposed by actors

of configurations is limited. It can point to situations where foresight is able to say something – where networks are stable at least in the short term (the monopoly) or where future developments will depend on the conditions formulated by actors to choose between one of a few options (oligopoly, monopsony). It also points to all those situations where networks are not configured at all and where such an approach – formal or based on sociotechnical scripts – can offer no direction. Foresight can then only provide an inventory.

CONCLUSION

This chapter argues that three lessons derived from innovation studies are important for foresight. First, innovation processes do not unfold in a linear sequence from science to market. Rather, innovations describe a whirlwind pattern and consist of the establishment of links between different actors. Foresight should account for this collective character. Second, innovation is social as well as technical – the two are simultaneously shaped and constantly entangled. Consequently, research priorities put forward with the help of foresight exercises imply certain sociotechnical configurations. Third, innovations are path-dependent, and path-dependence can occur very early. Hence one of the roles for foresight should be the identification of the situations where 'small events' tend to make the trajectory of innovations irreversible.

The concept of techno-economic network accounts for these three observations. The relation with foresight is that potential future trajectories are inscribed by actors through their attempts to stabilize new techno-economic networks. Earlier work has led to a formalization that serves to identify such stabilization attempts, rendering explicit the scripts and the *de facto* scenarios put forward by actors. Foresight processes can hence be seen as the constitution of hybrid fora where formal scenarios of the foresight practitioners (for example, policy makers) and the formalized scenarios of others (for example, researchers) meet. It consists, then, of actors' *coups de force* to have their scenarios accepted, that is, incorporated in scenarios made by others. Thus one of the effects of foresight processes is to promote (or push or organize) a confrontation between scenarios. In the foresight exercises recently carried out by CSI, four typical situations of such scenario confrontation were encountered. They can be characterized by economic metaphors.

In the monopoly configuration one network dominates and all actors integrate this feature as they elaborate their own scenarios. Proposed new networks do not aim at substituting the principal one but operate in a complementary manner. In the oligopoly configuration a few incompatible and incommensurable networks oppose themselves to each other. They define radically different futures, with regard to both end-state and path. Criteria have not yet been built enabling their comparison or weighting. When this is done, however, the winning network will achieve a (local) monopoly position. In the third configuration, indicated as monopsony, within one forum the same end-state is anticipated, but proposed paths are slightly different. Finally, the last configuration is one of pure competition. Here, future worlds proposed by actors proliferate, without end-states or paths being shared by others. Networks are hardly inscribed, and fora to debate them eventually are only partially constituted. The first three configurations represent relatively stabilized networks for foresight. In the last case, however, although it is often the main reason for conducting such exercises, foresight can only provide an inventory of all potential future worlds.

Integrating lessons from innovation studies drives the focus of foresight exercises from a predictive to a procedural conception. It insists on the foresight *process* – a movement that in practice is already largely observed. It might result in significant changes in the way policies are formulated both by leading to a formalization of the predictions actors make through the networks they construct, and by organizing hybrid fora where networks and the future worlds defined through them can be brought into confrontation with each other. This process enables all situations to be identified where only a small number of scenarios dominate and organizes the debate around the trajectories that are about to stabilize. It also enables an inventory to be made of hypothetical claims for the emergence of radically new techno-economic networks. Like innovations, if such processes are to play a role in policy formulation, it is thus important to analyse how they unfold over time. This calls for a new research agenda, focusing less on how to construct foresight processes than on their effective development and stabilization.

NOTES

1. The term 'articulation' is used here in the French sense, meaning the connection between two entities. In the French meaning of the word the entity/ies articulated or the joint itself are not necessarily concrete (e.g. as in 'hip joint', an articulation between two lorries, or 'articulated speech'), but can be abstract, which is the case here. Similarly, the word 'stake' is used to translate the French word 'enjeu' – meaning 'what is at stake' – since no better English term seemed to be at hand.
2. See for instance Coates et al. (1994).
3. See Larédo and Mustar (1996).
4. Barbier (1994), Barbier and Larédo (1994), De Laat (1996) and Rémy and Larédo (1995), respectively.
5. See, respectively, Georghiou (1996), Grupp (1993), MESR (1994) and OCV (1996).
6. This upswing went along with the rise in research programmes, which we cannot discuss here. See for instance Larédo and Mustar (1996), or the special issue of the journal

Research Evaluation, edited by Luke Georghiou, which gives an overview of recent European national efforts in research evaluation (vol. 5, no.1).

7. Rip, for instance, writes: 'evaluation studies traditionally resolved this problem [of the objectives against which to evaluate] by conserving the (initial) objective of the policy maker' (Rip, 1995, p. 116, our translation).

8. A tendency existing during the 1980s but only now developing fully. See Adelson (1989), Amara (1989), Dror (1989), Geurts (1993), Godet (1979), Irvine and Martin (1984, 1989) and Whiston (1994).

9. Linstone (1989) speaks of the 'chasm between the analyst and the real world'; in Linstone (1994) he adds that 'the reductionist paradigm ... proved frustratingly inadequate to deal with complex systems' (p. 2), and pleads for a more integrated approach which links 'technology', 'organization' and 'individual'.

10. Although the authors use the term 'forecasting', normally associated with prediction, their article gives quite a complete synthesis of what at least in Europe are more commonly known as 'foresight activities'.

11. One of the foresight projects managers we interviewed remarked that the (social) networking aspect has become so important for public technology policy that in some cases it had come to overshadow technical content itself: 'they only put people together since they think that's what makes the innovation run ... it seems as if they have altogether forgotten about the technical choices that could eventually be made and the impact on society these might have'.

12. See, for instance, Bijker and Law (1992), Dosi et al. (1988), Freeman and Soete (1990), Jasanoff et al. (1994) and Rip et al. (1995b).

13. See De Laat (1995). The instrument is based on Callon's translation sociology (cf. Callon, 1986) and makes an analytical distinction between (1) the translation of political stakes into envisaged technical, and other, objects, (2) the intervention in TENs to realize them, and (3) the anticipation of future networks that they express.

14. See Coombs et. al. (1987) for an overview of the demand-pull/science-push debate.

15. Von Hippel (1988); see also Bijker (1992) for a case of 'invention' during the 'diffusion' stage of a product.

16. For instance the oft-cited chain-link model of Kline and Rosenberg (1986). For other models see Forrest (1991).

17. In Porter et al.'s recent (1991) handbook on foresight techniques and methods one reads, for instance: 'the supply of scientific knowledge and technological principles [vs.] economic and societal demand' (p. 21); and although the authors admit that 'unfortunately the growth of technologies is strongly affected by the social/political context in which they are embedded [and hence there is] *no single growth pattern that describes the development and diffusion of all technologies*' (p. 58, their emphasis), nevertheless a seven–stage linear model is proposed (p. 59) as a 'general concept of how technologies develop' (p. 58).

18. See, respectively, Akrich (1993), Bijker (1987), Latour (1993a), Law and Callon (1992). Mangematin (1996) is also very illustrative with regard to the simultaneous shaping of organization and technology *within* a research project.

19. Callon (1987).

20. For a full-fledged account of this argument see Latour (1994).

21. Cf. Winner (1980).

22. This does not imply that the detailed effects of such a choice will or can always be fully understood beforehand. We would even like to emphasize that such choices and the constructions are not fixed once and for all – they can and will be contested by actors and hence will stabilize (see next paragraph) only temporarily. See Latour (1993b, 1994).

23. Dosi (1982), Nelson and Winter (1977, 1982), Sahal (1985). Whereas they focused on typical products/technologies, such regimes are said to exist on the level of generic technologies (Perez, 1983), countries (Lundvall, 1988) or social groups (Bijker, 1987) as well.

24. David (1986) explains that in the case of QWERTY, the arrangement of the keyboard was the best way to prevent the compacting of type-bars behind one another. For the manual

act of typing itself better solutions might have existed (by 1867 there were more than 50 patent attempts describing a commercial typewriter). Moreover, Remington was nearly broke when it bought the manufacturing rights from the inventor. Nevertheless, schools for novice typists based themselves on the Remington machines. Likewise the early manuals. Consequently the operators were trained in QWERTY, which influenced buyers and suppliers. QWERTY's final standardization in 1890 owed to the expectations that the buyers of typewriting machines had with regard to the equipment users, who were now used to the system. Despite the fact that in 1890 new machines had been developed with both a better key arrangement and a better way of preventing the type-bars from compacting, it was already too late: now, some 100 years later, the greater part of the world still finds itself typing on a QWERTY keyboard. For the other countries a similar story can probably be told (France, for instance, uses 'AZERTY' keyboard). Note that observations of the sociologists cited in the preceding paragraph and the economists cited here converge: the QWERTY story shows very well that the simultaneous stabilization of both social and technical elements accounts for irreversibility.

25. Rip (1995).
26. Cf. 'lock-in', the adoption of some technologies more rapidly than others, determined by network externalities, scale economies in production, increasing returns in information and technological interrelatedness (Arthur, 1988, 1989). See Callon (1991) for a sociological account.
27. Cowan (1990).
28. See Porter et al. (1991), chs 9 and 10 for an overview. See Marchetti (1991a, 1991b) for applications of such methods to technological developments. See Irvin (1993) for a lucid comment on the pros and cons of such techniques. Moreover, it can be remarked that the cited methods analyse technology in isolation from the social domain.
29. Williamson (1983), Karpik (1996).
30. Callon (1991).
31. The argument put forward here is the same as in innovation sociology (see above): an object stabilizes when the actors linked to it align and converge. In other words, stabilization (or irreversibility, as mentioned above) is indicated by the fact that the shape of the technical object does not change any more, even in association with new actors. The same goes for a research project: it becomes more and more successful when it links more actors without changing its definition and with actors sharing the definition – otherwise the project will end up where Aramis, the French individual subway train, ended – in a museum (Latour, 1993a).
32. The French environment and energy agency. This work is described in De Laat (1995, 1996).
33. Following Akrich (1992b), it concerns the future (and as yet fictive, cf. De Laat, 1995, pp. 71ff.) script of the object, that is, the users and other elements, such as infrastructure, compatibility with other techniques, industrial sectors, and so on, *inscribed* in the objects promoted through the projects at the agency.
34. After the results with the formalization exercise internal to the organization, ADEME chose to associate itself with its Dutch homologues NOVEM (the Netherlands agency for energy and environment) and SENTER (the Dutch agency for the stimulation of innovation). The three decided on four fields in which to conduct a common exercise to further work out the approach. One of them (biomass) will be dealt with in a later section of this chapter.
35. See, for these notions, respectively Akrich (1992b), Callon (1987) and Law and Callon (1992).
36. As most of the traditional forecasting methods (Delphi, Cross-Impact Analysis, Relevance Trees, and the like) have. See Jantsch (1967).
37. Examples are the Dutch foresight steering committee OCV, using scenarios as the heart of its foresight exercises (see OCV, 1994, Tijink et al., 1994); ADEME's huge scenario study in the field of housing (Bourdeau et al., 1992); or again Shell, known for being the first company systematically using scenarios for strategic planning (Bouvier and Olivier, 1983, Leijten, 1989).

38. The term 'obligatory passage point', originally a military term referring to strategic positioning, is used in translation sociology to designate the problems which an actor (for example a scientist) states have to be solved in order to realize a given goal (Callon, 1986, pp. 205–6). See also Vissac-Charles (1995) for the use of this concept in project management.

39. A symmetrical argument is to say that a formal scenario must also gain the interest of the actors it envisages involving. So instead of fighting to be accepted by the 'officials' of scenario making, actors could also try to ignore or change the scenario. Although this point deserves further elaboration, it appears that once a set of actors agrees that a scenario, having been generated by foresight exercises, should serve as a guide to future actions on, for instance, a national level, it will probably be more effective to act in accordance with such a scenario than try to reformulate it. Indeed, much depends on the 'force' of the scenario: the more allies it has, the more associates (Latour, 1986) and the more power it has (see our earlier note on alignment and stabilization). This is also the result of a process, and is not given beforehand. Cf. Dinkelman (1995) who describes how, although scenarios were established 'scientifically' for acid rain and global warming, it took rather a long time and a lot of effort before they appeared on political agendas – now both these scenarios as well as the underlying methods have been stabilized, however, they have quite a high mobilizing power.

40. See Callon and Rip (1992).

41. See Callon (1981), Collins (1985), Latour (1987) and Pickering (1992).

42. Commissariat de l'Énergie Atomique, the French nuclear energy research institute.

43. To give an impression: the CEA has over 18 000 employees and Framatome is – in terms of absolute expenditure – among the top 20 of French R&D performing companies (*Le Monde*, 3/8/95).

44. Hughes (1983).

45. The AFME is the former French energy agency.

46. Intuitively one might expect that there would be commonly shared technical limits to the power generated by, for instance, a windmill (perhaps maximum blade size). However, even the maximum unit size of renewables is contested, and thus the type of networks that can or should be constructed is not a fixed item, but subject to discussion, as Jørgensen and Karnøe (1995) show.

47. Cf. the multitude of French concerted actions related to energy technologies in the 1960s and 1970s.

48. For the economic concept of monopoly, see Perry (1989), pp. 191–6 and, for monopolistic competition, pp. 199ff.

49. See Mangematin and Callon (1995) for a fuller account of such 'acteurs incontournables'.

50. We here rely on the enlargement of our approach from ADEME to its Dutch counterparts NOVEM and SENTER. See note 34 and de Laat (1995).

51. Which, as the reader by now should realize, are themselves temporarily stabilized results of long chains of translations which we will not go into here.

52. Callon (1981).

53. The International Energy Agency. Discussion on the types of biomass to promote went on between the two (and other) countries in meetings organized through the IEA. Such expert meetings typically take the form of *formalized* hybrid fora since they are loci where actors propose scenarios, and fight (techno-scientific) battles in order to establish which path to choose as well as the criteria for their selection.

54. Lévy (1993); see also Chartier and Mauguin (1993).

55. Hence not for electricity, confirming the uncontested monopoly of nuclear energy as outlined above.

56. In French, this is called an active 'veille technologique' – an active competitive intelligence – which 'keeps awake' research, whereas a passive one would have only consisted in scanning competitors' activities, through, for instance, patent analysis.

57. As indicated by the recent publication of a new methodology to decide on options in the field of 'energy crops' (Biewinga and Bijl, 1996).

58. Within the framework of the establishment of its biomass programme. See NOVEM (1992).
59. Interviews held with spokespersons of DLO confirmed that the embargo held until Spring 1995.
60. P. 295. The report was published June 1995. See DLO (1995).
61. As the reader will understand, the story is a bit more complicated than this. For instance, in the meantime a gasification plant for organic waste has been built, and this TEN around gasification of organic waste is now associated with the new DLO programme. We have not been able to investigate how, for instance, its results have served as an *intéressement* device. Whatever the situation, within less than one year emerging networks have been amalgamated so that they now share an end-state.
62. For the different economic theories of the oligopoly see Shapiro (1989).
63. Market is meant here not in the restricted sense of the locus where supply meets demand, but as the universe of users, with their needs, hierarchies of preferences, and so forth (Callon et al., 1992, p. 221). Hence in our examples several such markets might be distinguished besides the market for electricity: a market for genetic techniques for trees, a market for harvesting machines, and so on.
64. One might even think that this was a result of the previous 'battle' about energy and the will of actors – many of which participated in the energy debate – not to give room to one monopoly situation.
65. Respectively: hollow and flat plastic containers and organic waste.
66. Apart from technologies competing for the same goal, it offers good examples of an enlarged definition of users, with the proliferation of spokespersons representing, for instance, besides end-users and their preoccupations, air pollution, health, or beauty (Barbier, 1994).
67. For the economic notion of monopsony and backward vertical integration see Perry (1989), pp. 196–9.
68. The study referred to here was conducted by Rémy and Larédo (1995). An international survey was conducted under the auspices of the Association Descartes in Paris and will be published in due course.
69. Latour (1987).
70. '*Intéressement is the group of actions by which an entity ... attempts to impose and stabilise the identity of the other actors it defines through its problemisation*' (Callon, 1986, pp. 207–8). See also note 38, above, on obligatory passage points.
71. Latour (1989). This is cited to remind the reader of all the previous constructions a scenario at any moment encapsulates. It is Joliot's construction in the 1930s, which explains, following the Second World War, his ability to convince policy makers as early as 1945 of the need for a specific institution dedicated to nuclear energy, the CEA, which brings the reader back to our first configuration, the nuclear monopoly.
72. A problem to which constructive technology assessment (Rip et al., 1995a) seems only one among many potential solutions.
73. Callon et al. (1992). See also Marsh et al. (1996) annex C, in which ADEME explains how it uses the concept of TEN in its strategy formulation.
74. Even the use of the traditional term 'scenario-writing' (Jantsch, 1967, pp. 201–2), more or less fallen into oblivion, could be reconsidered. It would now not only concern writing potential future developments down on paper, but the various inscriptions made on other materials, representing *de facto* future anticipations.
75. Inversely, the existence of a demonstration programme might be a good indicator of a monopsony configuration being actively looked for. Public actors are no different; they participate in the co-constructing of scenarios and fora.

REFERENCES

Adelson, M. (1989), 'Reflections on the Past and Future of the Future', *Technological Forecasting and Social Change*, **36** (1–2), 27–37.

Akrich, M. (1992a), 'Beyond Social Construction of Technology: the Shaping of People and Things in the Innovation Process', in Dierkes, M. and Hoffmann, U. (eds), *New Technology at the Outset*, Frankfurt/New York: Campus/Westview, pp. 173–90.

Akrich, M. (1992b), 'The Description of Technical Objects', in Bijker, W.E. and Law, J. (eds), *Shaping Technology/Building Society. Studies in Sociotechnical Change*, Cambridge, MA: MIT Press, pp. 205–24.

Akrich, M. (1993), 'Essay of Technosociology: a Gasogene in Costa Rica', in Lemonnier, P. (ed.), *Technological Choices: Transformation in material cultures since the Neolithic*, London: Routledge, pp. 289–337.

Amara, R. (1989), 'A Note on What We Have Learned About the Methods of Futures Planning', *Technological Forecasting and Social Change*, **36** (1–2), 43–7.

ANRS (Agence nationale de recherche sur le SIDA) (1995), *Prospective SIDA 2010. Le SIDA en France. État des Connaissances en 1994*, Paris: ANRS.

Arthur, W.B. (1988), 'Competing technologies: an overview', in Dosi, G., Freeman, C., Nelson, R., Silverberg, G. and Soete, L. (eds), *Technical Change and Economic Theory*, London: Pinter Publishers, pp. 590–607.

Arthur, W. B. (1989), 'Competing technologies, increasing returns, and lock-in by historical events', *The Economic Journal*, **99**, 116–31.

Barbier, R. (1994), *Étude sur l'Implantation des UIOM en Milieu Urbain*, Paris: CSI École des Mines/ADEME.

Barbier, R. and Larédo, P. (1994), *Il y a du neuf dans les poubelles*, Paris: CSI École des Mines/ADEME.

Biewinga, E.E. and Bijl, G. v. d. (1996), *Sustainability of Energy Crops in Europe. A methodology developed and applied*, Utrecht: Centre for Agriculture and Environment.

Bijker, W. (1987), 'The Social Construction of Bakelite; Towards a Theory of Invention', in Bijker, W.E., Hughes, T.P. and Pinch, T.J. (eds), *The Social Construction of Technological Systems*, Cambridge, MA: MIT Press, pp. 159–87.

Bijker, W.E. (1992), 'The Social Construction of Fluorescent Lighting, or How an Artifact Was Invented in Its Diffusion Stage', in Bijker, W.E. and Law, J. (eds), *Shaping Technology/Building Society. Studies in Sociotechnical Change*, Cambridge, MA: MIT Press, pp. 75–102.

Bijker, W.E. and Law, J. (eds) (1992), *Shaping Technology/Building Society. Studies in Sociotechnical Change*, Cambridge, MA: MIT Press.

Bourdeau, L., Angioletti, R. and Haguenauer, G. (1992), *Bâtiment 2030. Quels Bâtiments pour l'avenir? Quatre scenarios et leurs configurations*, Sophia Antipolis: ADEME/CSTB.

Bouvier, M. and Olivier, M. (1983), 'La planification stratégique et Shell française', *Futuribles*, **72**, 23–8.

Callon, M. (1981), 'Pour une Sociologie des Controverses Technologiques', *Fundamenta Scientiae*, **2** (3/4), 381–99.

Callon, M. (1986), 'Some elements of a sociology of translation: domestication of the scallops and the fishermen of St Brieuc Bay', in Law, J. (ed.), *Power, Action and Belief. A New Sociology of Knowledge?*, London: Routledge & Kegan Paul, pp. 196–233.

Callon, M. (1987), 'Society in the Making', in Bijker, W., Hughes, T. and Pinch, T. (eds), *The Social Construction of Technological Systems*, Cambridge, MA: MIT Press.

Callon, M. (1991), 'Techno-economic networks and irreversibility', in Law, J. (ed.), *A Sociology of Monsters*, London: Routledge & Kegan Paul, pp. 132–61.

Callon, M., Larédo, P. and Mustar, P. (1995), 'Introduction générale', in Callon, M. Larédo, P. and Mustar, P. (eds), *La gestion stratégique de la recherche et de la technologie. L'évaluation des programmes*, Paris: Economica, pp. 9–24.

Callon, M., Larédo, P., Rabeharisoa, V., Gonard, T. and Leray, T. (1992), 'The management and evaluation of technological programs and the dynamics of techno-economic networks: The case of the AFME', *Research Policy*, **21**, 215–36.

Callon, M. and Rip, A. (1992), 'Humains, non-humains: morale d'une coexistence', in Theys, J. and Kalaora, B. (eds), *La Terre Outragée. Les experts sont formels!*, Paris: Editions Autrement, 140–56.

CEA (1992), *Energy Data Book. France in the World 1992*, Paris: CEA.

Chartier, P. and Mauguin, P. (1993), *Agence Nationale pour la Valorisation des Cultures Énergetiques: Rapport final du groupe d'études*, Paris: ANVCE/ADEME.

Coates, J.F., Mahaffie, J.B. and Hines, A. (1994), 'Technological Forecasting: 1970–1993', *Technological Forecasting and Social Change*, **47** (1), 23–33.

Collins, H.M. (1985), *Changing order: Replication and induction in scientific practice*, London: Sage.

Coombs, R., Saviotti, P. and Walsh, V. (1987), *Economics and Technological Change*, London/Basingstoke: Macmillan.

Cowan, R. (1990), 'Nuclear Power Reactors: a Study of Technological Lock-In', *Journal of Economic History*, **3**.

David, P.A. (1986), 'Understanding the economics of QWERTY: the Necessity of History', in Parker, W.N. (ed.), *Economic History and the Modern Economist*, Oxford: Basil Blackwell.

Dinkelman, G. (1995), *Verzuring en broeikaseffect. De wisselwerking tussen problemen en oplossingen in het Nederlandse luchtverontreinigingsbeleid (1970–1994)*, Utrecht: Jan van Arkel.

DLO (1995), *DLO onderzoekplan 1995*, Dienst Landbouwkundig Onderzoek, Wageningen, The Netherlands.

Dosi, G. (1982), 'Technological paradigms and technological trajectories', *Research Policy*, **11** (3), 147–62.

Dosi, G., Freeman, C., Nelson, R., Silverberg, G. and Soete, L. (eds) (1988), *Technical Change and Economic Theory*, London: Pinter Publishers.

Dror, Y. (1989), 'Policy Reasoning for Forecasting', *Technological Forecasting and Social Change*, **36** (1–2), 99–104.

Forrest, J.E. (1991), 'Models of the Process of Technological Innovation', *Technology Analysis and Strategic Management*, **45**, 439–53.

Freeman, C. (1982), *The economics of industrial innovation*, London: Francis Pinter.

Freeman, C. and Soete, L. (eds) (1990), *New explorations in the economics of technological change*, London: Pinter Publishers.

Georghiou, L. (1996), 'The UK Technology Foresight Programme', *Futures*, **28** (1).

Geurts, J.L.A. (1993), *Omkijken naar de Toekomst. Lange termijn verkenningen in beleidsexercities*, Alphen aan den Rijn: Samson H.D. Tjeenk Willink.

Godet, M. (1979), *The crisis in forecasting and the emergence of the 'prospective' approach*, New York: Pergamon Press.

Grupp, H. (ed.) (1993), *Technologie am Beginn des 21. Jahrhunderts*, Berlin: Physica-Verlag, Springer Publishers.

Hauptman, O. and Pope, S.L. (1992), 'The Process of Applied Technology Forecasting. A Study of Executive Analysis, Anticipation and Planning', *Technological Forecasting and Social Change*, **42**, 193–210.

Heuvel, C.M. van den (ed.) (1994), *Chemie in Toekomstperspectief. Drie scenario's van Chemie in een veranderende wereld*, Amsterdam: Dutch Foresight Steering Committee OCV.

Hippel, E. von (1988), *The sources of innovation*, Oxford: Oxford University Press.

Hughes, T. (1983), *Networks of Power: Electrification of Western Society*, Baltimore, MD: Johns Hopkins University Press.

Irvin, D.J. (1993), 'Technology Forecasters – Soothsayers or Scientists', *IEEE Technology and Society Magazine* (Spring), 10–17.

Irvine, J. and Martin, B. (1984), *Forecasting in Science. Picking the Winners*, London: Francis Pinter.

Irvine, J. and Martin, B.R. (1989), *Research Foresight: Creating the Future*, The Hague: Netherlands Ministry of Education and Science.

Jantsch, E. (1967), *La Prévision Technologique (Technological Forecasting in Perspective)*, Paris: OECD.

Jasanoff, S., Markle, G.E., Petersen, J.C. and Pinch, T. (eds) (1994), *Handbook of Science and Technology Studies*, London: Sage.

Jørgensen, U. and Karnøe, P. (1995), 'The Danish Wind-Turbine Story: Technical Solutions to Political Visions?', in Rip, A., Misa, T.J. and Schot, J. (eds), *Managing Technology in Society. The Approach of Constructive Technology Assessment*, London: Pinter, pp. 57–82.

Karpik, L. (1996), 'Dispositifs de confiance et engagements crédibles', *Sociologie du Travail*, 4, 527–550.

Kline, S.J. and Rosenberg, N. (1986), 'An overview of innovation', in National Academy of Engineering (eds), *The positive sum strategy: Harnessing technology for economic growth*, Washington, DC: The National Academy Press.

Laat, B. de (1995), 'Strategic analysis for technological research agencies – a tool for making implicit choices explicit', in Bennett, D. and Steward, F. (eds), *Technological Innovation and Global Challenges. European Conference on Management of Technology*, Aston University, Birmingham: Aston Business School/International Association for the Management of Technology, pp. 669–76.

Laat, B. de (1996), *Scripts for the Future. Technology foresight, strategic evaluation and socio-technical networks: the confrontation of script-based scenarios*, PhD, University of Amsterdam.

Larédo, P., Kahane, B., Meyer, J.-B. and Vinck, D. (1992), *The Research Networks built by the MHR4 Programme*, Brussels: Commission of the European Communities.

Larédo, P. and Mustar, P. (1996), 'The techno-economic network: a socioeconomic approach to state intervention in innovation', in Coombs, R., Saviotti, P., Richards, A. and Walsh, V. (eds), *Networks and Technology Collaboration*, Cheltenham, UK: Edward Elgar, pp. 143–64.

Latour, B. (1986), 'The powers of association', in Law, J. (eds), *Power, Action and Belief. A New Sociology of Knowledge?*, London: Routledge & Kegan Paul, pp. 264–80.

Latour, B. (1987), *Science in Action. How to follow scientists and engineers through society*, Milton Keynes: Open University Press.

Latour, B. (1989), 'Joliot: l'Histoire et la Physique Melées', in Serres, M. (ed.), *Éléments d'histoire des sciences*, Paris: Bordas, pp. 493–513.

Latour, B. (1992), 'Where are the Missing Masses? The Sociology of a Few Mundane Artifacts', in Bijker, W.E. and Law, J. (eds), *Shaping Technology/Building Society. Studies in Sociotechnical Change*, Cambridge, MA: MIT Press, pp. 225–58.

Latour, B. (1993a), 'Ethnography of a "High-Tech" Case. About the Aramis case', in

Lemonnier, P. (ed.), *Technological choices – transformations in Material Culture since the Neolithic*, London: Routledge and Kegan Paul, pp. 372–98.

Latour, B. (1993b), *La clef de Berlin et autres leçons d'un amateur de sciences*, Paris: La Découverte.

Latour, B. (1994), 'On Technical Mediation – Philosophy, Sociology, Genealogy', *Common Knowledge*, **3**, 29–65.

Law, J. and Callon, M. (1992), 'The Life and Death of an Aircraft: A Network Analysis of Technical Change', in Bijker, W.E. and Law, J. (eds), *Shaping Technology/Building Society. Studies in Sociotechnical Change*, Cambridge, MA: MIT Press, pp. 21–52.

Leijten, A.J.M. (1989), 'Materialenonderzoek bij Shell', in Ministry of Science and Education (ed.), *Verkennen in Nederland. Deel 2. Vijf case-studies*, Den Haag: SDU, pp. 43–66.

Levy, R. (1993), *Les biocarburants (dit 'rapport Levy')*, Paris: Assemblée Nationale.

Linstone, H.A. (1989), 'Twenty Years of TF&SC' (Foreword to the Twentieth Anniversary Issue, 'Forecasting A New Agenda'), *Technological Forecasting and Social Change*, **3** (1–2), 1–13.

Linstone, H.A. (1994), 'New Era – New Challenge', *Technological Forecasting and Social Change*, **47** (1), 1–20.

Lundvall, B.A. (1988), 'Innovation as an interactive process: from user–producer interaction to the national system of innovation', in Dosi, G., Freeman, C., Nelson, R., Silverberg, G. and Soete, L. (eds), *Technical Change and Economic Theory*, London: Pinter Publishers, pp. 349–69.

Mangematin, V. (1996), 'The Simultaneous Shaping of Organisation and Technology Within Co-operative Agreements', in Coombs, R., Saviotti, P., Richards, A. and Walsh, V. (eds), *Networks and Technology Collaboration*, Cheltenham, UK: Edward Elgar, pp. 119–42.

Mangematin, V. and Callon, M. (1995), 'Technological competition, strategies of the firms and the choice of first users: the case of road guidance technologies', *Research Policy*, **24**, 441–58.

Marchetti, C. (1991a), 'Modeling Innovation Diffusion', in Henry, B. (ed.), *Forecasting Technological Innovation*, Brussels and Luxembourg: ECSC, EEC, EAEC, pp. 55–77.

Marchetti, C. (1991b), 'Technological innovation in transport', in Henry, B. (ed.), *Forecasting Technological Innovation*, Brussels and Luxembourg: ECSC, EEC, EAEC, pp. 201–19.

Marsh, G., Staunton, G.M., Wart, R. van der, Valant, P., Clément, D., Smeers, Y. and Kebler, K. (1996), *Methodologies for advising on the formulation of an EU Energy R&D strategy. PANEL Project*, Brussels: European Commission, Directorate-General XII Science, Research and Development.

MESR (1994), *Consultation Nationale sur les Grands Objectifs de la Recherche Française*, Paris: Ministère de l'Enseignement Supérieur et de la Recherche.

Nelson, R. and Winter, S. (1982), *An evolutionary theory of economic change*, Harvard: Harvard University Press.

Nelson, R.R. and Winter, S.G. (1977), 'In search of useful theory of innovation', *Research Policy*, **1** (6), 36–76.

NOVEM (1992), *De haalbaarheid van de produktie van biomassa voor de Nederlandse energiehuishouding*, Utrecht: NOVEM.

OCV (1994), *Koersen op kennis: voortgangsrapport van de Overlegcommissie Verkenningen*, Amsterdam: OCV.

OCV (1996), *A vital knowledge system. Dutch research with a view to the future*, Amsterdam: Foresight Steering Committee.

Perez, C. (1983), 'Structural change and assimilation of new technologies in the economic and social systems', *Futures* (October), 357–75.

Perry, M.K. (1989), 'Vertical Integration: Determinants and Effects', in Schmalensee, R. and Willig, R.D. (eds), *Handbook of Industrial Organization*, Amsterdam, New York, Oxford, Tokyo: North-Holland, pp. 183–255.

Pickering, A. (ed.) (1992), *Science as Practice and Culture*, Chicago: The University of Chicago Press.

Porter, A.L., Roper, A.T., Mason, T.W., Rossini, F.A. and Banks, J. (1991), *Forecasting and Management of Technology*, New York: Wiley Interscience.

Rémy, E. and Larédo, P. (1995), *Étude de prospective dans le domaine de l'environnement*, Paris: CSI Ecole des Mines/Association Descartes.

Rip, A. (1995), 'Le poids des phases initiales dans le déroulement des programmes', in Callon, M., Larédo, P. and Mustar, P. (eds), *La gestion stratégique de la recherche et de la technologie. L'évaluation des programmes*, Paris: Economica, pp. 111–124.

Rip, A., Misa, T.J. and Schot, J. (1995a), 'Constructive Technology Assessment: A New Paradigm for Managing Technology in Society', in Rip, A., Misa, T.J. and Schot, J. (eds), *Managing Technology in Society. The Approach of Constructive Technology Assessment*, London & New York: Pinter, pp. 1–14.

Rip, A., Misa, T.J. and Schot, J. (eds) (1995b), *Managing Technology in Society. The Approach of Constructive Technology Assessment*, London & New York: Pinter.

Robinson, G. (1994), 'The inhibitors that could stop foresight working', *Research Fortnight*, 2 November, p. 13.

Sahal, D. (1985), 'Technological guideposts and innovation avenues', *Research Policy*, 14, 61–82.

Shapiro, C. (1989), 'Theories of Oligopoly Behavior', in Schmalensee, R. and Willig, R.D. (eds), *Handbook of Industrial Organization*, Amsterdam, New York, Oxford, Tokyo: North-Holland, pp. 329–414.

Tijink, D., Heijden, R.E.C.M. van der and Thissen, W.A.H. (1994), *Scenario's op het OCV-toneel. Reflectie op OCV-toepassingen van scenario-workshops*, Faculteit Technische Bestuurskunde, Technische Universiteit Delft.

Vinck, D. (ed.) (1991), *Gestion de la Recherche*, Bruxelles: De Boeck-Wesmael.

Vissac-Charles, V. (1995), *Dynamique de réseaux et trajectoires de l'innovation*, PhD thesis, École des Mines de Paris.

Whiston, T.G. (1994), Book review of: Brian Twiss, *Forecasting for Technologists and Engineers: a Practical Guide for Better Decisions* (Peter Peregrines, London, 1992), *Research Policy*, 23 (2), 231–2.

Williamson, O.E. (1983), *Markets and Hierarchies: analysis and antitrust implications. A study in the economics of organizations*, New York: Free Press.

Winner, L. (1980), 'Do artifacts have politics?', *Daedalus*, 109, 121–36.

10. Cultural and institutional determinants of national technological advantage

Paolo Guerrieri and Andrew Tylecote[1]

INTRODUCTION

This chapter seeks to help explain the nature and origins of national technological advantage. It has been influenced by the literature on the national
systems of innovation (for example, Nelson, 1993; Lundvall, 1993) but it
differs in its approach. It pays relatively little attention to the systemic nature
of innovation at the national level. Instead it seeks to cut the Gordian knot,
and impose a brutal simplicity on the analysis. We have set out to identify
two patterns of difference: first, how countries differ in the extent to which
they have the characteristics that may be required for success; second, how
industries differ in what they require for success. The working assumptions
were that countries exhibit reasonably stable and substantial differences in
cultural and institutional 'endowments', which are rather uniform across
industries; and that industries exhibit reasonably stable and substantial differences in cultural and institutional requirements, which are rather uniform
across countries. We then discuss how far the match of patterns can account
for, and predict, the technological advantage of nations, and how far such an
approach can be reconciled with a recognition that technological advantage is
path-dependent, and that systems of innovation are increasingly international.

A MICROECONOMIC HYPOTHESIS ON TECHNOLOGICAL ADVANTAGE

Thirty years ago Burns and Stalker (1966) argued persuasively that innovative firms in general needed a different ('organic') style of management from
the received 'mechanistic' wisdom, which would still serve slowly changing
firms very well. What we then had, in effect, was a continuum contingency
theory of innovation: the higher the technology of an industry, the faster its
rate of change, and the more offensive the strategy of a given firm within it,
the more organic that firm needed to be. Apart from that, the main thrust of

the work on the requirements for successful innovation, such as that of Freeman (1974, pp. 171–94) giving the findings of the SAPPHO project at Sussex University, was for long to establish commonalities of best practice. More recently there have been important contributions to the literature which have suggested differences among (and within) industries: examples are Ansoff and Stewart (1976), Teece (1986), Pavitt (1984, 1988), Hobday (1994) and perhaps also Tylecote and Demirag (1992). Without attempting to do justice to this work here, we shall attempt some generalizations of the differences in requirements among industries. First, however, we shall try to generalize about what, in any industry, is likely to be required for successful innovation, and the extent to which different countries meet these requirements. What follows builds on Guerrieri and Tylecote (1994, 1997).

BEHAVIOURAL REQUIREMENTS FOR TECHNOLOGICAL ADVANTAGE

We begin with the behavioural core of our theory. First we shall set out aspects of managerial behaviour which (it is generally agreed) are normally required, in some measure, for successful innovation. We shall then argue that the cultures and traditions of the different countries with which we are dealing predispose managers of those nationalities, and firms based in those countries, to meet those behavioural requirements to varying degrees.

We propose that the fundamental behavioural requirement for successful technological innovation is interaction of various kinds:

1. Functional – among the different functions and departments within the firm, normally focused on the R&D department.
2. Vertical – up and down the line of command within and below management.
3. External – particularly with other firms, for example with customers and suppliers, and other firms (even rivals) in the sector (with whom there may be common interests in training, research, government actions, and so on – see Lundvall, 1988).
4. In large divisionalized firms, where there are technological synergies among divisions, there is also a requirement for divisional interaction.

Each of the first two categories requires subdivision:

1. Within functional interaction the most interesting distinction is between a general inclination to cooperate across functions, and a specific inclination for other functions to cooperate with the production department

(on which see, for example, Bergen, 1983). The first is clearly favoured by 'organic' as opposed to 'mechanistic' styles of management, in Burns and Stalker's terms (1966). So is the second, but it also depends on the degree of respect for production; see below.

2. Within vertical interaction there is again a distinction between a general inclination to communicate among different hierarchical levels, and a specific inclination to form a good relationship between managers and managed, that is, good industrial relations.

NATIONAL PREDISPOSITIONS

Tylecote (1996) has undertaken a historically based cultural typology of the nations of West and Central Europe. He finds one dimension of difference, or dichotomy, similar to that found in a Franco-Dutch comparison by d'Iribarne (1989), which distinguishes aristocratic from bourgeois culture. The 'aristocratic' group is that of the Western kingdoms, of England, France and Castile, which have long been centralized states dominated by aristocrats where the dominant culture had little respect for the arts of manufacturing and where society has tended to become stratified and segmented into 'orders' which aped medieval professions like the lawyers and like them sought ennoblement by cultivating refinement and exclusivity. (English and French aristocrats differed: the former maintained continuity of dominance, and with it the dominance of their anti-industrial culture; French aristocracy was reborn after the Revolution as a meritocracy of engineers – very refined, elitist engineers who had little to do with the humble arts of manufacturing, but still, engineers. Thus for industrial purposes France counts as only semi-aristocratic.) The 'bourgeois' group contains mainly the successor states of the Holy Roman Empire: Germany, Northern Italy and The Netherlands. There the failure (until the nineteenth century) to establish centralized kingdoms allowed a separate development of city (bourgeois) culture in which the arts of manufacture were central. In Scandinavia, the kingdoms, though centralized, were never really dominated by the aristocracy (Sweden) or that dominance was thrown off (Denmark); and all were deeply influenced by German city culture as spread by the Hanse. Southern Italy developed a decidedly anti-industrial variant of aristocratic culture.

For all the aristocratic dominance of the Tokugawa era (till 1868), modern Japanese culture can be squarely placed in a 'super-bourgeois' category: the Meiji restoration involved a total commitment to industrial success which made the arts of manufacture even more important than for the bourgeois Europeans. The United States is harder to categorize: it may have been a chip off the English block, but the dominant culture in the northern states was that of dissidents from the aristocratic society of seventeenth-century England, and their respect for the arts of manufacture would have been supported later by the influence of Scottish and German immigrants – two groups which had a disproportionate impact on industry. Any US disrespect for production would clearly lack the deep cultural roots that such an attitude has in England and France; but there is some evidence for it recently (see Dertouzos et al., 1989). We have to leave the US in an intermediate category.

We borrow from Hofstede (1983, 1984) two other dimensions of difference: power distance ('the degree of tolerance of inequality in wealth and power indicated by the degree to which centralisation and autocratic power are permitted') and individualism ('the extent to which the individual expects personal freedom versus the acceptance of responsibility to family, tribal or national groups (i.e. collectivism)') (both quoted from 1983, p. 49). For our countries' scores, see Table 10.1, which shows that power distance diminishes roughly from south to north in Europe.

Table 10.1   Individualism and power distance in eight countries

	Power distance index	Individualism index
France	68	71
Germany (FR)	35	67
Italy	50	76
Japan	54	46
Sweden	31	71
Switzerland	34	68
UK	35	89
USA	40	91

Source: Hofstede (1983), p. 52.

Individualism could also be described as 'marketization': the belief that individuals are free to operate for their own interests on labour and other markets. Hofstede treats this as a one-dimensional continuum but we believe it is more V-shaped: individualism is at the apex of the inverted V in Figure 10.1, but the 'groupism' or 'collectivism' which is the alternative is divergent: in North/Central Europe, following the Teutonic tribal tradition (d'Iribarne, 1989) there is a weak tendency to the sort of groupism which tends to unite firms as communities (thus Hofstede's moderate scores for Germany, Switzerland and Sweden). On the other hand there is in all European countries (and the USA) a tendency for groupism on the basis of discipline or function

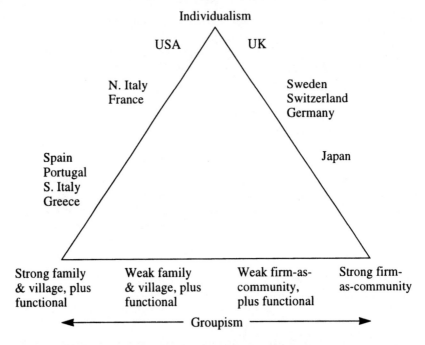

Figure 10.1   Individualism and the four types of groupism

(engineers, accountants, lawyers). This has a tendency to divide firms later-
ally, balancing the Teutonic unifying effect. In Southern Europe this kind of
groupism merely compounds the effect of another sort – loyalty to family and
(small) local community – which is also divisive within any large firm.
Japanese groupism is an extreme form of the unifying 'firm-as-community'
tendency, not offset by any concern with discipline or function; see for
example Clark (1979).

IMPLICATIONS OF NATIONAL PREDISPOSITIONS FOR BEHAVIOURAL REQUIREMENTS

Functional interaction will of course be discouraged by functional groupism
but encouraged by 'firm-as-community' groupism. It will be discouraged by
the 'family and village' variety. It will be mildly encouraged by lower power
distance since that makes it easier for employees at lower levels to form the
lateral relationships required by the 'organic' style of management. Functional
interaction with production will be particularly encouraged by bourgeois and
discouraged by aristocratic culture. This is confirmed by Bergen (1983) and

Lawrence (1980) comparing the UK and Germany. The greater respect for culture in the bourgeois cultures is confirmed by the pay statistics quoted by Guerrieri and Tylecote (1994) for departmental heads: only in Germany, Switzerland, Belgium and The Netherlands is the production director the highest paid; in France and Britain that honour goes to the finance director. (We have no comparable data for the USA; for Japan, such data would be largely meaningless in view of the custom of job rotation among departments.)

We might then calculate quantitative scores for countries as follows:

- Score for 'favourable groupism' by subtracting individualism percentage from 100 and making the score positive for firm-as-community, zero for firm-as-community with functional, and negative for other groupism.
- Score for 'low power distance' by subtracting Hofstede's percentage from 100 and dividing by 2. For functional interaction with production only score 25 for bourgeois (50 for Japan) and −25 for aristocratic, 0 for intermediate.

For the results see Table 10.2. Note that predisposition to vertical interaction can simply be scored as 100 less the power distance score.

Industrial relations can be scored as above for groupism, except that functional groupism does not count one way or the other: so all the Teutonic countries as well as Japan get a positive score. (The distinction between the firm-as-community countries and the rest corresponds exactly to Alan Fox's (1974) distinction between high-trust and low-trust industrial relations, and to strike statistics over the last 30 years or so.)

Table 10.2   Scores for national predispositions to interaction

	USA	UK	FRG	Japan	Sweden	Switzerland	Northern Italy	France
Functional interaction	21	21.5	32.5	77	34.5	33	1	−13
FI with production	21	−3.5	57.5	127	59.5	58	26	−13
Vertical interaction	60	65	65	46	69	66	50	32
Industrial relations	−9	−11	33	54	29	32	−24	−29
External interaction	25	0	50	75	50	50	50	25
Divisional interaction	21	21.5	32.5	77	34.5	33	1	−13

External interaction with other firms will be facilitated by bourgeois culture, particularly at local and regional levels. We rate it simply according to the aristocratic/bourgeois score.

Finally, the predisposition to divisional interaction can be assumed to be similar to functional interaction. This is because much the same determinants are relevant, and because a firm which has little difficulty in achieving good functional interaction can give more attention to encouraging its divisions to interact well.

EXTERNAL REQUIREMENTS

There are also three underlying external requirements for successful innovation, which will also vary among sectors: a science base, technically trained labour and finance.

Industries clearly require a science base in terms of the appropriate expertise in the external research system. Elsewhere (Guerrieri and Tylecote, 1994, 1997) we have considered variations in the inclination and ability of firms to make use of their own and others' science bases, but, for brevity, we do not do so here. On the strength of the science base in the eight countries, we have reasonably trustworthy empirical data, based on output measures (as opposed to input, that is, spending measures).

For the period 1978–80, Arunachalam and Manorama (1989, p. 395) give data for the number of scientific papers published, and observed and relative citation rates. We show these output measures, with the number of papers divided by the population in millions, in Table 10.3.

Germany's publication and citation rate (and perhaps that of others) is depressed *vis-à-vis* the UK's by language difficulties (most of the journals surveyed are in English); it is significant that its relative citation rate – allowing for the relative neglect of non-English-language journals – is higher than the UK's.

Table 10.3   Science base: output measures, 1978–80

	Sweden	Switzerland	UK	FRG	France	Italy	Japan	USA
Papers published per person	2949	2353	1746	1109	1030	394	606	1790
Observed citation rate	3.42	3.77	2.93	2.60	2.32	2.19	2.35	3.82
Relative citation rate	1.23	1.23	1.17	1.03	1.08	0.98	0.93	1.03

We have disaggregated data only for the UK, France, Germany, Japan and the USA. Output data are from Martin et al. (1990, Tables 7 and 9) for 1986, shown divided by population in millions (Table 10.4).

Table 10.4   Percentage share of world citations, divided by population in millions, by discipline, 1986

	UK	FRG	France	Japan	USA
Clinical	0.19	0.06	0.06	0.04	0.23
Biomedicine	0.15	0.08	0.07	0.04	0.24
Biology	0.20	0.08	0.05	0.04	0.19
Chemistry	0.141	0.147	0.103	0.095	0.145
Physics	0.109	0.147	0.121	0.056	0.186
Engineering	0.142	0.113	0.061	0.089	0.196

Note: The quantity of papers published by English-speaking nations is slightly overstated because their journals tend to be more cited.

We conclude from the aggregate data in Table 10.3 that the Swiss and Swedish science bases are generally strong, and the Italian weak. For the other five countries we can tentatively disaggregate the disciplines into biology-based, chemistry-based and physics-based sciences, treating engineering as belonging mostly to the latter, and using the citation measure (Table 10.5). Note that our crude scoring system understates the striking difference between Germany and Britain in the relative positions of biology-based and chemistry-based sciences, to which we return below.

Table 10.5   Strength of science base, mid-1980s, inferred from citation measure

	UK	FRG	France	Japan	USA
Biology-based	High	Moderate	Moderate	Low	High
Chemistry-based	High	High	Moderate	Moderate	High
Physics-based and engineering	Moderate	High	Moderate	Moderate	Moderate

A related but distinct issue is the supply of technically trained labour. This can be roughly divided into graduates and those with intermediate skills. We shall assume that (since graduates and postgraduates are a joint product, with research, of higher education institutions) the pattern of supply of graduate labour mirrors the pattern of the science base as shown in the tables. As to intermediate skills, Soskice (1991) shows how German firms have acted to create an excellent supply of adequately educated and well-trained skilled workers and technicians, and how British firms have abjectly failed in this respect. As we have tended to do under other headings, he is inclined to place other North European countries near to Germany, (Northern) Italy not far below, and France in a separate category in which a reasonable degree of success has been achieved using a different, state-dominated route. Dertouzos et al. (1989) point out the serious deficiencies of the USA with respect to the mathematical and scientific education of the mass of the population – shared with the UK; the contrast is with Continental Europe and Japan (see Table 10.6).

Table 10.6   Availability of non-graduate technically trained personnel, mid- to late 1980s

Japan	USA	FRG	Sweden	France	UK	Italy
High	Low	High	High+	Moderate	Low	Moderate

Every financial system provides, in some measure, a supply of new finance and corporate governance or control (Tylecote, 1994a, 1994b). Innovation obviously requires a sufficient quantity of finance at acceptable terms. It also requires corporate governance, control of the firm and within the firm, which is supportive of innovative effort and expense (rather than disapproving because current profits are reduced). Financiers and 'governors' have to cope with two problems: low visibility and novelty. (For a fuller account of what follows see Tylecote, 1994a, 1994b.)

Technological innovation requires investment of various kinds which can be ranked according to their 'visibility' to external sources of finance, ranging from 'fixed investment' in machinery, buildings and so on (highest visibility); through R&D expenditure; training; in sales/marketing, market research, distribution and servicing, advertising and low initial pricing; in production, on pre-launch cooperation with R&D (or indeed 'hidden' R&D by production personnel) and on post-launch 'teething troubles' (lowest visibility). Another determinant of the visibility of innovative effort is the level at which it is administered: the most visible is that which is administered directly by a main board director in a central staff function (for example, R&D labs); the least visible is that which is devolved to the middle manager in charge of an obscure profit centre in a large diversified firm. Industries in which innovation requires heavy investment in low-visibility categories or at low-visibility levels will require finance and governance which display firm-specific perceptiveness. This is traditionally evident in 'insider-dominated' systems in which there are stable relationships between managers and large shareholders (often founding families), and between managers and banks; they can also be called bank-based systems. Continental Europe and Japan come into the insider/bank-based category, which can be subdivided into private bank-based, where the state is broadly speaking in the background (Germany, Sweden and Japan, in our sample) and state bank-based, where, because of the weakness of private capital, the state has come into the foreground both as owner of financial institutions, and as owner of major manufacturing enterprises (France and Italy). Only the private bank-based system is capable of firm-specific perceptiveness in industry in general; the state bank-based system is too centralized to provide it in more than a limited number of high-profile enterprises. (We look in more depth at France and Italy in the section below on the role of the state.)

The private bank-based system has, however, two important weaknesses:

1. The first is almost inherent: dealing with novelty. Insiders are perceptive precisely because the firm they are dealing with is not new and is thus a known quantity. A new firm, particularly in a new industry, can have no insiders: it will be unfamiliar and disturbing to financiers who are used to stable relationships. Neither adequate finance nor adequate governance will be provided.
2. The second weakness is contingent: it develops for large firms as a bank-based system matures. Founding family shareholders lose touch, grip and interest, and can no longer provide good managers or intelligent control. The banks which have provided finance and in one way or another have helped to monitor and control the firm also lose interest because with maturity large firms in general cease to need their loans. Here it is adequate governance, not finance, which is the problem.

Let us now consider the alternative: the stock-exchange-based, outsider-dominated system. Banks conduct their business and make loans on a transactional rather than relational basis, and their role is limited both in terms of finance and (even more) of governance. Shareholders (now increasingly financial institutions or pension funds) avoid large shareholdings in any individual firm, thus limiting the information and power which can develop. What this system can *not* provide is firm-specific perceptiveness, except in a limited number of cases. It may, however, cope with the two weaknesses of the bank-based system:

1. Novelty. The stock exchange as an institution is no better able to cope
    with novelty than a bank, but within the looser structures of an outsider-
    dominated system venture capital may develop, as it has in certain geo-
    graphical areas and new industries in the USA. Venture capital provides
    or should provide both finance (directly, and through the reassurance it
    gives to other financiers) and a measure of governance to new firms in
    areas in which it has expertise. It has, in fact, what novelty needs: (new)
    industry-specific expertise.
2. Governance of mature large firms. Outsiders can exercise indirect gov-
    ernance of large firms through (a) the threat of hostile takeover if they
    become dissatisfied and the share price falls, and (b) the inconvenience
    of a low share price even without takeover threat. They may alternatively
    form coalitions in order, briefly and by exception, to intervene directly to
    oust the board.

The weakness of the stock-exchange-based system is inherent – its lack of
firm-specific perceptiveness. This tends to lead to shortage of finance for
small firms, and short-term pressures on large firms, in low-visibility industries – but it can be kept in check for large firms through deliberate management policy, aimed at

- maintaining a clear focus on a limited number of closely related sectors so that they are well matched to the expertise of specialist investment analysts in the stock exchange or financial institutions,
- cultivating their relationships with 'the markets' so that their innovation strategies are as well understood as possible.

Under these circumstances even 'outsiders' who hold only a small proportion
of a large firm's shares may well find it worth their while to invest the time
and money necessary to understand it. As with venture capital, however, it is
mainly in the highest-technology sectors that the returns on such a policy will
seem adequate both to the managers and to the 'outsiders' concerned.

Two 'deviant' countries are of interest:

1. The UK: This is a stock-exchange-based country which has not devel-
    oped an adequate venture capital industry (the large flows of 'venture
    capital' which flowed into UK industry during the 1980s mostly went to
    fund management buy-outs in established firms). Its record of indirect
    governance of mature large firms is also rather poor, with the possible
    exception of pharmaceuticals.
2. Japan: The governance of mature large firms is less problematic in Japan
    because of the implicit (and not absolute) 'lifetime employment' com-

mitment to the core labour force. As the firm matures, this provides a continuing, indeed increasing, pressure for organic growth and thus for product innovation. At the same time the willingness of young core workers to accept low wages in the early part of their careers, and the large element in workers' earnings tied to profits, provide in effect a large fraction of the finance needed for innovation.

THE ROLE OF THE STATE

The state always has the role of providing most of the hard and soft infrastructure (the latter discussed above). It also provides a legal and regulatory framework; and to varying degrees it acts as buyer, financier and owner. For reasons of space we have to be highly selective here, and discuss three roles: shaping the market, as regulator and buyer; financing innovation; and as owner.

Shaping the Market

Regulation of pricing
This role is most important in pharmaceuticals. In most countries, with the exception of the USA, pharmaceuticals prices are to some extent regulated. Notably beneficial is the UK regime, under which price control is designed to give a certain rate of profit (from which R&D can as usual be deducted – providing an incentive for R&D); notably unfavourable is the Japanese, under which price ceilings for existing drugs are progressively lowered, providing an incentive for a stream of pointless 'me-too' variants from the producer.

The state's role as defence buyer
Governments, mainly the home government, are the main buyers in defence industries. The role of defence spending has been discussed elsewhere (Guerrieri and Tylecote, 1994, 1997) in terms of the diversion of skilled labour, which tends to have a highly adverse effect on the culture and structure of firms. As Burns and Stalker (1966) showed for UK electronics in the 1940s, the practices suitable for supplying the military are quite different from those appropriate to civilian markets. In our terms, functional interaction with marketing and production can be almost irrelevant when the government is the customer. The provision of finance for innovation by government makes it unnecessary to cultivate a relationship with the stock markets in which the latter understand the process of innovation – which appears largely to account for the failure of UK electronics to do so (Demirag, Tylecote and Morris, 1994). The rate of spending on defence-related R&D as a percentage

Table 10.7   Defence-related R&D as a percentage of GDP, 1985

USA	UK	France	Sweden	FRG	Italy	Japan
0.85	0.67	0.46	0.30	0.14	0.08	0.02

Source: Patel and Pavitt (1991), Table 3.3.

of GDP gives a good indication of the role of defence procurement in high-technology industries, and is shown in Table 10.7.

The principal industries affected by defence procurement are electronics and aerospace. There seems at least some degree of civil–military symbiosis in the latter – much less in the former. During the 1980s the level of military spending, generally and on R&D, began to fall, particularly in the USA and the UK, and as it did so the manner of spending also changed – towards competitive tendering and fixed price contracts. Thus both diversion of resources and distortion of behaviour are diminishing rapidly, in the high-spending countries; but the effect on performance will not yet have become apparent in our data.

The state's role as buyer in civilian industries
As we saw above, the state has an extensive role in industry in France and Italy. Elsewhere in Europe – in Sweden, Germany and the UK – utilities (telecoms, electricity supply, and so on) are or were until recently state-owned. There is an important role in such cases for the state as buyer, which it may play well or badly, to the benefit of (mostly large) firms in the upstream industries affected. The strong, highly centralized French state apparatus, dominated by the elite engineers referred to earlier, has since the 1940s consciously sought to use its position as buyer to move French industry up-market; and might, given its qualities, have been expected to be largely successful, where the firms concerned were large and with high-visibility innovation. (For the outcome see below.) The Swedish and German states, less committed to industrial strategies but responding to well-organized 'bourgeois' business cultures, provide modest assistance in this role. The German government is generous to a few selected areas, mainly through nationalized industries, notably telecommunications and the railways.

The UK and Italian governments could not have been expected to perform this role successfully. The UK state apparatus (and politicians) belong to a technologically ignorant aristocratic culture (the sole exception is the Department of Health, which deals with the pharmaceutical industry). In the UK government support of all kinds has long been very low except for defence activities. The central Italian state apparatus has very serious and well-known deficiencies.

The State as Financier of Innovation

The state plays a role as financier of innovation almost invisibly, through the taxation of profits. Innovation is largely financed through the retention of profits, and even more through the reduction of profits (since most innovative expenses cannot be capitalized, or begin depreciation well before a return begins to appear). Thus for an established, profitable firm, the higher the marginal rate of taxation of profits, particularly distributed profits, the more its innovative expenses benefit from an implicit loan from the tax system. The main country in which high marginal taxation of profits, and higher taxation of dividends, persists is Japan, although Sweden had such a system until recently. There is a range of tax treatments of R&D expenditure: that in Germany is very generous, that in the USA is not. Since 1975 Italy has provided substantial subsidy for the purchase of machine tools and other equipment. The Swedish government has been generous in providing subsidy for R&D for process but not for product innovation.

The state's role as visible financier depends largely on its role in the banking system. The French government has mainly supported private firms' innovation through selective cheap long term loans for 'modernization' of all kinds, taking advantage of its control of the banking system. A large proportion of state-owned financial institutions in Italy are regional and local, and their loans play an important role in financing small and medium-sized businesses; in Germany too state-owned regional and local banks play an important role. (In spite of state ownership these regional and local banks may show 'firm-specific perceptiveness'.)

The State as Owner

As indicated above, the extent of state ownership ranges from high (for the moment) in France and Italy to newly low in the UK to virtually non-existent in the USA. The criticisms of the Italian and UK governments as buyers can be repeated as regards their role as owners, although at all events they provide (or, rather, used to provide) adequate finance: it is (or was) the governance which is defective. Again, the effectiveness of the French state has depended on visibility.

The importance of the French state (at national level) is well known: certain areas regarded as of strategic importance (for example, electronics/ informatics, nuclear energy, civil aerospace and, of course, defence) are targeted for massive support mainly through subsidy to state-owned 'national champions' in each area. The Italian central state is as important as the French, though less coherent, as a provider of funds. For a long period, the Italian approach to industry has been dominated by public intervention, and extensive protection of public sector companies, as in the case of chemicals.

SECTORAL CHARACTERISTICS

We now examine the different sectors in order to distinguish them by their different emphases on the behavioural and external requirements discussed above. There are a number of 'surface' characteristics by which one can categorize industrial sectors, for our purposes. We shall depend mainly on four:

1. Membership of 'technological families', electricals/electronics, chemicals and mechanicals being the chief ones, as proposed by Patel and Pavitt (in Freeman et al., 1991, p. 45).
2. Technological level, as defined by R&D intensity. (However, the use of this measure to indicate technological level can be misleading, particularly in small firms and the mechanicals 'family'.)
3. Position in Pavitt's taxonomy (Pavitt, 1984) of firms: as scale-intensive, science-based, specialized supplier or traditional.
4. Character of output and market: capital, intermediate or consumer (final) good; private or state purchasers.

These taxonomies are interrelated. Thus 'science-based' is almost inevitably highest R&D-intensive and 'traditional' is lowest, though the other two categories are not so easily placed. Less obviously, the technological families can themselves be given an average position in terms of other characteristics: the electricals/electronics is somewhat higher in R&D than the chemicals and decidedly higher than the mechanicals. Again, the electricals/electronics is (relatively) dominated by consumer/final output, the chemicals family is (overwhelmingly) by intermediate output, and the mechanicals family has an exceptionally high commitment to capital goods.

We now consider the behavioural and other requirements of the 'technological families' in general.

Mechanicals

This is the oldest and slowest-growing family, and the least science-intensive, with the lowest R&D. As we said above, it lays particular emphasis on capital goods, and capital goods industries tend to be relatively high-technology, in terms of the skill requirements for manufacture and for new product development. The requirement in these areas for current expense for future improve-

Table 10.8 Percentage distribution of innovation costs, USA, 1985

Industry	Applied research	Preparation of product specifications	Prototype or pilot plant	Tooling and manufacturing equipment and facilities	Manufacturing start-up	Marketing start-up	Total
All	18	8	17	23	17	17	100
Chemicals	29	7	13	22	13	17	100
Electrical and instruments	16	8	11	26	18	21	100
Machinery	6	11	23	20	21	18	100
Rubber and metals	15	4	15	45	15	6	100

Source: Mansfield (1988b), Table 6.

ment of products and processes is much greater than the R&D would imply, and is concentrated in and around the production function (see Machinery in Table 10.8).

Mechanical capital goods has a high requirement for functional interaction with production, low for other functional interaction (with marketing); and high for industrial relations and vertical interaction. Moreover, although its measured R&D intensity is not high, there is a requirement for finance such as one would normally associate with high R&D intensity: finance with the firm-specific perceptiveness to recognize largely invisible piecemeal innovative effort, mainly in columns 2, 5 and 6 in Table 10.8.

To the extent that mechanical intermediate goods has a lower technological level, it will have a lower need for vertical interaction and firm-specific perceptiveness in finance; since a large proportion is scale-intensive and therefore the manual workers – numerous throughout the mechanicals family – are in larger groups, the requirement for good industrial relations is particularly strong. It otherwise resembles mechanical capital goods. Mechanical consumer goods, for example, cars and washing machines, are similar: although they need a quantitatively large marketing function, given the relatively slow rate of change of the industry, in practice functional interaction in general need not be better than fair. On the other hand, given the complexities of assembly and sub-assembly, external interaction must be excellent: the only difference here from intermediate and capital goods is that external interaction here is with suppliers (through purchasing) rather than customers.

Electricals/electronics

This family, as the name implies, is readily divisible into two sub-families, electricals and electronics; and indeed the latter can be further subdivided into 'hardware' and 'software'. It is hard to see much in common technologically or in any other way between (say) equipment for the generation, transmission and distribution of (bulk) electricity, and the microelectronic equipment used in computing; however, there are some 'grey areas' we can identify halfway between them. Another obvious connection is that a large number of major companies are involved in both sub-families. The electricals sub-family is very similar to the mechanicals family in the 3–D character of the product, the pace of technological change and in its distribution along the 'stream' of production – with a high concentration in capital goods. In consumer goods, electricals and mechanicals seem to merge – in washing machines, for example. The behavioural and other requirements are accordingly very similar.

The electronics sub-family is clearly the youngest, fastest-growing and fastest-changing of the (sub-)families; it is also more dominated by consumer markets than chemicals, mechanicals or electricals. There used to be a rather clear distinction between consumer electronics, which was scale-intensive, and electronic capital goods (like computers), which were science-intensive. Although consumer electronics needed to be responsive to scientific and technological advance, it was not in itself science-intensive. Its speed of change and mass-production character meant that it needed good functional interaction of all kinds, including production, and industrial relations. These same characteristics meant a need for good divisional interaction, since although it was best to set up new divisions to develop new families of product, they needed access to competences and resources held by older divisions – electrical as well as electronic. As an assembly-based industry with a network of component suppliers, it needed excellent external interaction. It also needed finance which was perceptive, because of its innovations' low visibility. Meanwhile, electronic capital goods could be roughly divided into (at least) two categories: (1) those such as controls for machinery in which perhaps the key requirement was good interaction with the users of the controls – divisional or external, depending on whether they were within the same firm; (2) those at the cutting edge of new technology, such as computers and scientific instruments, whose science intensity meant that the key requirements were for science-based, industry-specific expertise in finance (including venture capital), and vertical interaction.

Over the last twenty years two important changes have taken place in this pattern. First, the relative importance of software in the industry as a whole and in most products has been increasing rapidly. Software has no production function as normally understood: design is, in effect, production. It has thus no requirement for functional interaction with production and industrial relations (at least with manual workers) is unimportant. Second, over the last decade the computer and associated industries have become scale-intensive and sold increasingly to consumer markets – without losing much of their science intensity.

Chemicals

The chemicals industries have changed profoundly since the 1950s. They were originally a reasonably coherent family of industries, dominated by the paradigm of continuous flow process (achieved wherever scale was large enough) and quite science-, that is to say chemistry-, intensive. They accordingly required a strong science (chemistry) base and quite high scores on functional interaction with production and vertical interaction. Their central emphasis on intermediate goods meant that little functional interaction with marketing was needed, and as commodity producers, they needed little external interaction either. Although generally scale-intensive, the relatively small proportion of manual workers meant they had only a modest requirement for industrial relations.

This technological family is in the process of dividing into two largely distinct sub-families: 'chemicals' and 'bio-chemicals'. The chemicals sub-family has a new emphasis on 'effect chemicals', which require a strong concern with the use to which they are put and thus a high external interaction (with a limited number of industrial customers), in addition to the other requirements mentioned. The 'biochemicals' sub-family comprises the pharmaceuticals and agrochemicals industries; it has, as the name implies, a different (but even more demanding) requirement in terms of science base, including, besides chemistry, biology, molecular biology and the medical sciences. It has had little need for functional interaction with production since production costs are (particularly in 'ethical' pharmaceuticals) a minor fraction of value-added and production decisions can be taken separately from the others. (This is now changing, as our case studies indicate.) The unimportance of production implies a negligible requirement for industrial relations. Its customers are not few and industrial, but hundreds of thousands of doctors and farmers – industrial customers, but too numerous to deal with through external interaction – and the marketing function is accordingly much more important; over the last two decades good functional interaction with marketing has become of decisive importance. A great deal of finance is required, concentrated in the rather visible area of R&D. (See Table 10.8 for the relatively high fraction of applied research in innovation costs in the chemicals sectors generally. Pharmaceuticals has a decidedly higher fraction since the manufacturing costs are much less than in the rest of chemicals.) Established companies can generally provide the finance required out of cash flow, and their main need from the financial system is a modest measure of industry-specific expertise such as a stock-exchange-based system can easily provide. Over the last decade, however, new start-up companies in biotechnology have made an important contribution to pharmaceuticals. They need venture capital, only available in the appropriate quantity and quality in the USA. They also need entrepreneurs, who are often academics.

THE IMPORTANCE OF SIZE

We have already pointed out that the need for divisional interaction depended on the size (and diversity) of the firm: if you have no divisions you do not need divisional interaction. Some other requirements become at least less pressing, or easier to satisfy, in a small firm. This is the case for vertical and functional interaction. However deep class differences are, however great the deference owed to the boss, interaction among different levels in the hierarchy will probably be quite good in any firm with less than (say) 50 employees. Likewise, small firms may not even have separate functions, and if they have they will be too small and close to each other to form separate cultures: so functional interaction will be good whatever the predispositions of individuals, or their national cultures. (As we suggested above, this may have been one of the reasons for the decentralization of UK engineering firms.) Other requirements, on the other hand, become more pressing. The smaller the firm, the more it depends on outside finance and outside sources of technology, services and components, and skilled personnel; and the less able it will be to draw any of these from outside its own national frontiers. So external interaction of all kinds, the science base, the supply of trained personnel, and the various roles of government become more important.

However, we should not go too far and argue, conversely, that multinational firms are not affected at all by the factors which have just been mentioned as more important for the small firm. Patel and Pavitt (1991) have shown how very limited is the internationalization of most multinationals' R&D activities; and the key activities of innovation may be still more concentrated at home than R&D employment. (It can, for example, be argued that the foreign R&D labs of Japanese firms are largely a development of their long-established policy of scanning foreign science and technology.) Relatively low concentration at home is shown by the multinationals of small countries, predictably, and UK multinationals, less predictably. Likewise, a large multinational may be able to raise all the *finance* it needs wherever it is convenient; but its *governance* will almost always remain rooted in its domestic financial system – however small the country.

Nor dare we suppose that multinationals which employ many different nationalities can thereby easily escape from the cultural traditions of their home base. How multinational will any such company be at the top? Lorenz (1989) shows that Electrolux, for all its official policy of communicating in English, remained dominated by Swedes. How much less 'multinational' must Japanese firms be! None the less, long-established multinationals may well learn to accommodate themselves to, and even take advantage of, national differences of all kinds, behavioural and other. The history of Unilever (Wilson, 1968) provides examples of this; though one might expect particular enlightenment from Unilever as one of the few firms which is genuinely multi- (at least bi-)national in its origins – British and Dutch.

At any rate the difference in requirements between large and small firms has an important implication – that apart from really scale-intensive industries where only big firms may play, countries may succeed in the same industry with different industrial structures. If a country's predisposition for vertical, functional and divisional interaction is high, its structure may be weighted towards big multiproduct firms. If, on the other hand, it is weak in these respects, but it has the characteristics required by a small firm in that industry, it may develop large clusters of small firms in the sector.

THE HYPOTHESIS AND THE EVIDENCE: EUROPE, THE USA AND JAPAN

In Guerrieri and Tylecote (1994), the objective was to draw a 'European map' of competitiveness for the entire range of manufacturing industries. We chose as the best measures of countries' competitive advantages indicators for both trade and technological performances. To compute them we used an original database (SIE-Technology-Trade Database), that includes data for trade flows and patents granted in the USA (technology output), in 38 sectors from 1970 to 1990. The countries considered were: France, Germany, Italy, Switzerland, Sweden and the UK. For each country, four performance indicators were derived: (i) the share of world exports as indicator of absolute trade advantage; (ii) Balassa index for trade specialization as revealed comparative trade advantage indicator; (iii) a second trade specialization indicator, the contribution to trade balance, which takes both imports and exports into consideration; (iv) a revealed technological comparative advantages indicator, that is the Balassa index for technological specialization. More recently we extended this procedure to Japan and the USA and presented comparisons on the basis of a compressed list of 13 sectors (Guerrieri and Tylecote, 1997). While no single indicator can provide an adequate view of a country's competitive advantage, it is possible to draw fairly reliable results if various indicators are considered together and over a long period, as in the present chapter.

We found, first, that sharp differences exist among the eight countries. Each major country has a very different sectoral pattern of technological and trade advantage, and the national patterns show considerable stability over time. Second, most differences date back to the early 1970s, and over the past two decades, if anything, they have become sharper. The growing internationalization of industries and competition seems to have increased – up to now at least – the national specificities in terms of national competitive advantage. Third, each country succeeds not in isolated sectors, but in clusters of sectors connected through vertical and horizontal relationships at technological and production levels. So, a nation's competitive advantage includes a set of related groups of industrial sectors, which seems to play a key role in affecting the overall dynamics of technological accumulation and trade performance in each country. This enables us to summarize the pattern of technological advantage in ways which can be easily related to our explanatory framework. It should be borne in mind that the patterns of advantage which we describe are essentially relative to the country's average: they take no account of the fact that, for example, Italy has a very poor record on patenting in general, relative to its population or output, while the UK has experienced falls in market share in the large majority of the 38 sectors. We compare countries by technological family and sub-family.

Mechanicals and Electricals

In the mechanicals family and electricals sub-family, Japan and Germany are pre-eminent, with strength also in Switzerland and Sweden, and in certain areas also (Northern) Italy. The first four countries have all the key requirements emphasized for these sectors: functional interaction with production, industrial relations, external interaction, good supply of engineers and intermediate skills, and firm-specific perceptiveness in the financial system. Note, however, that the requirement for external interaction can no longer be well satisfied within one small country, and thus Sweden's relative remoteness has become something of a disadvantage, as has the diversion of engineers to defence. Northern Italy is a marginal case here: it lacks good functional interaction with production and industrial relations, and this accounts for its weakness in the scale-intensive parts of this group. It is, however, strong in capital goods, where specialized supplier firms need not be large enough for functional interaction with production or industrial relations to pose a problem; they depend absolutely, on the other hand, on good external interaction with customers, which within Italian industrial districts does exist. France is deficient in all the characteristics mentioned, except where external interaction with government purchasers is concerned, and it is therefore unsurprising that the main exceptions to its weakness in these areas are aircraft and railroad equipment. The 'Anglo-Saxons', the UK and the USA, bring up the rear. Their low scores on functional interaction with production, industrial relations and external interaction are a serious handicap here.[2] Diversion of the science base to defence compounds the problem, except in aircraft – and aircraft is the main exception to the weakness of both.

The electronics sub-family shows a quite different pattern. No European country shows real strength: the field is dominated by the USA and Japan (and of course increasingly other East Asian countries not considered here). Within that duopoly, the consumer electronics areas are dominated by Japan, with the exception of products such as personal computers and printers which have only recently become consumer goods. We have noted that these products are particularly demanding in just those areas – functional, external and divisional interaction – in which Japan is supreme. Japan has also great strength in 'commodity chips' where the engineering skills of volume production, emphasizing functional interaction with production and industrial relations, are vital. The USA holds the field in most of the highest-technology areas in electronics, where the science base requirement – its forte – is highest; also in software, where the industrial relations and functional interaction with production requirements are virtually nil, and which feeds off links with advanced hardware. Both these high-tech areas benefit from the industry-specific expertise of venture capital. All the European countries have some vital deficiency – not always the same – in all these areas; and because of the external interactions among sectors within this sub-family, weaknesses in one contribute to weakness in another.

The area of greatest European strength is the chemicals family. Germany, France, Switzerland and the UK all have three or four chemicals sectors in their best eight. The USA is also strong; Japan woefully weak. As argued above, however, it is important to split the family into the two sub-families of chemicals proper and biochemicals. Chemicals proper are moving from 'volume' products to 'effects', and with that from an emphasis on functional interaction with production to external interaction; the science base remains important. Since all those factors are strong in Germany and Switzerland, it is easy to understand that these countries remain strong there. French and UK strength in chemicals proper is the more difficult to understand, given their weakness in functional interaction with production and external interaction. Their strong science bases at least help, however, and since chemicals, lacking assembly lines and so on, does not require good industrial relations, one weak point is spared. In biochemicals, on the other hand, the UK excels, with both drugs and agrochemicals in their best eight; drugs is in the French best eight. In this area functional interaction with production and external interaction were never important, while the science base in the biosciences – the UK's strongest scientific area – is of great importance. In both sub-families, particularly biochemicals, graduate skills are more important than intermediate – favouring the UK (particularly) and France against Germany. (Remember that the military distraction which blights UK and French physics-based industries has little impact on the chemistry- and biology-based ones.) The absence of biochemicals from Germany's best eight is easily linked to its relative weakness in biosciences. (Lacking figures, we believe Swiss bioscience to be strong.) The explanation for the US strength in both sub-families is similar to that for the UK, with venture capital helping to explain its strength in biotechnology. Japan is relatively weak in science base and graduate skills in both chemistry and biosciences, and gains nothing from its good industrial relations and little from its functional interaction with production and external interaction.

THE ROLE OF HISTORY AND CUMULATIVE CAUSATION

The general emphasis of the explanation has been on requirements common to a given sector now, or recently, in all countries, and cultural and institutional features now, or recently, prevailing throughout a given country. Although history has been used or implied to explain variations among countries in culture and institutions, it has not been used to explain the development of specific industries in a particular country. Yet clearly industry A will not be strong now in country X, just because cultural and institutional conditions which now happen to favour such an industry happen to prevail there. Causation is cumulative: the most important precondition for strength tomorrow is strength today. In technology, specifically, the more you know about today's state of the art, the easier you will find it to master – or create – tomorrow's, although where technological discontinuities occur it is important to be ready to dump old expertise. (In one respect our explanation can easily be adapted to recognize this: we have identified industry-specific variations in the science base among six of our eight nations. One major factor in this is of course the past pattern of industrial strength and weakness, which both feeds into and feeds off the science base.) There are undoubtedly (hi)stories to be told which will contribute to our understanding of the present technological advantage of nations. A very simple and well-known story relates to aircraft: defeat in war led to the destruction of the German and Japanese aircraft industries, and that and their low military spending afterwards explain their weakness in that sector now – cultural and all other institutional factors have nothing to do with it. More complex and longer (hi)stories are needed to explain how favourable or unfavourable cultural and institutional specificities have developed in a particular industry of a particular country. If we were to offer many such, we would be in effect abandoning our project; but used sparingly we may be able to account for a good proportion of the relatively few mismatches between our theory and the facts.

The UK Chemicals and Pharmaceuticals Industries

The strength of the UK chemicals and biochemicals industries remains somewhat under-explained. At the beginning of the century it was rather the other way about (which begs a question we have no space to answer). The collapse of the native UK chemicals industry at the end of the nineteenth century merely led to its replacement by Continental immigrant entrepreneurs and Continental multinationals: the UK market and supply of inputs were too attractive to ignore. The First World War led to the confiscation of the German-owned firms, which formed the core of the misnamed Imperial Chemical Industries, under the renamed Lord Melchett (alias Alfred Mond, a German

Swiss). This new 'UK' firm, which dominated the UK chemicals industry (as it still does, in chemicals proper), was run, of course, on sound German principles, which naturally included the encouragement of the local science base and skills at all levels, and a respect for the position of engineers. The science base was further improved, both absolutely and relatively, by events on the Continent during the 1930s and 1940s. Thus in the postwar period the UK chemicals industry became and remained much stronger than one might have expected, particularly given its requirement for functional interaction with production. However, this account relates mainly to chemicals proper, since ICI has never been dominant or even particularly important in pharmaceuticals. (It – now its offspring Zeneca – *is* strong in agrochemicals.)

The rise of UK pharmaceuticals, from a very low base in 1940, is still more remarkable. The industry benefited somewhat from the improvement of the British science base in chemistry during the 1930s, and much from the rather later rise of UK biology (*vide* penicillin). After that, according to George Teeling-Smith of the UK Office of Health Economics (personal communication), two factors were crucial: the incursion of US companies, and the National Health Service. It was the US firms which, around 1950, introduced the industry to properly organized sales campaigns, and forced the UK firms in self-defence to copy them. (There were no such pressures on the German and French firms until much later.) By the 1970s, the UK firms had marketing departments of much higher status than their French and German rivals, and it was this learned difference in corporate culture, rather than any innate difference in national culture, which made the difference in functional interaction with marketing, when (as we believe) this became important for innovation in the 1970s and 1980s. Another parallel learning process began in the 1940s in the UK government. With the formation of the National Health Service a government department – the Department of Health – found itself taking detailed responsibility for a whole industry. It was obliged to develop a level of scientific and technological expertise quite foreign to the UK civil service (in peacetime). As in effect the only buyer from the young UK pharmaceuticals industry, it was at the same time obliged to develop a price regime for it; and it chose an extremely sensible, innovation-supporting one. A third learning process affected the chemicals and biochemicals industries together, and was perhaps the most remarkable: the UK industry, committed to technological innovation as it was, had managed by the 1980s to educate the City of London stock markets in the conditions for its success, and to persuade them – against their practice in other industries like electronics – to use technically qualified investment analysts to advise City fund managers.

US and UK Electronics

It is thus possible to stretch corporate culture and the behaviour of the relevant external institutions some way beyond what might be expected from the prevailing national characteristics. US electronics is another case in point. Given the huge advantage in its science base during the 1950s, 1960s and 1970s, and the great size of the potential market in the USA, US firms were bound to dominate the industry initially, but they were driven out of the mass market for consumer electronics by the Japanese; this was largely due – we would argue – to the latter's superiority in functional interaction with production, industrial relations, divisional and external interaction, and firm-specific perceptiveness. So far, so 'national'. Meanwhile the large size of the US industry, and its rapid technological advance, led to the development of a geographically concentrated and industry-specific venture capital industry, with industry-specific expertise, ideally suited to the requirements of small firms in emerging sectors of a high-tech industry. Now we come to the 'stretch': sector after sector matured and as it did so demanded more and more of the 'Japanese' characteristics listed above. Those firms which did not show a modicum of such characteristics went under; those which showed more than a modicum – for example, Hewlett-Packard – prospered. The process can be likened to the development of resistance to antibiotics among bacteria: if the initial dose is high or the population of bacteria small, none will survive, but if neither of these conditions holds, a degree of drug resistance will appear and progressively increase, meanwhile spreading through multiplication (in firms, growth) and gene transference (imitation, particularly through movement of personnel). The US firms which emerged successful from this process of accelerated evolution had corporate cultures plus external relationships (for example, with the science base) ideally suited to the combination of mass production with high technology which now obtains in much of information and communications technology (for instance, personal computers).

UK electronics provides a much less uplifting story, but one which puts less strain on our conceptual framework. In the 1960s, the UK electronics industries were second only to the US, having had a good start in the Second World War and having the second-best science base thereafter. They then withered. Part of the story was clearly the lack of functional interaction, particularly with production, but to some extent also with marketing, as exemplified in the failure of EMI in the scanner market which it had pioneered; and we are entitled to blame this at least partly on national culture. Part of it was failure in corporate governance, going from King Log – the inertia which allowed the great electrical firms, GEC, AEI and EE, to pursue technology without troubling much about profit – to King Stork: when governance was tightened under Arnold Weinstock during the 1960s it emphasized short-term profit with little attention to the long-term earnings potential of innovation. R&D and other innovative expenses shrank relative to the international competition. Again, we are entitled to blame this at least partly on the absence (inherent in the UK financial system) of firm-specific perceptiveness. A third factor, again easily linked with our framework, is the role of government. Military contracts not only diverted much of the electronics science base and skills away from civil innovation, but distorted the structure and culture of the businesses concerned away from that required to succeed there. This meshed with the trends in corporate governance: short-termist controls need not be challenged where innovation is paid for by government. Military funding is now much less abundant and less feather-bedding, but the damage has been done. The UK firms over the last 10–15 years have been like a small number of bacteria faced by a large dose of a new antibiotic: they have been unable to find answers in the time available.

CONCLUSIONS

In this chapter we have put forward a theory of national technological advantage which emphasizes cultural and institutional specificities of national economies and their fit to the requirements of technological innovation varying by technological (sub-)family. We have argued that successful innovation requires four broad behavioural characteristics (with subdivisions) – functional, vertical, divisional and external interaction – and appropriate support from four external groups of actors: government, financial system, education system, and science base. How high a score is required on each item varies among technological (sub-)families. Scores attained vary markedly among national economies. Assuming competitive success in medium- or high-technology industries depends mainly on process and product innovation, it is then possible to predict, by comparing sector requirements with country 'scores', a country's overall performance and its pattern of comparative advantage. We have shown that such an approach explains the pattern and direction of change of comparative advantage – in patenting and trade – among the USA, Japan and six European economies, rather well.

However, the approach is still open to question. Implicit in it is the assumption that countries exhibit reasonably stable and substantial differences in cultural and institutional (C&I) variables, which are rather uniform across industries. If country A has a pattern of C&I scores well matched to the requirements of industry 1 at a given period, it will tend to do well over that period. We say 'tend to' because there is clearly a degree of inertia in comparative advantage: if A is extremely weak in industry 1 at the beginning of the period it cannot become a front-runner within a decade. It is more plausible to argue that it will move up towards a (high) equilibrium position during that period. Of course, if the requirements change and its scores change little (or vice versa), its direction or speed of movement will change. This 'equilibrium' tendency is redolent of neoclassical economics, even though the forces posited are not. It neglects, as neoclassical economics tends to, the fact that industry often exhibits increasing returns, and that therefore success breeds success. Causation is cumulative and progress is path-dependent. Therefore, though cultural and institutional factors are important, they may not be enough to produce, by themselves, major shifts in international rankings in an industry. Indeed, in determining initial position, other factors – for example, effects of defeat in war on the Japanese and German aircraft industries – may have been more important. It was also necessary to concede that, at company level, culture and institutions are highly malleable, so that instead of national specificities imprinting themselves more or less uniformly on a country's industries, differences can evolve among those industries according to their circumstances. This view, which again implies path dependence, fits comfortably with an evolutionary and institutionalist approach to economics. We have shown, with a number of examples, how it is possible to construct a synthesis which retains some of the 'clear cutting edge' of our original approach but recognizes the truth of path-dependence in innovation.

NOTES

1. We are indebted to many individuals for their help and advice: notably to Lars-Erik Gadde, Hakan Hakansson, Istemi Demirag, Hanne Norreklit, John Groenewegen, Pascal Petit, Robert Salais and other fellow members of the Pan-European Project on Performance Pressures and Innovation; to the industrial managers who cooperated with the investigations by Tylecote et al.; and to Charles Edquist, Bart Nooteboom and others who commented on earlier drafts presented to the European Association for Evolutionary Political Economy conference in Paris, November 1992, and the Judge Institute of Management Studies, University of Cambridge, February 1993. We are also indebted for financial support to the Joint Committee on the Successful Management of Technological Change of the UK Science and Engineering, and Economic and Social, Research Councils; the University of Sheffield Research Stimulation Fund; the CNR (Consiglio Nazionale delle Ricerche) and the University of Naples.
2. Tylecote's UK research has found that UK engineering firms in general succeed in getting the necessary functional interaction with production and external interaction only by an extreme decentralization of managerial responsibility, so that the functional interaction required is that within very small units, and the external interaction is only with a very small number of suppliers and customers. The price they pay is a severe loss of synergies with other units, and almost complete invisibility of innovative investment to external sources of finance – indeed the visibility in many cases is very poor even from Head Office! This applies equally in electrical, electronic and mechanical engineering.

REFERENCES

Ansoff, Igor and Stewart, John M. (1976), 'Strategies for a Technology-Based Business', in Rothberg, Robert (ed.), *Corporate Strategy and Product Innovation*, New York: Free Press, ch. 6.

Arunachalam, S. and Manorama, K. (1989), 'Are Citation-Based Quantitative Techniques Adequate for Measuring Science on the Periphery?', *Scientometrics*, **15** (5–6), 393–408.

Bergen, S.A. (1983), *The R&D/Production Interface*, Aldershot, UK: Gower.

Burns, T. and Stalker, G. (1966), *The Management of Innovation*, London: Tavistock.

Clark, R. (1979), *The Japanese Company*, New Haven and London: Yale University Press.

Demirag, I., Tylecote, A. and Morris, B. (1994), 'Accounting for Financial and Managerial Causes of Short Term Pressures in British Corporations', *Journal of Business Finance and Accounting*, **21** (8), 1195–213.

Dertouzos, M., Richard, L., Solow, R. and the MIT Commission on Industrial Productivity (1989), *Made in America: Regaining the Productive Edge*, Cambridge, MA: MIT Press.

D'Iribarne, Philippe (1989), *La logique de l'honneur: Gestion des entreprises et traditions nationales*, Paris: Seuil.

Fox, A. (1974), *Beyond Contract: Work, Power and Trust Relations*, London: Faber and Faber.

Freeman, C. (1974), *The Economics of Industrial Innovation*, London: Penguin.

Freeman, C., Sharp, M. and Walker, W. (eds) (1991), *Technology and the future of Europe: Global competition and the environment*, London: Pinter.

Guerrieri, P. and Tylecote, A. (1994), 'National Competitive Advantage and Microeconomic Behaviour', *Economics of Innovation and New Technology*, **3**, 49–76.

Guerrieri, P. and Tylecote, A. (1997), 'Interindustry Differences in Technical Change and National Patterns of Technological Accumulation', in Edquist, Charles (ed.), *Systems of Innovation*, London: Cassell, ch. 5.

Hobday, M. (1994), 'Innovation in Semiconductor Technology...', in Dodgson, M. and Rothwell, R. (eds), *A Handbook of Industrial Innovation*, Cheltenham, UK: Edward Elgar, ch. 11.

Hofstede, G. (1983), 'National Cultures in Four Dimensions: A Research Theory of Cultural Differences Among Nations', *International Studies of Management and Organisation*, **13** (Spring–Summer), p. 52.

Hofstede, G. (1984), *Culture's Consequences: International Differences in Work-Related Values*, London: Sage.

Lawrence, P. (1980), *Managers and Management in West Germany*, London: Croom Helm.

Lorenz, C. (1989), 'The birth of a transnational: striving for balance', *Financial Times*, 19, 21, 23, 28 and 30 June.

Lundvall, B.-A. (1988), 'Innovation as an interactive process: User-Producer Relations', ch. 17 in Dosi, G. et al. (eds), *Technical Change and Economic Theory*, London: Pinter.

Lundvall, B.-A. (ed.) (1993), *National Systems of Innovation*, London: Pinter.

Mansfield, E. (1988b), 'The Speed and Cost of Industrial Innovation', *Management Science*, **34** (10), 1157–68.

Martin, B., Irvine, J., Narin, F., Sterritt, C. and Stevens, K.A. (1990), 'Recent trends in the output and impact of British science', *Science and Public Policy*, **17** (1), February, 14–26.

Nelson, R.R. (ed.) (1993), *National Systems of Innovation*, Oxford: Oxford University Press.

Patel, P. and Pavitt, K.A.R. (1991), 'Europe's technological performance', ch. 3 in Freeman, C., Sharp, M. and Walker, W. (eds), *Technology and the Future of Europe*, London: Frances Pinter.

Pavitt, K.A.R. (1984), 'Sectoral Patterns of Technical Change: Towards a Taxonomy and a Theory', *Research Policy*, **13**, 343–73.

Pavitt, K.A.R. (1988a), 'International Patterns of Technological Accumulation', in Hood, N. and Vahlne, J.E. (eds), *Strategies in Global Competition*, London: Croom Helm.

Soskice, David (1991), 'Institutional Infrastructure for Institutional Competitiveness: A Comparative Analysis of UK and Germany', ch. 3 in Atkinson, A.B. and Brunetta, R., *Economics for the New Europe*, New York: New York University Press.

Teece, D.J. (1986), 'Profiting from Technological Innovation: Implications for Integration, Collaboration, Licensing and Public Policy', *Research Policy*, **15**, 285–305.

Tylecote, A. (1994a), 'Financial Systems and Innovation', in Dodgson, M. and Rothwell, R. (eds), *Handbook of Industrial Innovation*, Cheltenham, UK: Edward Elgar, ch. 19.

Tylecote, A. (1994b), 'Financial Systems and Innovation', *European Association for Evolutionary Political Economy conference*, Copenhagen, 28–30 October.

Tylecote, A. (1996), 'Cultural differences affecting technological dynamism in Western Europe', *European Journal of Work and Occupational Psychology*, **5** (1), 137–47.

Tylecote, A. and Demirag, I. (1992), 'Short-termism: Culture and Structures as Factors in Technological Innovation', in Coombs, R., Saviotti, P. and Walsh, V. (eds), *Technological Change and Company Strategies*, London: Academic Press.

Wilson, C. (1968), *History of Unilever*, London: Cassell.

11. Innovation, diffusion and political control of co-generation technology in the UK since privatization[1]

K. Matthias Weber

INTRODUCTION

There has been a debate in Europe over the last few years concerning how to address the environmental challenges involved in the supply of energy, given the trend towards liberalization and the retreat of government from responsibility for energy supply. The expectations of an economically more efficient liberal framework bring the fear that a liberal approach might undermine action to protect our environment and resources and the move towards sustainable development.

Therefore a crucial question is: can governments manage the processes of technological change from environmentally hazardous to more sustainable technologies, even if this requires improvements in supply systems which are more than just incremental changes within existing technological regimes? To answer this, we need to know how processes of technological change come about in different types of organizational and regulatory frameworks in the energy sector, and how government actions fit into the system which determines the innovation and diffusion of energy technologies.

Despite the progress made in understanding technological change, there is in fact very little knowledge of the interrelationships between government activities and the evolution of technologies. Government policies are usually regarded as an exogenous force impinging on technological change. This chapter argues that, in order to draw useful conclusions for government intervention in the process of technological change, governments should be understood as an endogenous element of the system which drives technological change. To make constructive use of this perspective, as a foundation for problem- and policy-oriented diffusion studies, different single-disciplinary contributions to technological change have to be brought together to deal with politics, economics and technology (PET) simultaneously. This argument comes together in my presentation of what I call the 'PET systems approach'.

The evolution and (re-)emergence of combined heat and power (co-generation, or CHP) in the UK since the early 1980s can be used to test the usefulness of the PET approach. The case of the UK is particularly interesting. It is an example of the fast growth of CHP (which till the mid-1980s only played a negligible role in the UK) during and after a shift of the economic regime in the energy sector from a nationalized and monopolistic one to a liberalized and privatized one. This shift also implied a transformation of the interfaces between government and the energy supply industry. It is unclear whether the recent success of CHP is to be interpreted as a consequence of liberalization, whether it has been mainly technologically driven or whether it is the result of a unique coincidence of economic and environmental driving forces after liberalization which has only temporarily increased the interest in CHP.

The chapter briefly discusses existing disciplinary approaches and integrates their different levels of analysis (political, economic, technological) into a coherent approach for the study of diffusion and political control, the 'PET system'. This provides a vocabulary which allows the bridging of disciplinary gaps. The approach is used to structure and analyse case-study material on the diffusion of co-generation technology in the UK since the early 1980s. The conclusion discusses the usefulness of the theoretical perspective presented and its applicability in other contexts.

CONCEPTUALIZING TECHNOLOGICAL CHANGE AND POLITICAL CONTROL

Current Understanding of Technological Change and its Determinants

Substantial progress has been made in our understanding of the processes underlying technological change, from a variety of different economic and sociological directions:

- Evolutionary economics has pointed to the importance of looking at reinforcing feedbacks, path-dependent trajectories and both supply-side and demand-side factors in industrial development (Nelson and Winter, 1982; Dosi, 1988a, 1988b; Arthur, 1988).
- Revolutionary versus incremental notions of technological change are now understood within broader frameworks and practices, forming technological and techno-economic paradigms, or even techno-economic regimes (Dosi, 1982; Freeman and Perez, 1988; Metcalfe and Boden, 1992; Kemp, 1993).
- The notion of 'systems' is now used both in the sense of technical components and architectures (Henderson and Clark, 1990; Tushman

and Rosenkopf, 1992) as well as in an organizational and institutional sense of national innovation systems or technology support systems (Lundvall, 1992; Nelson, 1993; Niosi et al., 1993; de Liso and Metcalfe, 1994). This shows the complexity and interdependence of transformation processes related to technological change; it recognizes the importance of regulatory frameworks, of national structures and histories. Especially with regard to large technical systems, the consideration of technical and organizational issues is indispensable (Hughes, 1983; Hughes and Mayntz, 1988; Summerton, 1994).

- Organizational and social factors are at the core of many approaches to understanding technological development, coming under such terms as 'the social construction of technology' (Bijker, Hughes and Pinch, 1987; Bijker and Law, 1992), 'techno-economic networks' (Callon, 1992) and 'socio-technical constituencies' (Molina, 1993; Collinson and Molina, Chapter 6 in this volume). Although emphasis is put on the role of actors and the mental frameworks governing their behaviour, the underlying common logic points to the need to consider both the technical and the social in order to understand technological change. Differences still exist as to which is to be given the most importance: the 'technical' or the 'social'.

However, with very few exceptions (for example, Irwin and Vergragt, 1989; Krupp, 1992), the political dimension is either subsumed under the social, or neglected in favour of a deeper analysis of the impact of policies on innovation itself (Meyer-Krahmer, 1989), about which conclusions are then drawn for the political level. But progress has also been made in political sciences. Based on systems approaches (Görlitz and Druwe, 1990; Luhman, 1988; Mayntz, 1987) and on network approaches (Marin and Mayntz, 1991), the possibilities and limitations of political control of technology have been tackled.

Given that the conclusions of much research on technological change are addressed to government, it is surprising that these problems have not been dealt with. Anyway, like the other approaches mentioned, the political ones are very limited in their scope, concentrating on politics and policy-making processes, but neglecting several other facets of technological change. Consequently, if one accepts that technological change is a phenomenon which depends on a variety of interdependent social, techno-economic and political processes, that government measures affect all these levels, and that government is not an independent force but subjected to a multitude of feedbacks from other social and economic actors, then it is obvious that an integration of these perspectives in a coherent approach could provide a very useful foundation for analysing the role of governments in technological change – both in a retrospective and a prospective sense.

The PET System

System description

These insights will be made more explicit by proposing an approach which I call the 'PET system', PET standing for politics, economics and technology as the three main areas I try to consider endogenously. It is not intended to formulate a new theory of technological change, but rather to draw existing

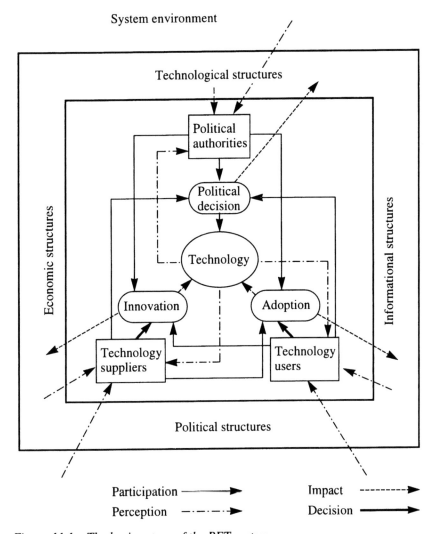

Figure 11.1   The basic set-up of the PET system

lines of research together as a foundation for structured problem-oriented research.

As shown in Figure 11.1, the PET system has five analytical levels, which cover both the micro perspective of actors and interactions, and the macro perspective of structural transformations. The system reflects the interdependence between technology and its selection environment as well as the interdependences between the different elements which constitute this environment. The five levels are:

1. Technology and technological options: this level is subjected to changes, transformations and improvements, or even to the emergence of substantially new options.
2. Actors and their motivations, interests and possibilities; in this case, mainly users and suppliers of technology, and political authorities.
3. Interactions which determine the generation and selection of technologies and of technology-related strategies in terms of innovation, adoption and political measures.
4. The endogenous environment of the technology and of the actors, constituted by the evolving structures of the system. Basically, these structural elements provide the settings and the institutions within which interactions take place and which in turn are the aggregate outcome of the interactions.
5. The exogenous selection environment which is understood as not being affected by the interactions in the system; rather, the system as a whole adapts to them.

Obviously, the history and evolution of different countries has an important role to play in determining both structural settings and actors' behaviour.

Technology – the object of investigation

Apart from the most simple examples, almost all technologies are made up of several components, thus representing a system in a purely technical sense.[2] Nowadays technical systems exist which are so pervasive in character that they cover whole countries (electricity supply) or even the whole world (communications).

Whereas technology is subjected to the limitations of what is physically feasible, any options are constrained by the immediate social, economic and political environment. This environment is heterogeneous, composed of different types of interests and actors who assess different dimensions of a technology in different ways, in line with their respective interests. These dimensions can be of a technical and economic nature, but can also embrace a technology's organizational implications, its longer-term impacts on the structure of power relations, or its environmental impact. Consequently, in such a multidimensional and multiple-actor framework for technological change, the notion of a technology's 'superiority' as used in earlier diffusion models needs to be reassessed in a more differentiated way.

Structures of the PET system

Technology develops inside a wider socioeconomic and technological environment, which can be divided into a few 'structures'. These structures are in a permanent process of change, mostly slow and incremental, but sometimes fast and revolutionary. Being the result of a historical process, these structures could be regarded as the accumulated result of decisions made by the actors in the course of time. I shall argue later how these structures then affect individual decisions, representing a feedback between the macro level of structures and the micro level of actors.

Economic structures refer to the types and sizes of companies in an industry, its organization (for example, monopolized/liberalized, private/public ownership), and the structures of its main market, both on the technology-supply side and the technology-user side. They also comprise what is usually defined as the regulatory regime.

Structures of the policy-making process determine to a large extent the outcome of the negotiation processes leading to the formulation and implementation of public policies and regulatory measures. The organizational interfaces between government and industry, in particular, play an important role in shaping and influencing political decisions.

Structures for the generation and supply of (technological) information have been recognized as increasingly important. They comprise elements such as the existence and the organization of R&D activities in a country or an industry, technology policies, channels of information dissemination and institutions like the patent system.

Technical structures are defined as the physical settings which limit how the diffusion of a new technology takes place, for example technical interdependences and constraints, or the structure of the existing capital stock.

Interaction arenas and decision making

Whereas structural transformations are used to represent the changes taking place at the macro level of the system, they build on the underlying processes at the micro level. On the one hand, accumulated individual decisions shape and determine what the structural settings look like (dashed arrows in Figure 11.1). (For example, the decision to adopt a new technology has an incremental effect on the technological structures of a country, and political decisions can affect its economic structures very markedly.) On the other hand, it is evident that the actual evolution of these structures has an effect on the positions of the different actors in respective decision-making processes. In other words, the perception of structural changes at the micro level (dashed/ dotted arrows) interconnects the observable structural transformations, and allows the driving forces of these dynamic processes to be captured.

I distinguish between 'decisions' and the 'interaction arenas' in which these decisions are reached through negotiation or bargaining processes. Although, for example, the decision to adopt a technology is taken ultimately by an individual company, this decision is the result of interactions with others, like technology suppliers, regulatory bodies, consultants and so on. A decision (thick arrows) is the synthesis of such a negotiation process in conjunction with the interests, goals and expectations of the actor who finally decides.

Although this is a simplification of reality, three main types of decisions and of related interaction arenas can be defined:

1. Adoption decisions, which are ultimately made by technology users, after having explored alternative options and the different requirements to be fulfilled.
2. Innovation decisions, such as the decision of a supplier to develop and market a new technology; this can be preceded by R&D, market explorations, cooperation with users, and so on.
3. Political decisions, to be taken by political authorities like governments, such as in the introduction of new regulations, or the structural reorganization of an industry.

Political choices regarding new control measures are hence analysed in a similar way to technological choices, namely as the result of a decision-making process involving not only government bodies but also representatives from industry or from other relevant social groups. Hence, one gets a picture in which both the diffusion of new technologies and the formulation and implementation of political-control measures are finally determined by overlapping groups of actors in similar processes of variation and selection, but taking place in different arenas of interaction where specific criteria of selection apply.

Furthermore, different means can be distinguished by which interactions can take place. I propose four different types of means, namely financial exchanges (expressed in money terms), execution of power (which usually takes the form of legal acts), information exchanges and transfer of actual things/artefacts.[3] The organizational settings in which these means can be used are markets, hierarchies or networks.[4]

Actors: objectives, perceptions, expectations

As outlined above, negotiation processes are distinguished from the final decision. What are the general motivations and processes through which an actor – be it a private company or a public organization – decides? I use the same representation of the decision-making process for the three main types of actors considered: users of technology, suppliers of technology and political authorities. Nelson and Winter's (1982) model of routines and satisficing behaviour under uncertainty is more useful than notions of maxi- mizing agents. This can be quite easily complemented by the concept of 'self-reference' for decision making in large organizations (Luhmann, 1988; Görlitz and Druwe, 1990). Based on perceived, but limited and filtered, information about changes and developments of available technical options, an actor (user, supplier, political authority) who is confronted with the neces- sity and the possibility of spending limited resources on different types of activities becomes involved in a negotiation process to reduce uncertainty about the best possible decision to be made (see Clark and Juma, 1992). In the course of this negotiation process the four different types of 'means' are used by the actors involved in order to affect the final decision so that they match their own perceived interests as well as possible. These interests can be seen as a combination of 'external' interests (in the sense of economic or political success) and of 'internal' interests, reflecting the self-referential aspects of decision making.

For perceiving and filtering information, it is important to take the con- straining role of expectations inside established regimes into account because they contribute to the reduction of uncertainty and the stabilization of the decision process by excluding unconventional options. Obviously, the notion of regimes applies equally to techno-economic and political aspects of tech- nology.

System dynamics

The overall description of technological change in terms of structures, actors and technological characteristics as schematically sketched in Figure 11.1 is useful for structuring empirical information. In addition, PET terminology can be used to structure and understand the dynamics of change and its underlying mechanisms. Basically, an evolutionary argumentation is applied to describe the system dynamics, making use of the different elements of the PET system.

The main driving forces of change and variation in such a system are, on the one hand, rooted in the auto-dynamics of technology, offering new opportunities for future development paths. On the other hand, different types of needs – technical, economic and social – can induce efforts to innovate. These needs can be imposed exogenously, for example by changing demands from society, but can also be rooted in the interests and objectives of the actors. 'Novelty' can hence be induced in the system by technology itself, but also by social forces. Uncertainty adds to the variation in the search for new solutions because *ex ante* there can be different possible paths which are regarded as worth exploring. Finally, the diversity of knowledge bases, skills and organizational features of novelty-generating firms contributes to variety.

These possibilities for variation are strongly constrained by dominant mental frameworks and designs (Tushman and Anderson, 1986) shared among the community of researchers, engineers and decision makers. The constraints include expectations concerning the operation of the different decision arenas and the structural interdependences in the system, that is, the expected constraints imposed by existing technological, economic, informational or political structures. In other words, there is a 'selective force of anticipated selection mechanisms', which contributes to the *ex ante* adjustment to certain technological trajectories, even before any effective decision is made. The crucial elements in this perspective are obviously the interests, goals and anticipations of the different actors which lead to decisions affecting other actors as well as the structural settings. Inside the system there are different elements which mutually affect each other. The transformations of information and impulses into decisions by the actors are usually the most difficult and least explored elements of every specific study.

Hence, the notion of selection environment being used here is much broader and more differentiated than the initial definition used in economics, which was mainly confined to adoption decisions in a competitive market. In PET, all actors potentially participating in the three interaction arenas (innovation, adoption, policy making) contribute to technology selection, using all the means of interaction defined (information, money, legal measures, artefacts). From a different angle, political measures can also be regarded as being subjected to selection processes in a quite similar way to technologies. Such measures are determined by the interests and representations of pressure groups, by financial constraints and by competing political goals in the policy-making process. All the decisions which are made shape and affect the changes of the structures in the end, and in particular the content and the use of technology. To put it in even more general terms: objects of selection and (endogenous) selection environment shape each other mutually.

The 'selection environment' of a technology is constituted at a first level by these interdependent processes among the actors, but at a second level also by the embedding structural transformations. Technology may be set in the centre of our perspective, but these two levels of selection environment as described by PET are co-evolving with the technologies in a kind of symbiotic interrelationship – including government policies and political structures. Beyond these two levels, one can distinguish a 'system environment' which represents the exogenous driving forces of change in the system.

In addition to the aforementioned anticipation by existing mental frameworks, the interdependence between the elements of the system is also an important stabilizing mechanism, corresponding to the evolutionary element of continuity. A number of others can be identified, especially reinforcing effects between technologies and different types of structural settings (for example, network externalities), durability of technical hardware (for example, vintage effect), complementarities among technologies (economies of scale and scope, system architecture), and learning and epidemic effects.

In order for a technology to diffuse successfully, it has to 'match' with the rest of the system which itself is changing – not only in the technical sense, but also with regard to organizational and cognitive aspects. In addition, the path-dependence of technological change and lock-in effects (Arthur, 1988) as the result of reinforcement also require a 'temporal match' for a change of established trajectories or even paradigms – the right decisions at the right time are needed.

The preceding model implies the notion of a smooth co-evolution, rather than that of discontinuous jumps and technological revolutions. In large interrelated technological systems it is obviously very difficult to introduce fundamental changes due to a variety of resistances, but once the right matches are established a fast process of change with pervasive impacts can be triggered. The change of the dominant paradigm in terms of structural settings (technological, economic, informational and political), of mental frameworks and of related sets of interests can be regarded as a process requiring a very high activation impulse in order to trigger self-reinforcing processes for the establishment of a new and consistent evolutionary path.

THE DIFFUSION OF CO-GENERATION TECHNOLOGY IN THE UK

Co-generation has not been a success story in the UK, but liberalization seems to have changed its prospects. Studying the UK is therefore also a test-case for the liberalization plans in other countries, especially in those where CHP is already well established, and where in a liberalized framework the specific requirements of CHP ought to be respected. According to PET, these requirements encompass economic and political considerations, but also the technical configuration and specificities of CHP.

Co-generation Technology: Characteristics, Implications and Improvements

In general, co-generation (or combined heat and power, CHP) works on a very simple and straightforward principle: the simultaneous generation of useful heat when generating power. The importance of this apparently simple principle lies in the gains in efficiency and the reduction of emissions and CO_2 which can be achieved in comparison with conventional separate production of electricity and heat. Although the detailed environmental and resource advantages are still a matter of dispute among promoters and opponents of CHP, it is widely recognized that they do exist and that reductions in the order of 15 per cent on average should be regarded as realistic (Sirchis, 1990; Enquete-Kommission, 1995). The controversy about co-generation thus focuses on the balance between its environmental and long-term economic advantages, on the one hand, and the additional organizational and investment costs, on the other.

Three main types of CHP technology can be distinguished, namely those based on steam turbines (which are typically large in scale), gas-turbine systems for medium-size, and reciprocating engines for small-scale applications. Three main types of applications correspond to these technologies, namely district heating, industrial processes and small-scale applications for individual buildings or group heating. Obviously these are three very different contexts for applying CHP, and due to the particularly dynamic developments in industrial and small-scale applications and the negligible role of district heating in the UK, I shall concentrate on these two.[5]

Applying CHP technology has a number of important implications which are crucial for understanding the constraints on its use. First of all, in order to be able to exploit its economies of scope it must be a 'decentralized' technology, since heat can only be distributed over short distances. A wider use of CHP needs thus to be seen in relation to the historically developed centralized power-generation structure, exploiting large economies of scale. Second, cogeneration links two chains of energy supply (heat and electricity) and requires a high level of horizontal coordination in order to exploit the efficiency benefits of co-production as expressed in corresponding fuel savings. Usually, the limited flexibility of heat supply implies that CHP plants operate according to the requirements of the heat load. In other words, CHP can usually be used only to cover the base-load of a site and needs to be complemented by additional boilers and a connection to the power grid. Here, the crucial issues are technical grid connection conditions and the economic terms of exchange, that is, tariffs for importing and exporting power.[6] The third point is that CHP is not a simple technology; it requires a good deal of specialized knowledge for designing, planning and operating plants. Despite attempts to standardize equipment at the low end of the power scale, the systems need to be adapted to the entire energy context of a site. Finally, although CHP is based on established technical knowledge, it is a step towards a decentralized energy supply system. Hence, whereas it is technically in line with the dominant technological paradigm of power-supply technology, organizationally it can be seen as part of a new trajectory of decentralized power generation.

CHP as part of the established power-technology trajectory is a rather mature technology; the principle was already applied at the beginning of this century. Targeted research and development on CHP has been carried out during the last decade only, and the improvements achieved were important factors for its wider diffusion. Apart from technical characteristics like efficiencies, the crucial innovations were of a rather mixed technical and organizational nature. Packaging units for small applications and the exploitation of economies of scale by small series production have reduced installation and unit costs. Remote on-line monitoring, computerized control systems and preventive maintenance have increased reliability to a level which has fulfilled the users' expectations while reducing operation costs. Information technology also helped solve the technical and economic problems related to grid connection and the control of decentralized generation. A learning process during the 1980s led to integrated design, planning and operation methods which were adequate to deal with the complexity of the schemes and to optimize operation, for example by integration of other processes like cooling, heat pumps, waste incineration, heat storage and so on. Finally, the performance in terms of emissions was gradually improved. The different improvements and refinements are still going on, but a level of quality has been achieved which makes the technology stable and reliable in its present configurations. The next major changes are expected to come from the introduction of fuel cells, but the timescale of their introduction is still unclear.

Consequently, a variety of technological improvements and breakthroughs of both the architectural and component type can be identified (Henderson and Clark, 1990); these widened the potential for applying CHP, challenging the established arguments in favour of a centralized power production – arguments such as the benefits of economies of scale and the natural monopoly character of power supply. These improvements in CHP outweighed the improvements achieved in separate generation, tipping the balance in recent years in favour of CHP.

Exogenous and Structural Changes

After the first oil crisis in 1973, security of supply raised interest in CHP in the UK, but the availability of North Sea oil dampened that interest. The environmental question did not play a major role in the discussion on energy policy and technology options in the 1980s either – in contrast to most other EU states. Economic arguments and, in the context of district and community heating, social arguments were much more important.

This effect was further reinforced by the economic recession which limited the possibilities for investment both in the public and private sector. In addition, the financial and legal resources of municipal authorities, which are one of the main potential investors in CHP, have been cut considerably during the past decade. In industry, a reduction of activities in heat-intensive production technologies changed the requirements for large amounts of heat. Whereas the relatively low level of fuel prices in the last years has not been conducive to a switch to highly fuel-efficient technologies like CHP, the possibility of using natural gas for power generation considerably facilitated the implementation of CHP.

Changing economic and regulatory structures

Although privatization of the electricity supply industry (ESI) in 1990 may have been the most important energy industry event of the last decade, the Energy Act of 1983 had already opened up the possibilities for non-utility power production with CHP; it obliged the electricity boards (as they were then) to accept power sales from independent power producers. Consequently, some first, if difficult, attempts were made to establish new CHP plants which not only generated power for the site's own needs but also exported power to the grid. Privatization and liberalization in 1990 completely overturned the structure of the electricity supply industry in England and Wales by breaking up the Central Electricity Generating Board (CEGB) and the regional boards into two major generating companies (National Power and PowerGen), 12 independent regional electricity companies (RECs) for supply, whilst transmission came under the responsibility of the National Grid Company. Almost all of these companies have also been privatized. The key element of the UK system is the electricity pool, an artificial market for power, which is regulated and supervised by the Office of Electricity Regulation (OFFER). Both generation and supply have been opened stepwise for other private companies, including the successors of the CEGB members, which have started to compete with each other. During the first years of the new system there have been substantial problems of uncertainty, instability and adjustment.

The changing organization of the ESI has also triggered the emergence of a new type of company – integrated energy services companies (IESC). These fulfil the task of bridging between final service users on the one hand and equipment suppliers and power generation on the other. Privatization put an end to the strict organizational separation of energy-supply chains, offering the opportunity to integrate generation and supply of different energy services and exploiting potential economies of scope by these new companies. Finally, all major companies in the sector have started to move in this direction – RECs, large generators and private-contract energy-management companies. These developments towards service integration follow the outsourcing trend of utility services by industrial and public energy users, especially when these services are becoming increasingly sophisticated and require a higher level of specialized knowledge.

This integration of technology supply and use functions in one organizational unit has been complemented by a corresponding extension of the activities of suppliers of traditional energy-system components, who extended the range of their services to maintenance and financing, especially for packaged small-scale CHP systems.

The political decision structures
Although a study was carried out in the late 1970s on the possibilities of city-wide CHP-based district heating, energy policy in the UK was concerned with other issues, especially the nuclear debate (Department of Energy, 1979). CHP was in effect a 'non-subject'. Given the main players in UK energy policy at the time, it also becomes evident that there was hardly any powerful interest group supporting CHP. The large power generators and suppliers did not have any interest in decentralized power generation, which could only have weakened their influential position; due to the horizontal separation of energy-supply chains, they could not even potentially benefit from its economies of scope. Heat supply was not their business just as power supply was not the business of British Gas. The strong ties between the established energy-supply industries and government excluded the influence of potentially interested parties like local authorities, universities, hospitals and industry, the latter being still the most powerful and influential among these candidates. However, any interest of industrial heat and power users in CHP was furthermore distracted by beneficial tariffs and by technical barriers, keeping CHP in its infant state.

Given this strong influence of the large energy companies, the decisions of 1983 and 1990 represented quite surprising ruptures, because government managed to carry on with its privatization despite the resistance of established power constellations. The ideological background of privatization and liberalization as well as the lamentable performance of UK power generation may help to explain these developments. Since 1990, government has been very reluctant to interfere in the energy-supply industry and the links with the ESI have become relatively weak. The regulator, the Office of Electricity Regulation (OFFER), has become a focal point of interest, because its decisions in the last few years have had considerable impacts on the uncertainties and hence on the investment decisions for power generation. Instability and unpredictability of electricity prices add to these uncertainties.

Information Supply on CHP

Co-generation has long suffered from the bad reputation acquired in former decades, especially in relation to district heating which is usually associated with it. Low reliability and poor economics were the main prejudices against CHP. Often this was just due to mistakes in sizing the plants, which required different estimations from those for heat-only equipment.[7] Hence the supply of information on new and improved equipment as well as on the advantages of CHP in the light of changing priorities with regard to environmental issues was crucial for making potential investors aware of this option and its potential benefits.

In the early 1980s there were only very sporadic activities in favour of CHP. In the mid- and late 1980s, the Combined Heat and Power Association (CHPA) and especially the Energy Efficiency Office (EEO) became key nodes in promoting CHP, mainly by supplying information on technical issues and on successful applications. In addition, the trend towards energy service integration also modified the informational links between service users and technology/service suppliers: installing and operating a CHP system requires detailed information about heat and power loads on the sites, a type of information which is only supplied if a considerable level of trust exists between the partners. Hence, especially in the late 1980s, when several new types of applications were customized, very close relationships had to be established in order to gain and build up the necessary competences for CHP. In other words, the information supply network which allowed the benefits of learning effects on a wider scale comprised government institutions, technology suppliers and technology users.

Diffusion Patterns of CHP in the UK Energy Supply Context

Like other European countries, the UK has experienced stagnation of its energy demand since the late 1970s, with a slow but constant growth of electricity demand. The bulk of electricity was generated in coal-fired and in nuclear power stations. However, since the beginning of the 1990s, a switch of fuel sources has taken place, enabled by the release of gas as a fuel for electricity generation ('dash for gas'). As a consequence, the construction of additional combined-cycle gas-turbine plants (CCGT) has led to a substantial overcapacity, but despite their high electrical efficiency, their overall efficiency remains far below that of CHP.

Table 11.1   The diffusion of co-generation in the UK (in MW and percentage of electricity generation capacity)

	1977	1983	1988	1991	1993	1994
Total CHP capacity (MWe)	2790	2250	1790	2310	2890	3140
Industrial (MWe)	~2500	~2000	~1700	~2040	~2600	~2770
Small-scale (MWe)	<5	~20	~30	together	180	230
District heating (MWe)	~70	n.a.	n.a.	270	~110	~140

Source: Digest of UK Energy Statistics 1995, HMSO/DTI 1995. Data for the three types of applications have been estimated based on a variety of sources.

The re-emergence of CHP from its decline till 1987/88 (see Table 11.1) needs to be seen in relation to these structural changes. Since then, there has been a relatively fast uptake, and the latest available statistical data (for 1994) indicate a total CHP capacity of about 3150 MW (5 per cent of overall capacity). This capacity is distributed through about 1150 CHP sites, so the decentralization effect is quite significant. The contribution of small-scale CHP to power generation is still quite low but it represents the vast majority of sites.

The Level of Actors: Motivations, Perceptions, Interactions and Decisions

Technology-supply side

With the first step towards liberalization of power generation in 1983, several companies identified the market opportunities of CHP, especially for small reciprocating engines and gas turbines. The first generation of CHP engines were just derivatives of other existing reciprocating engines to which a heat recovery system was added. The reception about the poor performance and reliability of these units which, furthermore, were often badly designed for the requirements of the site, confirmed the relatively negative reputation of CHP among many engineers.

This first generation should be regarded as an intensive learning phase for the suppliers, because they needed to understand the requirements of their potential customers which could not be easily satisfied by just selling hardware to them; their new customers did not possess the knowledge and skills to operate CHP systems properly. Through the intermediary role of the EEO's information and financial support schemes, a number of smaller projects were then promoted in order to improve available technology and also the reputation of CHP. A couple of very close cooperation agreements between large users of small-scale CHP equipment (for example, hotel chains) and manufacturers allowed the design of CHP systems which were well adapted to user needs. As a second step, the experiences gained through these exemplary projects fed back into other applications, for which economies of scale through packaging and standardization of equipment could be achieved in the end, contributing to the technological improvements mentioned earlier.

Apart from these technical aspects, CHP suppliers showed a fast response to the non-technical needs of their customers, who were interested in financing and full-service solutions. It was only after liberalization that these innovative offers could be made. This has led to a great variety of contractual arrangements for the installation, operation and maintenance of the plant on the customer's site, including the direct sale of electricity and heat services from a plant on site (these types of service are sometimes referred to as 'contract energy management', or CEM). In principle, the same arguments hold for gas-turbine applications, although they are usually larger and more site-specific in character. Reliability and maintenance were less crucial issues than in the case of reciprocating engines, due to experience in other fields, but several transfer problems from aero and off-shore applications to CHP required changes in the user–producer relationships.

Technology-user side
On the user side, one can distinguish a variety of types of firm: service end-users, intermediary companies like contract energy-management firms, and utility companies for distribution and generation, the latter having an additional specific function because they also provide and control the interface between end-users and the electricity grid as a kind of gate-keeper.

The main alternative to CHP for heat and electricity service end-users is the separate and individual generation of heat only on site, and the import of electricity from the grid. This is also the option which requires the lowest initial investment, but CHP promises to offer lower operation and fuel costs. In general, the main interest in CHP is based on the potential fuel cost savings it can provide and on the independence from the RECs. On the other hand, because energy supply does not make up part of their core business for most companies, CHP must promise very good payback times in order to be approved – especially in periods of shortage of financial means. Public users are less strict in this respect, but still have limited financial possibilities. A second aspect of in-company electricity generation is that most companies do not want to worry about it and do not want to build up additional competences to operate such plants. CHP being a more complicated, less standardized and less proven technology, firms are often reluctant even if the calculations are very promising. These detrimental effects can be compensated for by the general trend towards outsourcing of secondary and utility activities, offering the opportunity to specialized companies to provide well-designed co-generation systems.

Environmental arguments play a complementary role when deciding on energy supply but, especially in the private sector, this is often in the sense of reputation building and of showing environmental commitment. In the public sector, environmental arguments play a greater role due to political commitments, but usually the persistent support of an individual promoter seems to be needed to make CHP projects go ahead over the years. Environmental regulations were not regarded as being of any substantial impact for small- and medium-size CHP.

Uncertainties concerning the very rough estimations of fuel and electricity prices have a rather negative impact on CHP because a solid planning base is missing. The market niche for the emerging energy-service companies exactly fits this need, because they often take over the risk of investment in CHP, keeping a good share of the potential savings of the plant for bringing in their expertise and for bearing the risks of a long-term contract. The combination of financing, packaging, maintenance and construction was also compatible with the outsourcing trend in industry as well as in public companies. Hence the fact that the needs of the end-users could be matched by an extended range of services provided by the suppliers was helpful for CHP, but on the other hand there is still a great deal of uncertainty whether these long-term contracts will be beneficial in the end or not.

Not only have some of the technology suppliers extended the range of their services to CEM, but also some traditional energy-service companies, especially the former public electricity utilities, have started to occupy this field. Privatization and liberalization were again the forces behind this change of attitude on the side of the utility companies because they obliged them to expand their activities to other areas and also consider horizontally neighboured activities like gas supply, co-generation and all the services related to it. Whilst they were very reluctant with regard to co-generation till privatization, actively undermining the intentions of the Energy Act 1983 by informal means through their key position at the interface of the grid, they are now trying to set up their own CHP activities, forced to do so by the fear that others might provide these services to their established electricity customers. In their regions, the RECs still occupy a strategic position because they control the conditions for grid connections for those CHP operators who do not deal directly with the pool. Although the behaviour of the individual RECs differs, they are still able to obstruct projects which are not beneficial for themselves, but recent regulation has weakened their power in this respect.

The large generators, who are operating the major share of the centralized technical infrastructure, have started to look at decentralized options as well, but are still constrained by their capital stock and maintain an interest structure which favours traditional large-scale and centralized generation of power only.

Similar arguments hold for gas suppliers. Due to the change in the organizational structures of both electricity and gas supply, the established boundaries between the two systems have been opened up. Here, the necessity to match technology and organization becomes particularly obvious. As long as a company works in gas supply only or electricity supply only, there is hardly any scope and interest for a technology which combines both and questions the traditional business territories.

To sum up: the key development should be seen in service integration and horizontal coordination of heat and power supply. It provides the gateway for matching CHP with the existing technical and organizational structures. However, CHP is still a rather marginal activity for the RECs as well as for the large generators and the gas companies. Their interests and positions with regard to major regulatory issues are dominated by their core activities, namely power supply for the RECs, power generation for the large generators and gas supply for the now competing gas companies. In addition, the shorter-term investment logic applied by all users and introduced by liberalization favours economic-only criteria and the neglect of environmental and other long-term sustainability criteria – a trend which is rather detrimental to CHP.

Government Policies

Although the Energy Act of 1983 made it easier to start self-generation of electricity, complaints about the nationally owned electricity-generating boards continued. These complaints came predominantly from large industrial electricity users and strengthened the growing arguments for privatization and liberalization of public services in the UK. A strong coalition in favour of a revolutionary change of the economic regime in energy supply emerged despite the resistance of the established electricity industry organizations.

Although there has been some specific lobbying in favour of CHP by associations like the CHPA, CHP was hardly a topic on the political agenda. Only in recent years has it been considered relevant, following positive experiences from other countries. The official position of the UK government since 1990 has been that there is no need for any active energy policy, just limited regulation of a competitive system by the Office of Electricity Regulation (OFFER) and by Her Majesty's Inspectorate of Pollution (HMIP) in order to protect the consumers, to guarantee the efficient operation of the market and to protect the environment. The issue of security of supply, which had been on the political agenda for decades, is not regarded as a major concern nowadays, and thus not of major importance as a factor in favour of energy efficiency. Again in contrast to other EU states, support for CHP at the political level has hardly emerged as part of environmental and greenhouse gas discussions. In any case, environmental regulation in the UK has not been perceived as a constraint on investment decisions till now, especially for small-scale CHP applications. Due to the BATNEEC principle (best available technology not entailing excessive costs) applied by HMIP, both standards and environmental innovations are driven by developments on the European mainland, where stricter controls are in place.

An Integrated Representation

The structure of relationships described in this account of CHP in the UK can be shown by using a graphical representation of the PET system as in Figure 11.2. In the figure, the technology of CHP with its different dimensions and characteristics is represented in the centre square. These features change with the impacts of the three types of decisions, such as R&D (innovation), practical experiences (adoption, investment) and government research or research support, for example, the best practice programme (political decisions).[8] The three types of decisions made by the actors (manufacturers, users, government) not only affect CHP technology in its characteristics, but also the four structural aspects of the system (technical, economic, informational, political). Government activities for creating information-supply networks are one example of this; others are liberalization as a measure transforming economic structures, the emergence of new companies in the field of integrated energy-service supply, or the establishment of industrial associations for information exchange and for the transmission of political interests. The technical structures are directly affected by the adoption of and the investment in new energy-supply equipment.

These decisions are finally the results of interactions of a variety of actors. Investment by CHP users is dependent on inputs from the manufacturers and on information support from government and other users. Different industrial associations like the CHPA have been involved to varying degrees in the political and regulatory decisions. The actors' attitudes depend on the perception and assessment of their individual environment, including the decisions and interactions of the others. In the case of the UK, this environment has been predominantly shaped in recent years by liberalization, but driving

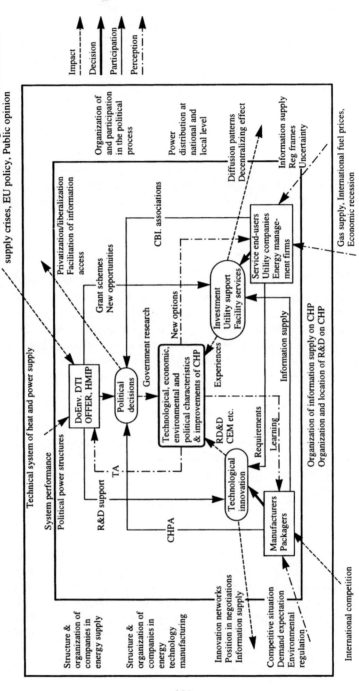

Figure 11.2   Co-generation in the UK according to the PET system

forces from outside the system boundaries also played a major role; for example the import of technological know-how, European environmental regulations or the fuel prices on the world markets. The changing situation in the UK was perceived by many manufacturers as an opportunity to engage in new development work for CHP, as it was by many users who realized new options in the liberalized framework.

CONCLUSIONS

The Dynamics of CHP Diffusion in the UK and its Implications

In the UK, the potential for applying CHP was blocked till 1983 by the positions of the horizontally separated national monopolies for electricity and gas supply. This situation changed in two steps (1983 and 1990), and the Electricity Act in 1990 subjected the existing ESI to a real structural shock. The new economic and regulatory regime allowed for more variety, changed the selection parameters throughout the whole system and broke up many of the continuities and inflexibilities of the old system. In this process, an important enabling role was played by government policies and by politics: the interfaces between energy policy and the energy-supply industry were broken up. This required first of all the establishment of the topic of liberalization on the political agenda, driven by strong ideological motivations in favour of a reduction of government influence in the economy and also by the poor performance of the UK energy-supply system. Obviously, CHP was not a real topic on the agenda, and thus the re-emergence of CHP was rather a by-product than a target of the reforms. In addition, CHP did not have strong backers. This political process of establishing and shaping energy policy can be interpreted as an evolutionary process in a similar way as for technology.

The diffusion process of CHP itself should be seen as the result of a complex interplay of structural changes, their perception by the different actors and their decisions on adopting CHP, on developing the technology and on providing adequate legal and regulatory rules. It was part of a transformation process of the entire energy system, covering technological, economic, informational and political changes, and embedded in a number of external developments which were conducive to CHP in the UK, such as the release of natural gas for power generation. Others, like the rather low level of environmental concern in the UK, had a detrimental influence. The systemic character of CHP and its organizational implications further add to this complexity.

In evolutionary terms, the transition to the liberalized system enabled the generation of more variety in terms of energy-supply systems by reducing several regulatory and administrative barriers and thus increasing the incentives for innovative approaches, both in terms of technology and organization. A critical role was played by the introduction of computer control systems to monitor and coordinate heat and power supply. Also at the different levels of selection the conditions changed, although in rather diverse ways. The stricter investment criteria applied by technology users made the case for CHP more difficult in many cases, as did some of the economic conditions, such as falling and fluctuating electricity prices. In other words, the longer-term benefits of CHP are not highly valued in the liberalized system. At the level of public utilities – which fulfil a gate-keeping function for all generation systems connected to their grid – the initial reluctance towards all types of CHP applications has given way to a more favourable stance, thus lowering the selection barrier. Whereas, in other countries, substantial financial support has been given to CHP, government policies after 1990 have been mainly restricted to the provision of information as a contribution to improving the conditions for variation and selection.

With regard to interest structures, the reforms have improved the situation for CHP because its double link to heat and to power supply can now be more easily exploited by the different users. But still, the basic structure of the UK ESI is not very amenable to the use of CHP. There is still a mismatch between the centralized and horizontally separated generation and supply system and the horizontally bridging principle of CHP which could only be resolved in the course of the slow replacement of the capital stock vintages over the next decades. The relative complexity of the co-generation system, the need for specialized knowledge of the technology and the subtleties of the regulatory system, as well as remaining prejudices and detrimental mental frameworks, contribute to the stability and continuity of the existing structures. In all these respects, the first steps towards service orientation in energy supply should be seen as the key element which could overcome these obstacles.

One could say that, despite the retarding influence of the historically grown structures and institutions, a sequence of events and decisions as reactions to liberalization was induced which finally enabled the wider adoption of CHP systems. Nevertheless, the overall effect is rather contradictory and double-edged, due to the dominance of short-term commercial interests over long-term and sustainability-oriented ones, and the high degree of uncertainty prevailing. There certainly was the opportunity in the early 'turbulent' post-privatization phase to induce more actively a transition to a decentralized and sustainable trajectory, but this would have required an active political commitment. This window of opportunity was missed because of this mismatch with the liberal ethos.

I would conclude that liberalization is certainly not the panacea for improving energy supply systems, but in the case of the UK it was a rather helpful influence. Whether it would be a helpful solution in other countries with already well-performing systems, with CHP possibly making a substantial contribution, can at least be doubted. The crucial disadvantage is the short-term logic introduced by a highly competitive framework which underestimates the long-term aspects relevant for energy supply. A variety of additional measures would have to be integrated in a liberalized framework, ranging from economic instruments like taxes and emission permits, to regulation and the reinforcement of organizational patterns conducive to an efficient supply. Also, technology policy can be helpful by promoting and protecting specific new technologies which are regarded as beneficial in the longer term but which manufacturing companies would be willing to consider only if they promise to survive in a competitive environment after having undergone a learning phase.

The Analytical Advantages of PET for Retrospective and Prospective Analysis

The analysis in this chapter has clearly pointed to the importance of including political structures and processes as an additional dimension to be considered in understanding technological change. In the case of CHP, they are in fact indispensable for explaining the inertia of the energy supply sector, for understanding the reasons for the sudden break-up of the entire sector by imposing the structural shock of liberalization and for analysing the instability and unreliability of the regulatory regime under OFFER since 1990.

Support is thus lent to the hypothesis that in order to manage technological change by means of government policies, the whole range of aspects implied by what I have called PET should be taken into consideration in an analysis of the transformation process. Consequently, six main points of intervention can be identified as potential targets for political measures, corresponding to different levels of the PET system:

1. Stimulation of the generation of alternative options on the technology-supply side, and the dissemination of technological knowledge. This includes the provision of opportunities for the technology to be the subject of a sufficiently long learning process in order to compete effectively with established options.
2. Modification of the direct utilization context, that is, of the factors which directly determine the decision to adopt or reject an option in its present state. This covers all facilitating and enabling activities of utility and energy-management companies.
3. Improvements in the informational interface between the actors for the provision of reliable information on the benefits, shortcomings and experiences with different options.

4. Reforms of the economic and technological structures in which the decisions to use or develop new technologies are embedded.
5. Adjustment of the specific regulations which apply to the sector or industry in question.
6. Opening of the structural settings for public policy making in order to facilitate the input of innovative ideas and avoid the lock-in between economic and political interests. This is an element of political control which also comprises the compartmentalized structure of policy making.

From a methodological point of view, PET provides a well-structured pattern for studying processes of technological change, which covers both the behavioural and the structural level of analysis in an interrelated way, thereby enabling a dynamic analysis of change. Not only are the main technological and economic aspects contained in the approach, but also the role of policy-making processes in relation to them. PET thus goes further than usual energy-policy studies which help to provide insights into the impacts of political measures, but do not help to address the problems and limitations imposed on politics in the course of implementation, especially with regard to the organizational interfaces between the political and economic realms. Despite this particular advantage for political analysis, PET is not restricted to it. Any of the actors considered in the system can use the approach to analyse their interplay with the others, their strategies and decisions.

PET is also particularly useful for prospective applications, allowing an exploration of the interplay and influence of a variety of factors in the analysis. Obviously, such a prospective analysis must be preceded by a retrospective one in order to understand the detailed operational mechanisms of the system, the ongoing developments and the unexpected events. Consequently, rather than developing specific testable hypothesis, the purpose of PET is to guide exploratory research. Given the complexity of systems like energy supply, the testing of general hypotheses would not even be a sensible goal. What can be achieved is an analysis of the mechanisms and switch points of change inside the system for a 'client' who is interested in the impacts of his behavioural options on other actors and their reactions to them.

Also at a more general level, the PET perspective has a number of important implications concerning the possibilities of managing change politically. Diffusion becomes part of a wider picture of system evolution which cannot be separated from it. They both develop in parallel in an organic way, encompassing the fields of technological, economic, social and political organization. The different areas mutually affect and constrain each other, inducing adaptations which operate through the nodes of actors' perceptions, mental frameworks and decision-making processes. Consequently, there is no central driving force and control of change, but a distributed and decentralized decision system. However, in periods of instability in which relatively small efforts are sufficient to induce considerable transformations, political decisions can have a decisive impact. Government – which is regarded as in charge of guaranteeing the efficient operation of the system as a whole – has a wide range of means at its disposal to affect the system and the path of technological change. Given the complexity and high uncertainties involved, the creation of the right matches and timing remain very difficult tasks, and political control needs to take into account its limited but potentially critical influence as one of the control centres of change in order to develop efficient measures.

NOTES

1. The research reported here was carried out at the Institute for Prospective Technological Studies, Ispra/Sevilla, and funded by the European Commission's 'Human Capital and Mobility' Programme. Much of the empirical information on which it is based was collected during a research stay at the Programme of Policy Research in Engineering, Science and Technology (PREST), University of Manchester, in 1995. It consisted of more than 30 interviews with representatives of CHP users, technology manufacturers, utility companies and government officials. An earlier version was presented at the Third International ASEAT Conference in Manchester, September 1995. Special thanks for their critical and helpful comments to Yvette Taminiau, Thomas Heinemeier, Donald Bain and especially Ken Green who had to struggle with my limited English skills.
2. 'Technological' and 'technical' are often used in unclear ways. Here, 'technical' is used when referring to the embodied elements (the artefacts) of a technology, whereas 'technological' is the more encompassing concept which includes both embodied and disembodied elements of technology, that is, artefacts *and knowledge.*
3. Callon (1992) uses 'intermediaries' in a similar way to the use of 'means' here. He distinguishes four types of intermediaries: texts, technical artefacts, human beings and their skills, and money.
4. We are using here the 'narrow' definition of network, in contrast to markets and hierarchies. For discussion of this and other definitions, see Thompson et al. (1991).
5. The history of and the reasons for the negligible role of district heating in the UK till the mid-1980s have been investigated in detail by Russell (1993).
6. Tariffs have been the subject of very controversial negotiations in recent years, mainly due to different interpretations of the avoided costs which should be remunerated. Whereas the fuel costs are undisputed, capacity terms, back-up and complementary power and security issues remain controversial between CHP operators and regional electricity companies.
7. One of the crucial errors made with the first small CHP plants was to size them according to the peak load of a site, that is according to a procedure which is followed for boilers. This decision was not only environmentally but also economically disastrous: due to the fluctuating load, the plants did not run efficiently.
8. In a more sophisticated representation, the comparison with competing technological options would have to be added.

REFERENCES

Arthur, B.W. (1988), 'Competing technologies: an overview', in Dosi, G. et al. (eds), *Technical Change and Economic Theory*, London: Pinter.

Bijker, W.E., Hughes, T.P. and Pinch, T. (eds) (1987), *The Social Construction of Technological Systems. New Directions in the Sociology and History of Technology*, Cambridge, MA: MIT Press.

Bijker, W.E. and Law, J. (eds) (1992), *Shaping Technology/Building Society. Studies in Sociotechnical Change*, Cambridge, MA: MIT Press.

Callon, M. (1992), 'The dynamics of techno-economic networks', in Coombs, R., Saviotti, P. and Walsh, V. (eds), *Technological Change and Company Strategies*, London: Academic Press.

Clark, N. and Juma, C. (1992), *Long-Run Economics. An Evolutionary Approach to Economic Change*, revised paperback edition, London: Pinter.

COGEN Europe (ed.) (1995), *The Barriers to Combined Heat and Power in Europe*, Brussels: COGEN.

David, P. (1992), 'Heroes, Herds and Hysteresis in Technological History: Thomas Edison and "The Battle of the Systems" Reconsidered', *Industrial and Corporate Change*, **1** (1), 129–80.

Department of Energy (ed.) (1979), *Combined Heat and Electrical Power Generation in the United Kingdom*, Energy Paper No. *35*, London: HMSO.

Department of Trade and Industry (ed.) (1995), *Digest of United Kingdom Energy Statistics 1995*, London: HMSO.

Dosi, G. (1982), 'Technological paradigms and technological trajectories: a suggested interpretation of the determinants and directions of technical change', *Research Policy*, **11**, 147–62.

Dosi, G. (1988a), 'Sources, Procedures and Microeconomic Effects of Innovation', *Journal of Economic Literature*, **26**, 1120–71.

Dosi, G. (1988b), 'The nature of the innovative process', in Dosi, G. et al. (eds), *Technical Change and Economic Theory*, London: Pinter.

Enquete-Kommission (ed.) (1995), *Mehr Zukunft für die Erde. Nachhaltige Energiepolitik für dauerhaften Klimaschutz, Enquete-Kommission 'Schutz der Erdatmosphäre' des Deutschen Bundestages*, Bonn: Economica.

Freeman, C. and Perez, C. (1988), 'Structural crisis of adjustment: business cycles and investment behaviour', in Dosi, G. et al. (eds), *Technical Change and Economic Theory*, London: Pinter.

Görlitz, A. and Druwe, U. (eds) (1990), *Politische Steuerung und Systemumwelt*, Pfaffenweiler: Centaurus.

Henderson, R. and Clark, K. (1990), 'Architectural Innovation: The Reconfiguration of Existing Product Technologies and the Failure of the Established Firm', *Administrative Science Quarterly*, **35**, 9–30.

Hughes, T.P. (1983), *Networks of Power: Electrification in Western Society, 1880–1930*, Baltimore, MD: Johns Hopkins University Press.

Hughes, T.P. and Mayntz, R. (eds) (1988), *The development of large technical systems*, Frankfurt/Boulder, CO: Campus/Westview.

Irwin, A. and Vergragt, P. (1989), 'Re-thinking the Relationship between Environmental Regulation and Industrial Innovation: The Social Negotiation of Technical Change', *Technology Analysis & Strategic Management*, **1**, 57–70.

Kemp, R. (1993), 'Technology and the Transition to a Sustainable Economy', paper for the 'Greening of Industry' *Conference*, Boston, 14–16 November.

Krupp, H. (1992), *Energy Politics and Schumpeter Dynamics. Japan's Policy Between Short-Term Wealth and Long-Term Global Welfare*, Tokyo: Springer.

Liso, N. De and Metcalfe, J.S. (1994), 'On Technological Systems and Technological Paradigms. Some Recent Developments in the Understanding of Technological Change', Paper presented at the Fifth Conference of the International J.A. Schumpeter Society, Münster, 17–20 August.

Luhmann, N. (1988), *Die Wirtschaft der Gesellschaft*, Frankfurt: Suhrkamp.

Lundvall, B.A. (ed.) (1992), *National Systems of Innovation. Towards a Theory of Innovation and Interactive Learning*, London: Pinter.

Marin, B. and Mayntz, R. (eds) (1991), *Policy Networks. Empirical Evidence and Theoretical Considerations*, Frankfurt am Main/Boulder, CO: Campus/Westview.

Mayntz, R. (1987), 'Politische Steuerung und gesellschaftliche Steuerungsprobleme – Anmerkungen zu einem theoretischen Paradigma', in Ellwein, T. et al. (eds), *Jahrbuch zur Staats- und Verwaltungswissenschaft, Band 1*, Baden-Baden: Nomos.

Metcalfe, J.S. and Boden, M. (1992), 'Evolutionary epistemology and the nature of technology strategy', in Coombs, R., Saviotti, P. and Walsh, V. (eds), *Technological Change and Company Strategy*, London: Academic Press.

Meyer-Krahmer, F. (1989), *Der Einfluß staatlicher Technologiepolitik auf industrielle Innovationen*, Baden-Baden: Nomos.

Molina, A. (1993), 'In Search of Insights into the Generation of Techno-Economic Trends: Micro- and Macro-Constituencies in the Microprocessor Industry', *Research Policy*, **22**, 479–506.

Nelson, R. (ed.) (1993), *National Innovation Systems. A Comparative Analysis*, New York/Oxford: Oxford University Press.

Nelson, R. and Winter, S. (1982), *An evolutionary theory of economic change*, Cambridge, MA: Belknap Press.

Niosi, J. et al. (1993), 'National Systems of Innovation: In Search of a Workable Concept', *Technology in Society*, **15**, 207–28.

Rosenberg, N. (1982), *Inside the black box. Technology and economics*, Cambridge: Cambridge University Press.

Russell, S. (1993), 'Writing energy history: explaining the neglect of CHP/DH in Britain', *British Journal of the History of Science*, **26**, 33–54.

Saviotti, P. and Metcalfe, J.S. (1984), 'A theoretical approach to the construction of technological output indicators', *Research Policy*, **13**, 141–51.

Schot, J. (1992), 'Constructive Technology Assessment and Technology Dynamics: The Case of Clean Technologies', *Science, Technology & Human Values*, **17**, 36–56.

Sirchis, J. (ed.) (1990), *Combined Production of Heat and Power (Cogeneration)*, London: Elsevier.

Summerton, J. (ed.) (1994), *Changing Large Technical Systems*, Boulder, CO: Westview.

Thompson, G. et al. (eds) (1991), *Markets, Hierarchies & Networks. The Coordination of Social Life*, London: Sage.

Tushman, M.L. and Anderson, P. (1986), 'Technological Discontinuities and Organizational Environments', *Administrative Science Quarterly*, **31**, 439–65.

Tushman, M.L. and Rosenkopf, L. (1992), 'Organizational Determinants of Technological Change: Towards a Sociology of Technological Evolution', *Research in Organizational Behavior*, **14**, 311–47.

Index

absorption of technology, 128, 132–8, 140–42
accessing technology, 128–9, 133–4, 140–42
acquiring technology: NTBFs and, 132–42
Activity Stage Model, 82
actors
  perceptions and expectations in PET system, 214, 217
  CHP in the UK, 225–8
  sociotechnical alignment of perceptions and goals, 93–4
adaptation of products, 48, 50–51
adaptive R&D units, 46
Adelson, M., 151
ADEME, 155–6, 159
administrative heritage, 53–4
adoption decisions, 216
adoption of scenarios, 166–9
agriculture: set-aside policy, 160–63
Akrich, M., 157
Alcatel, 44–54 *passim*
alignment, sociotechnical, 89–98
  'diamond of alignment', 89–90
  inter-company level, 95–8
  intra-company level, 90–95
  promoting at Sony, 98–101
alternative energy scenarios, 159
Amara, R., 156
Amit, R., 19
Anderson, P., 110, 218
Aoki, M., 35
Aoshima, Y., 83
Apple: Newton, 93
architectural technologies, 91–3
aristocratic culture, 182–3, 184–6
Arrow, K., 21
Arthur, B., 14, 219
Arunachalam, S., 186
AT&T, 13, 44–54 *passim*

Autio, E., 125, 126
autonomous firms, 137–42 *passim*

bank-based/insider-dominated systems, 189
banking system, 193
Barbanti, P., 33
Barbier, R., 151, 163
Barley, S., 34
Barney, J., 19
Bartlett, C.A., 42
behavioural requirements for technological change, 181–2, 184–6
Bell, M., 129
Bell Laboratories, 12–13
Bergen, S.A., 184–5
Beta-Max, 10, 11
biochemicals, 198, 202, 203–4
biomass, 159, 160–63
blind variation, 13–18
Boden, M., 119
Boehmer, A. von, 39
Bollinger, L., 126
Bosworth, D., 117
bounded cognition, 13–18, 22–3, 24
bourgeois culture, 182–3, 184–6
Bowonder, B., 84
British Technology Foresight Programme, 152
Brockhoff, K., 39
Burns, T., 180, 182, 191
Byé, P., 28, 29, 30, 32

Callon, M., 30, 152, 157
Campbell, A., 67–8, 71
Campbell, D., 14–15
capabilities
  and the firm, 18–23
  innovation, knowledge and, 8–27
  organization, innovating firm and, 2–5
  in specific contexts, 5–6

239

history and cumulative causation,
203–6
importance of size, 198–200
microeconomic hypothesis, 180–81
national predispositions, 182–6
role of the state, 191–4
sectoral characteristics, 194–8
Nayak, P.R., 61, 82
NEC, 44–54 *passim*
Nederhof, A.J., 34
Nelson, R., 13, 21, 110, 119, 154, 217
Netherlands, 160–63
new technology-based firms (NTBFs), 5,
124–49
as an element of a process, 126–7
in less advanced countries, 127–30
Portugal *see* Portugal
roles, 124–8, 131–2
technological dynamism, 124–6, 128–
30
Newby, H., 110
Nobel, R., 39
Nobeoka, K., 83
Nonaka, I., 83
Northern Telecom, 44–54 *passim*
novelty: finance and, 188–91
NOVEM, 161, 162
nuclear power, 158–60, 166

objectives/goals, 93–4, 217
Odagiri, H., 112–13
OECD, 129
Office of Electricity Regulation
(OFFER), 222, 223–4, 229, 233
Ohga, Norio, 91
oligopoly, 160–63, 166–9
Olleros, F.J., 125
operating NTBFs, 140–42
organization: capabilities, innovating
firm and, 2–5
organizational short-termism, 112, 113–
14
Orsenigo, L., 33
outsider-dominated/stock-exchange-
based systems, 189–90
overvaluation of assets, 33
ownership: state, 193–4

paradigmatic perspective, 17–18
Parsons turbine, 12

Patel, P., 194, 199
path dependence, 2, 14, 153–6, 203–6
Pavitt, K., 1, 64, 69, 125, 129, 194, 199
payback period, 115, 116
PCs, 97–8
Pearce, R.D., 39, 41
Penrose, E., 22
perceptions, 217, 225–8
sociotechnical alignment, 93–4
Perez, C., 128, 129, 130
performance
control, 71–2
innovation's effects on, 113–14
Perrino, A.C., 41
PET system (politics, economics and
technology), 213–19
actors: objectives, perceptions and
expectations, 217
analytical advantages, 233–5
co-generation technology in the UK,
229–31
interaction arenas and decision
making, 215–16
structures, 214, 215
system dynamics, 217–19
technology, 214–15
Peters, T., 82, 119
Peugeot 106, electric, 157
pharmaceuticals, 11, 191, 198
UK, 203–4
Philips, 4, 76–107
CD-ROM-based project compared
with Sony's, 80–81
comparison with Sony, 78–80
Photo-CD, 4, 76–107
Pickering, J.F., 66
pioneering emerging technologies, 91–
3
Pitts, R., 67
planning
rapid technological change and, 109–
11
strategic, 67–8
political decision structures, 215, 216,
223–4
Polygram, 79
Pope, S.L., 151
population perspective, 8–9
Portugal, 130–46
foreign technology, 140–42